THE TRANSFORMATION OF MAN

THE TRANSFORMATION OF MAN

A Study of Conversion and Community

ROSEMARY HAUGHTON

PAULIST PRESS DEUS BOOKS

PARAMUS, N.J. NEW YORK, N.Y.
TORONTO LONDON

A Deus Books Edition of Paulist Press, originally published by
Geoffrey Chapman Ltd, London, 1967, and in the U.S.A.
by Templegate Publishing Co., Springfield, Illinois, 1967.

Library of Congress
Catalog Card Number: 67-22746

Published by Paulist Press
Editorial Office: 304 W. 58th St., N.Y., N.Y. 10019
Business Office: Paramus, New Jersey 07652

Printed and bound in the
United States of America

CONTENTS

CONTENTS

Introduction

Part One

I.

II. Europe

III.

Part Two

IV.

V. The reception of the Gospel

Foreword

FOREWORD

THERE can no longer be any doubt that the Church has entered into a period of profound confusion and disorientation. Far from curing us of all our ills, the Second Vatican Council succeeded mainly in revealing how deep-seated are the problems of contemporary Christianity. To be sure, the Council accomplished many valuable things. It set the Church directly on the way to a major liturgical, ecumenical and theological renewal. It spoke effectively on religious liberty, the Church in the modern world, the rôle of the laity, the renewal of religious life, and on sundry other significant issues. But neither the Council Fathers nor many others in the Church foresaw the difficulties which have developed in the aftermath of the Council. Almost everyone recognized that it would not be easy to implement the work of the Council; that such difficulties have appeared as predicted is no surprise. What is surprising is the way the concern over 'implementation' has given way, in many quarters, to concern over far more basic issues of Christian existence. Even if Christianity were renewed, would it have a future? Who is God? What, if anything, does the traditional doctrine of God—or of man, or of the Church, or of the supernatural—have to say to contemporary man?

One might call questions like these pre-institutional. Some are so basic one can hardly begin to deal with such matters as parish reform, liturgical changes and ecumenism until at least some preliminary answers have been discovered. As it happens, though, these are questions which arise now at the end of many centuries of a highly institutionalized Christianity. They are questions which we felt had been answered long ago. Now we

3

THE TRANSFORMATION OF MAN

are finding that even if they had been answered once, the answers are no longer very persuasive; they say little to us, tell us nothing about our existence here and now. I needn't emphasize how disturbing this discovery has been for many. What began some few years ago as a crisis of institutional relevance and reform has now turned into a crisis of faith.

Whether the Church likes it or not, it is being pushed back to its very roots. But what are its roots? Surely the Bible and the early Christian community. Surely, too, the writings of the early Church Fathers. Yet surely also, and even more broadly perhaps, the nature of the Christian experience, that experience which first came into being nearly two thousand years ago and which has been sustained ever since. It is hardly a cultural accident that questions concerning the nature of this experience should come before our eyes so vividly and inescapably at the present moment in history. For 'experience' has become a central concept in modern-day life. People want to know how to feel, how to see, how to listen; how, in brief, to experience themselves, the material world, the reality of other people, the culture which surrounds them. They want to reach bed-rock and they believe, correctly I think, that experience provides the tools with which to dig.

And these are the tools with which Rosemary Haughton has chosen to dig. In working with the very ordinary material of human relationships—with the experience of people who argue, who love, who desire—she tries to shows us the theological cutting-edge of these relationships: what they reveal of the human condition and what they point to as central in that condition. Even more, she tries to show us how much we have lost by neglecting to see the importance of human 'transformation'. For at the deepest level, a person who is enlightened by his experience, who begins to see patterns and pointers, is a person on the way to transformation. With brilliant persuasiveness and insight, she argues that transformation, rather than formation, provides the key to Christian existence.

One passage among many I should like to quote, a passage which cuts to the centre of the disorientation which has appeared since the Council. 'Theologians', Mrs Houghton writes, 'are trying to adapt traditional theological structures to the existential attitudes of "modern man". But in fact the whole well-meaning labour is misplaced, because the thing about "modern man" is that people are not satisfied with classifications of themselves, modern or not. The more sensitive the person, the more he is suspicious of categories and evades them, looking for truth in the immediacy of personal experience. He isn't "modern man" but just himself.' In choosing to centre her account on 'the immediacy of personal experience', Mrs Haughton has stepped well beyond traditional theology. By choosing also to begin with particular experiences and concrete examples of human behaviour, rather than with general principles, she also displays an acute understanding of the way people actually experience themselves and others.

We don't, after all, live our daily lives on the high plateau of theological principles and axioms. We live, instead, in particular bodies, interacting with particular people in particular situations. The theology comes later. And that is one of Mrs Haughton's major points in choosing to approach human transformation in terms of specific people responding to specific situations.

Yet what does it mean, in the end, to be transformed as a human being? It is to enter into community, to discover who we are in relationship to other human beings, and, beyond that, to become aware, in Mrs Haughton's words, 'of being people living in relation to salvation'. In transformation and in community, then, we discover who we are. Mrs Haughton's book provides a sensitive, perceptive account of Christian self-discovery.

DANIEL CALLAHAN

INTRODUCTION

THE ideal of the formation of man is the process of using all the influences of culture—family affection, humane educational and political and social structures, and all the scientific know-how available—to help people to understand themselves and each other and the world they share, to adjust themselves to both without either undue aggressiveness or frightened conformity, and so to form satisfying and stable emotional and social relationships. This is to be done through a well-ordered community setting in which mutual responsibility and the care of the weak are taken for granted. All this, ideally, should produce the whole human being, the perfection of man. Nobody expects perfection in practice, but it is an imaginable ideal all the same, and one that seems worth striving for because even its imperfect attainment produces a verifiable amount of human happiness.

But there is another notion of the purpose or perfection of man—the idea of transformation. It is not imaginable at all, which is why we tend to place transformed man in a separate 'place' called heaven. Transformation is a total personal revolution. It begins with repentance—the rejection along with actual sins of the whole apparatus of natural virtue as irrelevant and misleading—and proceeds eventually to the desired dissolution of all that ordinary people ordinarily value in themselves or others. The result of this dissolution, this death of the natural man, is the birth of the whole human being, the perfection of man, meaning both man as an individual and man as a race, because the process is at once personal and communal. And it takes place in

7

Christ and nowhere else. It is what Christians call the resurrection, or eternal life.

This book is about such a transformation. Only a Christian can
write about this, because only a Christian can seriously entertain
the notion of transformation as a human fact, without meaning
by it any kind of gnostic or Buddhist separation of the eternal
soul from the perishable body.

Until recently, the Catholic tradition of Christianity appeared,
at least to those outside it, to be mainly concerned with the *formation* of man, as an ethical, social, political and even aesthetical
creature, rather than with his *transformation*. From the point of
view of the outside world, the Catholic Church is an educational
system that should produce civilized, high-principled, unselfish,
generous people, therefore its success or failure can be judged
accordingly. When the Catholic Church is condemned, it is for
manifest failure to produce the goods advertised, and Catholics
are compared to their detriment with non-Catholics in matters of
practical charity. When it is praised it is because it does turn out
people who are up to this standard—Pope John for instance, or
St Vincent de Paul, or St Francis.

The reformed tradition, on the other hand, has tended to play
down the formation aspect. It is faith that saves, blind trust in
Christ's redeeming act that makes a Christian, and no human
ethical achievements are relevant—they are even a distraction.
Formation is there, but it is let in by a theological back door and
kept in the kitchen. In the writing of Bonhoeffer, for instance,
the 'formation' type of values are simply non-existent, there is no
foothold for anyone trained to make ethical value judgments in
the tradition of western humanist culture. Writers of the Catholic
stream of European classical culture, however—Francis de Sales,
Newman, Claudel, Maritain, Belloc, Waugh—move in a recognizable world, and their specifically Christian oddness is acceptable
because it adds precisely the element of mystery and strangeness
which is missing from the Fabian-humanist tradition, and which
people want. The strangeness is strange and exciting precisely

because it occurs in a recognizable though richly obscure and complex cultural setting. It gives a feeling of safety and opportunity combined. But the strangeness of the Reformed tradition, when it is encountered 'pure' (that is, unmixed with humanist-Catholic accommodation as it is apt to be in the Anglican version) is the strangeness of nightmare, where nothing means what it seems to mean, solid ordinary things melt into vapour, and harmless ones take on terrifying significance.

This is how the situation does *still* appear to the majority of ordinary humanists—whether they are Christian-flavoured or not. But the appeal of Catholicism for reasons of this kind is fading. A generation has grown up that is suspicious of a rich tradition, scared by massive continuity, unwilling to acknowledge permanent ethical values, revolted by togetherness and the bland assurance that springs from the feeling of being part of a great whole. It is not only students and young intellectuals who reject the notion of human life implied in the concept of formation as I have described it. Middle-aged workmen in pubs, smart secretaries, adolescents in coffee bars and elderly women with dogs—all kinds and sorts of people betray an obscure awareness of life as uncertain, cut-off, undirected, and depending for its value (if any) on moments of purely individual heroism, insight, or love. The daily round, the rigid framework may be all the more essential to prevent the collapse of human life, but it is not authentic, it is not relevant to the real life which is always now but never present or graspable. This kind of awareness flowered, on the continent, in the various streams of existentialist philosophy, but as an undergrowth it is just as widespread in England where the sophisticated puritanism of logical positivism has had terrific snob appeal but not much more—appeal, that is to the half-informed intellectual hopefuls. The people who hammered it out are anything but snobs, and it is their obvious honesty and integrity that attracts people. It looks so *clean*.

The novels of the post-war years reflect this kind of awareness, both negatively and (occasionally) positively. It is combined with a characteristic and slightly panicky nostalgia for the strength and certainty of the formation values and loyalties: family affection, the continuing and earth-ing demands of home, land, business, social custom. The sequence of the two novels *Room at the Top* and *Life at the Top* shows particularly well this restless rejection and ruthless selfishness, and their inevitable counterpart in the need for continuity and stable, recognizable human values that eventually re-assert their pull. The inversion here is especially interesting because here the transformation-quest, hidden and distorted but real, is overtaken by the formation values it had disregarded, and their gravity-pull can be seen reshaping, after a fashion, a life that had tried to do without them.

This very widespread dissatisfaction with the values of classical humanism makes the appeal of the Catholic Church as it normally appears almost nil. And the same dissatisfaction is increasingly evident within the Catholic Church itself. The rediscovery of elements of a transformation theology has found a ready response, and the attraction of the ruthless Lutheran disregard for formation values is manifest in the unacknowledged influence of the Lutheran ethos by way of the existentialist philosophy which grew from Lutheran roots.

But, so far, although Catholic theologians are eagerly gathering from their Reformed colleagues elements for a renewed understanding of biblical and ecclesial theology, the main structures of Catholic theology (especially sacramental theology) remain immovable. A great deal of essential tidying and cleaning is going on, so that the structural beauty of the whole is more evident than it has been for centuries, but so far no one seems to have asked seriously whether these undoubtedly beautiful structures are suitable machines-for-living for people on this side of the atom bomb. And this question is becoming increasingly pressing as it becomes clearer and clearer that the challenge which seemed to be merely that of Reformed theology, a specialized study for ecumenists, is also the challenge of man as he knows himself, now, in terms of a culture doubtful of its roots, scornful of its traditions, and pessimistic about its future. In this uprooted state, when formation values are no longer self-evident, the living that must be done in theological structures is a living to which the abiding formation values enshrined in Catholic moral and dogmatic theology, and the way of life that expresses them, seem tediously irrelevant. The inevitable result of this has been an increasing tension within the Church between moral principles and dogmatic formulations as worked out by former generations and the pressure of the spirit of the age—to which indeed the Vatican Council bade us pay attention. But this spirit is the Spirit of God, and it is an explosive force.

This tension and unease shows itself throughout the Church, but the real cause of it is most clearly apparent, naturally, at the strictly theological level. And this is precisely where it is not being tackled. All that is happening is that theologians are trying to adapt traditional theological structures to the existentialist attitudes of 'modern man'. But in fact the whole well-meaning labour is misplaced, because the thing about 'modern man' is that people are not satisfied with classifications of themselves, modern or not. The more sensitive the person, the more he is suspicious of categories and evades them, looking for truth in the immediacy of personal experience. He isn't 'modern man' but just himself. The contradiction between man formed and man transformed is splitting the Christian consciousness at every level of community and personal life, and you *can't* adapt structures in such a way as to accommodate both, because structures are concerned solely with formation.

So if the division is to be healed, and the Word to be proclaimed in a theologically renewed awareness of the man who hears it (who is *both* the speaker *and* the hearer) the experience itself, that has made the division apparent, must provide the material for its healing. In that case the material of human experience must be presented in a way that makes clear the elements of the situation that are theologically relevant.

This book, then, attempts to show the elements of the human

theological crisis in which our whole culture is involved, and to interpret them in terms of the processes of formation and transformation. This ambitious project is brought down to earth (I hope) by the way in which I have chosen to pursue the discovery. It is not the only way, but it is a way which ensures that the discussion remains tied to the facts of experience and does not vaporize into a cloud of abstractions.

The 'material' for discussion must belong to human experience, but experience is particular, it is the actual interplay of real people in real settings. Therefore I have chosen not to begin with general ideas and illustrate them by examples, but to begin with particular examples of human behaviour and to try to discover in them the elements of the human situation as we are aware of it, now, in our particular culture.

The whole of the second part of the book is concerned with only one idea, which emerges as the focus of all the elements discovered in the earlier part. This is the idea of community, which turns out, not surprisingly, to be both the place where the division becomes apparent and the means whereby perhaps it may be healed and from which a new theology may grow—a theology which is radical in the sense of going to the roots and not being satisfied with mere weeding, but also in the sense of springing ultimately *from* the root, and growing according to the nature of the vine itself, which becomes apparent when the weeds and creepers are pulled away.

Part One

CHAPTER I

CONFLICT AND RESOLUTION

Two children are quarrelling. One is a boy, aged twelve, imaginative, touchy, withdrawn. The other is a girl aged eight, obstinate, impulsive, generous. It could have been any other two children, or any grown-ups, of any age and any assortment of temperaments. But people are never any age or any temperament, only their own at a given moment, and what is common is only real in what is particular. So these two particular human beings are engaged in that most frequent of human occupations—disagreement.

From this 'disagreement' and its results I hope to draw certain conclusions about the nature of human encounters in general, which will be examined in the rest of the book. In order to do this I am obliged to subject this very trivial incident to a degree of close analysis which is entirely out of proportion to the event. These very ordinary people in this extremely normal situation must bear a huge weight of significance about 'Man'. And this is, from one point of view, a distortion, even a torturing, of the reality. But from another point of view it is our normal dismissal of such events as trivial which is a distortion of their nature. They may be ordinary, but the whole sequence of such events, throughout a lifetime, does in fact determine the nature and destiny of man, and therefore of Man. These events, so common that they are forgotten as soon as they are over, do indeed bear the weight of the world, for they are what makes or unmakes the world—in St John's sense of the human world, the world humans make of themselves. So if this little incident seems fantastically overwrought it may be that our normal view is over complacent, too easily dismissive. I am not suggesting that we should think of, let alone *feel*, each tiny human event through such a lense of eternal significance. We would go mad—indeed people *do* go mad when they cannot help feeling too deeply the meaning of their own actions. But I do suggest that to correct our normal view from time to time may be salutary, in the sense of being, perhaps, a help to salvation.

The little girl, wanting to decorate her doll's house, has gone rummaging in the box under her brother's bed and, in his absence, taken his paint brushes and two tubes of paint. The boy, returning from an errand for his mother, wants to go on with a picture he had begun the day before; indeed it was only with great reluctance that he finally gave in to his mother's insistence that he should carry out an errand for her before settling down to his painting. He has not long had the paints, but he had long wanted them, for his picture-making is his precious and private world, in which he can say and discover all kinds of things, in which a constant and intoxicating dialogue takes place between himself as subject and himself as object, by means of a language which is that of familiar things around him, but changed and rearranged and encountering each other in always unexpected and yet controllable ways. It is his refuge from the demands of other human beings whom he does not understand and of whom he is afraid, and his means of growing in confidence and courage, so that he may not be so much afraid. Sometimes he paints in the kitchen, but he prefers the shed, when it isn't too cold, because he can shut the door. But, wherever he does it, it is hugely and savagely important to him, all the more because he has no idea why this is so, and would be mystified to have the situation described to him in my artificial and unnaturally intellectual version of quite ordinary feelings.

He comes back to his painting, therefore, with a mind both relaxed and attentive, expectant and relieved. Already, inwardly, he has laid aside the irritations of family commitments which are all the more irksome because he is beginning to be aware of them as more than external annoyances. He is beginning to know them as intimately involved in his own growth, as demands within him, to which, sooner or later, he must attend. But not yet, and in order to do so, sometime, he urgently needs at this moment to immerse his whole person in this work that he loves, but that he also fears, so that each time he comes to it he has to overcome a queer reluctance. This makes him especially irritable, but his need is strong enough to overcome the reluctance and so to add a liberating sense of victory to the other elements of feeling that surround his painting.

But the brushes are gone, two of his tubes of paint are missing. The promise is broken, the summons cannot be obeyed, the picture that he had begun lies there, wounded and crying out, and the wound and the cry are in himself.

Of course he knows at once what has happened to his brushes and paints. The ecstasy of anticipation that was ready to be transformed into the energy of loving dialogue—fervent enough and brave enough to battle with the hideous inertia of inadequate skill and intransigent tools—is changed instead to pure anger. And the blast of this anger opens up many doors in the boy's mind. These doors are usually kept closed, and what is behind them is usually unrecognized, and even disclaimed if it reaches the light of conscious thought. For what is behind those doors— in long, long corridors extending into deep darkness—is accumulated memories of rejection and estrangement, of insult and degradation, all inflicted by the huge power of the grown-ups. These stored but overlaid memories are not factual, they are completely contained in the boy's own reacting emotions of hatred and fear and despair and humiliation and desire for revenge, and also in pleasure in his own humiliation and in a strong desire to suffer outrage. All these are experienced only as unrecognized, un-named emotions and later, conscious, knowledge has modified the more recent and better remembered experiences by a wordless but workable understanding of grown-ups as people like oneself. They are people who do not always mean the hurt they inflict, who are not in control of thunderstorms and who do not

inflict burns or splinters on their son in revenge for his failure
to finish his porridge. So in the ordinary way the old hatreds and
fears remain safely tucked away, and affection reigns. But at this
crisis anger opens the doors of Bluebeard's room, and it is not one
room but many. As the boy goes to look for his sister, all those
doors are opening. But, because he cannot bear to know that the
real objects of his secret hates and lusts are the parents he loves,
the contents of those unlocked rooms will be poured out on his
younger sister. This is perfectly just, according to the inner
logic of the situation, for it is her action which has been responsible for unlocking the doors of the forbidden rooms.

The little girl is half prepared for her brother's attack. She
knows that she was to blame in taking his painting materials, and
she is obscurely aware of their importance to him as something
more than the convenience of having one's possessions immediately available when needed. She knows the deep absorption that
surrounds her brother when he paints and she has been, indeed,
baffled and irritated by it, and a little jealous of an experience that
excludes her. So the taking of his materials was not only dictated
by the need to carry out her own plans, but was also a small
gesture of defiance directed at the strange love her brother wor-
ships in secrecy, and an act of revenge for his faithlessness to her,
a sort of castration. Yet this is not, for her, the major ingredient
in her decision to help herself to his materials and risk his certain anger. She is, being the youngest in the family, sufficiently
confident of her own value to feel no very violent need to assert
her own claim to love against her brother's occasional unfaithfulness. She does not seriously doubt his devotion, and the revenge
aspect of her action is peripheral and incidental, though satisfying. The real need that dictated her action is one that would have
operated independently of whatever significance these particular
materials have in her relationship with her brother.

She has been arranging her doll's house, after a long period
when it stood neglected on the top shelf of the cupboard, and its
furniture is chipped and shabby after lying about for months at

the bottom of a cardboard box full of assorted toys and rubbish. Her housewifely sense of responsibility is sharpened by a sense of guilt, and the guilt of her neglect is all the more overwhelming because she does not know why she has neglected her doll's house. She is not nearly old enough to be aware of the transitoriness of her enthusiasms, all she knows is that, just now, it is vital that she should get her house in order and make amends for its previous disorder by extra loving care. The house should be neat and clean and bright, restful and inviting. Her spirit longs to relax in it, with a sense of accomplishment that opens the heart and makes it possible to offer welcome there to others. Until this work is done, and superbly done, she will not feel herself at liberty, free to offer her love generously to her friends or her mother, and for a person as naturally gregarious and affectionate as she is this is a severe deprivation. Hence the urgency that cannot bear any obstacles and brushes aside all difficulties, such as her brother's right to his own things. There are no other paints immediately available but his and she could have asked him for them if he had been in the house, but he was not. In fact she is glad of this because she knows, at the back of her mind, that he might well have refused, and that the scene she would be quite prepared to make in her efforts to get him to change his mind would almost certainly have ended in her defeat. (For the same reason she has taken the doll's house into her bedroom, instead of into the kitchen where her mother might be able to help.)

So she has been engaged for some twenty minutes in trying to paint the doll's house kitchen table a nice, bright blue. But the paints are not ideal for this task, and her efforts have produced disappointing results. She would not for a moment admit that this was inevitable, or even that she has not really got the effect that she saw so vividly in her mind's eyes—the vision that drove her to take the paints. But a lurking fear of final defeat is lending extra urgency and determination to her mood, and a smear of blue paint on her skirt has added an extra element of guilt. So the expectation (vivid, but unacknowledged out of defiance) of her mother's annoyance and reproach has sharpened her general state of defendedness and readiness for battle. In all sorts of ways she is in the wrong, and knows it, yet she is still possessed by a deep though inarticulate conviction that the demands of her doll's house for her total devotion are indeed as paramount as they seem, and that therefore *she* is somehow the ill-used, the mis-understood, the victim.

So brother and sister comfront each other, both possessed by an inner vision which is endangered, both injured, both afraid and both, in this moment, provided with a circumstantial bottle-opener that will let out the full power of the complex emotions that bubble within them.

It makes no difference which one is in fact to blame. To each, the other is the aggressor, the enemy. To each, the other symbolizes the destructive power of the unknown world—not merely the out-side world of baffling other people, but the inner world of the un-known and terrifying self. This inner world is not known as in-ward, but the struggle to keep its power at bay is part of this battle that now develops between brother and sister. They shout at and reproach each other, they insult each other with unlikely and irrelevant epithets, they accuse each other of things that are increasingly less related to the ostensible cause of the quarrel. In-deed the wretched painting materials are quickly forgotten, for they were only the trigger. Anyone listening to the quarrel might well find it difficult to discover what was its real cause. And in fact the immediate cause is not the 'real' cause, but the real cause is the human situation of each child, in its particularity.

Here, then, is my 'human situation', a familiar and recogniz-able one. Just because this is a particular one, having no exact duplicate, we can discover in it the elements of the wider thing, the human situation which has no existence except in this way, in each unique and unrepeatable event. But there it does exist.

This situation is one of ignorance striving for knowledge, of separateness striving for communion, of fear longing for safety.

Therefore it is a state of desire, which does not know what it desires, and of anger that does not know what to be angry with. It is subject to futility, and yet subject in hope, and this hope is precisely what makes the futility so painful. There is no way out of this situation, from within it. It is a self-perpetuating cycle of hope baffled and turning to vengeance, and vengeance frustrated and turning to fear, and fear seeking a way out and still hoping that there is one, and hope baffled.

But childish quarrels are as fleeting as they are frequent, and all other human events and encounters are equally transitory. The human situation is not static but only exists as its moments, that constantly change. And their changing character is not, after all, always the treadmill of the unalterable sequences of frustration. Although there is no way out from within the situation there is a release from without, and this simply means the intervention of some influence that is not totally contained in the situation itself. (Remember that the situation can only be particular, never general.)

It is the lack of any intervention, any new element in the vicious circle, that makes Pinter's play *The Caretaker* so absorbing and so claustrophobic. We feel that the situation, the round of mutually dependant self-deception, could so easily be broken. If only one of the two brothers had the courage to feel compassion for the tramp. But he is a threat to their frail structure of security, he is the threat of truth, so he must be pushed out, he must *not* be an intervention, but must be part of the structure of deception. When it becomes apparent that he can no longer support this structure, at the point where he begins to represent a challenge to the precarious self-approval of the brothers, he must go. The situation challenges *us* because it asks for compassion, but we are powerless, we can only watch while what might have been the saving intervention is rejected. The circle of frustration, vengeance, hope and frustration goes on. The emotions are not even violent enough to break out and cause some kind of débâcle, however horrible, that would break the circle.

In the particular situation I have described it is obvious that the quarrel will not continue indefinitely. Either something will happen to stop it, from outside, or the thing will work itself out by the inner law of its own composition.

In the latter case, if the children are left alone, the result may vary in the working out of its details, but the actual outcome is inherent in the situation as described.

The boy, being older, is able to wrest his paints and brushes from his sister by force and when he has used up most of his available store of insults and accusations he will do so. The girl's character makes it virtually impossible for her to admit defeat, therefore she will scream and kick and struggle with him, trying to get them back, and when he shuts and locks the shed door she will kick that, and throw things at it, and then anywhere at all, and may even smash the doll's house furniture for whose sake she began all the trouble. If she is still left to herself she will eventually fall asleep from sheer exhaustion, because nothing else but exhaustion can make her abandon the struggle. When she wakes up she will feel better, and a natural cheerfulness will enable her to carry on with her life, to meet her brother and talk to him quite happily, and ignore the quarrel for all practical purposes.

The boy, on his side, will ignore his sister's screams, deliberately shutting her out of his heart, for his own safety, for seriously to consider her feelings and needs would be to endanger all that he has tried to achieve. It would mean abandoning his painting, and with it his safety, his chance of discovering the meaning of self and life—or so it seems. And he is not yet whole enough to do that. He dare not give in because he is not sufficiently aware of himself to be capable of an act of giving at all. He will go on, behind his locked door, trying to paint, and probably this will not work, and he will blame his sister. He, too, will get over it, and forget, and make friends.

But in both children the fears and desires and needs that blew up into a quarrel will be unaltered. They will not be better understood, or less urgent. In fact a further difficulty will have been put in the way of eventually overcoming the fears or accomplishing the desires and supplying the needs, because now each is more than ever likely to use the other as a sufficient symbol of all that is wrong and that he or she does not understand. They may well learn, in time, not to offend each other in such obvious ways, and so avoid humiliation. They will gradually forget the intensity of feeling that characterized the encounter, and others like it, and come to laugh about it, perhaps together, for both of them will see only the triviality of the occasion and refuse to admit the importance of the underlying impulses. This they must do, in order to live in the same house and 'get on' together, and even at this age they are fully aware of the discomfort of *not* 'getting on' when you live at close quarters with other people. A lot of bitterness can be kept out of sight, from sheer necessity. But they may even come to disbelieve in the bitterness, and suppose that their kindly indifference to each other in later years is the norm of family affection. So the separateness and fear and distrust and frustrated longing lose their emotional character and can be disregarded. Only the results are left—a settled and contented and taken-for-granted lack of communication, the kind of stalemate that modern drama explores with such sickening truth, as in *The Caretaker*. The moral we are meant to point is, 'there is no way out, no intervention will happen'.

This is the kind of thing that happens when the basic ingredients of the human situation, as they are made evident in some such happening, are left to churn around together without any additions. For the purposes of argument so far, I have assumed that not only is there no intervention at *this* point in the children's lives but that no previous or subsequent intervention is of a kind that might, in practice, act as a real element in resolving the situation. It could do this either by occurring to one or other of the children as a memory, during the course of the quarrel, and so affecting his or her behaviour, or at some later date by affecting the memory of the quarrel, and so making it possible to modify its long-term results, although not, of course, the event itself. But this indirect intervention is still an intervention, and the discussion of this type of intervention is only excluded here in order to avoid complications. The same principles apply.

In practice, of course, the chances are great that some sort of 'intervention' will occur. This intervention is usually so spread out in time that it would be impossible to say exactly when it began to operate, and it is made up of things the children learn about living, through personal experience and perhaps from books as well, and of things that other people say to them, or simply *show* them, about how people live and 'get on' or don't. This kind of gradually accumulating influence is so much under-cover and so little recognized that it can be at work and yet not be sufficiently strong at any given moment to alter outward habits to a noticeable degree. Yet it does make a difference, and it can be recognized in gradually modified reactions to similar events. In order to show what this difference really is, therefore, I am describing some kinds of intervention that do really happen, but are more clear-cut and deliberate as events than the gradual infiltration of outside influences. Because they occur in a short time they are easier to analyse, but the basic process is the same. In real life the development over the years will probably be a mixture of the infiltration effect and the immediate impact effect, each reacting on the other. So the incidents described here are artificially extracted from their setting, but they can give a very good idea of what is going on in the whole process.

The importance of an intervention is that it introduces an ele-ment which is not totally contained in the situation itself. But it may, and probably will, be already involved in it to some extent. It may have been present as a formative influence on the child-ren, making them what they are at the time of the quarrel, and to that extent, therefore, being part of the situation. But when the intervention occurs it comes in from outside, as a power exterior to any that have been generated between the two participants.

It is, after all, likely that in a normal family a quarrel such as

I have described will be stopped, and the person who stops it will often be the children's mother. She hears the row going on outside the back door and abandons her baking with some irritation in order to do something about it. The 'something' she intends to do is to stop the quarrel. She has the power to do so, and she is sufficiently aware of her job as a mother to feel that this is not just a brute power but is her right, in virtue of her parental authority, and also her duty, as a parent who wants to bring up reasonably well-behaved people and not little savages. 'Awareness', here, does not of course mean that she thinks out all this. This is simply how some mothers *feel* about their jobs.

But the situation is not as simple as it seems. The purpose of her intervention is to stop the quarrel, because a quarrel is a noisy explosion of unruly emotion, and it disturbs the peace of the household in every possible sense. She wants to restore peace, and that is the real purpose of her intervention. But what is peace? On the answer she might give to this question depends the type of action she takes in exercising her authority to end the quarrel.

If the mother's notion of peace is an absence of overt strife, the matter is quite simple. This is in fact the usual definition (seldom defined, of course, in words, but rather in action) and in that case the ending of the quarrel is easy. The combatants are silenced, by the sheer weight of grown-up authority breaking through and overthrowing childish voices and childish emotions, and suppressing them. Then, if the mother is fair-minded and impartial, the paints and brushes are returned to their owner, some sort of an apology somehow extracted from both, and the girl is made to clean the paint off her dress. Some mothers would also punish the girl, or possibly both children, but this makes little difference to the essentials of the situation. What has happened is that the overt expression of emotion has been stopped, and if the family has a fairly well-established routine, and is accustomed to habitual norms of courtesy in speech and behaviour, these will carry the members of the family (including the former combatants) along with sufficient momentum through the next awkward hours, and make it difficult for the fight to break out again. Besides, the energy generated by anger has gone, there is no longer any zest for battle, only a certain awkwardness and shame, and these are quickly overlaid by the same benificent influence of custom and habitual affection. So peace is restored, everyone is friendly, and that is all that seems to be required.

This is a great deal better than the former alternative, when no one intervened at all. Both children have had to submit, but not to each other, therefore their resentment against each other is less. The sense of justice in both is to some extent satisfied ('fairness' is a very valuable source of a sense of security and peace). And although the children may resent their mother's arbitrary settlement of their difficulties, more especially if she punishes them, the very sense of being under authority is satisfactory. It lifts the burden of responsibility, harnesses for them emotions that frightened them and that they were not able to control for themselves. To some extent it frees them from the oppression of pent-up emotions by taking away the need to think about them or decide for themselves what to do about them. And in this freedom they can begin to make a new approach to each other.

But this approach can only be made by passing over the top of the emotional lava that has cooled and solidified since the eruption. The underlying causes of the quarrel, the elements of the human situation, are still present in all their potentially explosive power. A thick layer of habits of socially acceptable behaviour will make daily intercourse easy and friendly in spite of this, and it is only when this layer is broken by the impact of some new and violent emotion that the explosive elements are likely to get a second chance to come to the surface and be truly resolved. Meanwhile, there is friendliness but no real communication. There can't be, because of the antagonism and fear that still lies between the two, though they are no longer aware of it.

The assumption, here, is that all further conflicts will be dealt with in the same arbitrary manner. This is inevitably how most family quarrels have to be dealt with, but this does not mean that the lack of communication must remain total because, as I said above, the 'infiltration' method of intervention operates here, so that the actual stopping of the quarrel is in fact only one part of the total intervention. If this were not so the outlook would be depressing for busy parents with no superhuman patience or understanding. In practice we bash on with well-meaning if rough and ready responses, and succeed to a remarkable extent.

But for my present purpose it is necessary to see the effect of this kind of arbitrary, imposed ending of hostility, unmodified and 'neat'. And there are families where the total intervention is in fact of *this* kind, so that the more gradual influences *also* have the effect of keeping people separate rather than of finding ways (even undercover) of letting them meet. There may be, even so, slightly furtive 'meetings'. In moments of happiness, or of need, one may come to the other with real openness, but unless the emotion is strong enough to provoke a breaking of the barriers these meetings will be isolated and shamefaced contacts through cracks in the wall and lead to nothing more.

So, either from lack of articulation, or from real lack of contact, most human relationships are of this covered-up kind most of the time. This is the only kind of peace we normally know, and we expect no more than this peace that the world, when it is working efficiently, is well able to give.

The type of intervention so far described is based on a concept of peace as the cessation of hostilities, so that the daily work of human society may continue.

But it often happens that the person who has to stop a quarrel has a different notion of what peace is. If this person is, as in my example, the children's mother, the chances are she doesn't think about it as 'peace'—in fact doesn't think about it at all—but has the sort of 'feel' for the quality of human relationships that corresponds with what a Christian means by peace.

B

A mother with this kind of 'feel' uses her authority, as before, to make the children stop shouting at each other and pummelling and scratching each other. Even while she is being informed, repeatedly, loudly, and in two conflicting versions, about the occasion of the quarrel, she has a sense that much more is involved than the illicit borrowing of another's property. She knows, consciously or not, that this release of emotion is a challenge and an opportunity.

Things have come to the surface that are not normally seen. This is a nuisance, but also useful. It is not enough that the situation should return to what it was before the quarrel blew up, if indeed this were possible—and I have tried to show, above, that it is not possible.

Such an insight into the demands of the situation does not mean that the mother, the person in authority, must have detailed conscious knowledge of the underlying causes of each child's behaviour. I have sketched these causes here, in order to make clear how deep and far-reaching are the roots of human behaviour when it explodes into sudden action, but it is not necessary that they should be known in this way. It is only necessary that the mother should feel herself involved in the whole developing personality of each child, in his or her deepest longings and fears and hopes.

Their mother, then, will not need to go in for a lengthy Freudian delving, trying to uncover the past. She will take this past as her material, and look forward instead. She wants to help the little girl to see how important to him her brother's painting is, how he is discovering a world which is her world, too, and how she can help him by her interest, and herself learn and discover with him, by respecting his need, so that he may be able to accept her interest.

This is what, somehow, is achieved. It is done by actions rather than words—words of *this* kind not being relevant to most women in a hurry to get tea ready. But if words are not necessary to describe the inwardness of the situation, there are plenty of words that are available and relevant, words that make a bond between mother and daughter, from which security the child can view her brother with sympathy, because she no longer feels threatened. From this security she can begin to look at his pictures (literally, and metaphorically) with interest and even admiration. Once the child's imagination and sympathy are caught, some of the barriers to communication are already down. Then, in parallel with the new awareness of her brother as a person to be loved, the little girl can be helped in her own need to discover, in her own feminine and active way. Maybe more suitable paints can be bought tomorrow, and perhaps her brother will help her to redecorate the doll's house. Whatever happens, the little girl is able, now, to accept both herself and her brother. She is likely to show this by being busy about something with her mother—making biscuits, or laying the table.

The boy, older and more introverted, is more deeply wounded by his own actions and words. He is frightened by the strength of the power he has let loose. He is old enough to realize that his painting materials are not sufficiently important to merit such a violent reaction, but he is not aware of all the underlying emotions that added themselves to his resentment. There is in such a case no need that he should be aware. (In other, more extreme, cases awareness might help, and may sometimes be absolutely necessary.) He can be helped to realize that there is a power in him which he does not understand and to which he cannot dictate, but which can be used for good as well as for evil. It could have been used to make a picture, it can be used to make all kinds of things, and above all to make a new relationship between himself and other people. Just now, this means his sister. He is old enough to realize how strong was her need for the paints, and how her youth and her impulsive nature make it almost impossible for her to act more sensibly in accomplishing her urgent desires. He can begin to see that his need for solitude and self-discovery are legitimate, and that he need not be ashamed to want them, but that they are not incompatible with his sister's need for his friendship and guidance and practical help. A certain amount of his own time and privacy and convenience must be sacrificed, but he will gain, not lose, by the sacrifice. All this, as with the little girl, comes about without any of the elaborate explanations I have used to make clear what is happening. It comes about because he, too, is set free from his fear by the assurance of love. The transference of energy happens, the increased ability to be generous happens, just because he now knows he is loved.

This understanding of themselves and each other that the children gain can remove some of the barriers that they have erected against each other. Some of the suspicion and fear have gone. Not all, of course—they go too deep for that—but enough to enable these two people to see each other and recognize each other. This kind of recognition is not just 'knowing about', it is real knowing. There is, at this point, a true human encounter.

At this moment then, something new happens. It is not something that the mother can bring about; all she can do is help each child to lower the barriers. It is not something that either child can bring about, because left alone neither can even lower the barriers, but must depend on outside influence, past or present, to make this possible. What happens is not in one or other, but is both in and between them, is an activity, a joining, a current. It is a being-together, but it is not an essence in the sense of static components of each one that are somehow combined. It is something that can only occur in the exchange, in relationship, and can only flow from an authentic decision in the face of the demand of that relationship. It is the essential human thing and yet it is something that, as the situation shows, is difficult to elicit and cannot be made to order.

In this moment, when conscious human effort has prepared the way, there comes into being that which actually makes up each one's decision, and yet does not act except by this free decision. This activity is love, the traffic of man's essential self which is his spirit.

What follows? The decision of love, the moment of pure

knowledge in the spirit, produces characteristic results. The children may apologize to each other, if that is the way they have been taught to behave, but in any case now an apology seems almost superfluous, because the bitterness has completely gone. (But an apology satisfies them, because it is good to put into words their rejection of their failure of love.) They are truly ashamed of what happened, but their shame is not a burden to them, but has become the material of a new relationship, a closer and happier one. Both will want to do something for the other, to show that the repentance is real and heartfelt. If the boy offers to help his sister to decorate her doll's house next day it will not be from a need to satisfy the demands of justice, or to ensure his own subsequent privacy, but purely as a gesture of love. If the girl is careful to leave her brother in peace until teatime it will not be out of deference to his right to privacy, or out of fear of further anger, but purely as a gesture of love. When they meet at tea they will discover a new pleasure in each other's company, and also in the company of the other members of the family. There is a new bond between them, which is a secret conspiracy of love, for they cannot express it, even to themselves. It is a secret they share, but whose influence spreads outwards to the others with whom they share their meal and their lives. So there is a new state of affairs not only between the two children but between them and their brothers and sisters and their parents. This new state of affairs is peace and it grows directly out of the decision of love, which is the act of the spirit in man.

All sorts of things could prevent the outcome I have described, and in any case there will always be more quarrels, and their solution can never be perfect. My example is not a model for parents, who already have enough people trying to make them feel guilty, but a microcosm in which the elements of all human conflict can be seen at work.

The 'flashpoint' of decision is the moment when formation gives way to transformation. But the two have nothing in common at all, they do not even meet. Without the long process of formation there could be no transformation, yet no amount of careful formation can transform. Transformation is a timeless point of decision, yet it can only operate in the personality formed through time-conditioned stages of development, and its effects can only be worked out in terms of that formation.

The occurrence of the point of transformation can be called the salvation event, and in my example this occurrence clearly depends on the mother's success in reaching the 'spiritual' reality of the two children and communicating with it. This communication, then, is her giving of love, her personal decision of self-surrender. Whether she makes this gift of herself will depend on the way in which she has learned to think of herself as a mother. Are the children for her, or she for the children? Are her household tasks, her sense of achievement as a housewife, so important to her that a serious upsetting of her achievement, as represented by the quarrel, seems a real threat to her personal integrity? If so, has she acquired sufficient inner security of being, herself, loved to ignore and tread down this fear, to go out from herself in response to her children's need for her love? Unless her own formation has taught her to think of herself as primarily at the service of her children, spiritually as well as physically, she will not have the kind of 'feel' for the situation that makes possible the lowering of barriers, so that the communication of love can take place.

There is even more to the situation than this. It is possible for the mother to tackle the situation in very much the way I have described it, simply because her knowledge of psychology has taught her that this is the constructive and sensible method of dealing with it. If her personal formation has given her a strong sense of duty and of self-respect, these may overcome any incidental reluctance or irritation at the interruption of her own work. She will deal with the quarrel carefully and conscientiously, along the lines I have indicated, but for her there will be no decision of love, no real self-giving, no transformation. It may well be that in the process of carrying out this plan the power of love will find an opportunity because her efforts to achieve the desired result have brought her 'nearer' to the children than she actually intended to get. In that case the situation may be transformed, as it were, accidentally. But if it is not, if she goes through the whole process of reconditioning her children's minds simply as a duty, as due to herself as mother, or to God as ruler, then the chances are that reconditioning is all she will achieve. She will succeed in the more civilized formation of her children's minds, but she will not communicate to them her own spirit, and so help them to overcome their own fears and leap to life in response to the demand for decision. So the two children may be persuaded to behave in the outward ways I have described, but they will do so in relation to ideals of fairness, order, and enlightened self-interest, not in response to love. There will be no meeting, no transformation, only a better formation. This is perhaps part of the reason why rather muddly, inefficient, and quarrelsome families often seem to have more real unity and warmth than families in which the parents are better informed, more self-controlled.

Assuming, next, that the mother does bring to her children a real gift of herself, there is still a long way to go. Her success in reaching each child, in achieving a communication that will enable the children to reach each other, will depend on the kind of formation *they* have had. The kind of effort at bringing about a reconciliation that I have described fails, over and over again, because the estranged people are too closely wrapped in their fears and hatreds for the message of love to reach them. If the boy in my example had been, for instance, frequently ignored or bullied by his father, who made a favourite of the little girl, the resentment against her would probably have been much too strong to be broken down by one appeal, however loving. It would have taken a long time and perhaps the experience of adult love over a long period, to penetrate the armour this would have *had* to create, in order to protect him from consciousness of unbearable hurt. Or again, if the boy had been much petted and indulged, and taught to regard his talents and his wishes as the most important thing in life, his sister's attack on his privacy would have seemed so monstrous as to be almost unforgivable. His mother might, possibly, succeed in getting through to him, but her appeal would meet with very strong resistance because it would seem inconsistent with the priorities which had become embedded in his consciousness of life. Her appeal would have to contend not only with a natural reluctance to abandon a strong position of being in the right but with a certain moral revulsion, as if she were asking him to do something unethical, for the sake of peace. And the same sort of psychological blocks, varied according to her differing temperament, would operate in the case of the girl.

But these examples of the effect of formation in relation to the salvation opportunity have been conceived as the results of a formation which is clearly opposed to the lowering of barriers, and therefore to the communication of love. What about formation which is directed *to* the service of love? In discussing the mother's difficulties, I mentioned the type of formation in which self-respect can take over the functions of love. This is the kind of appalling deceit that made St Paul say, on the one hand, that the Law was spiritual—that is, directed to spiritual ends—and on the other, that it led to death. A person can carry out the works of the Law, in all conscientiousness and convinced (quite rightly) that the Law is of God, and is spiritual, and meant to give life. And yet such a person will be deceived and deceiving, headed for death, enclosed by sin.

This is the dilemma. A good formation, according to a sound customary and moral Law, is necessary if a person is to be able to respond to the demand for the decision to love. Yet if this formation is really good and really thorough it may, just because it is good, prevent the person from being aware of the need for repentance and decision. No need for repentance will appear, therefore no change of heart, no transformation, will be possible.

In my example, the two children came to a new life, a new experience of relationship, because they had sinned. There is no doubt about the sin—what they did was wrong. There is no doubt about the result—what came out of it was good. And there is little doubt that without the wrong the good would not have happened. The good formation they had been given broke down, and in that breaking down a power was released that was much more real, nearer to the 'heart' of each, than the good behaviour that went before. Yet, if there had not been good formation, directed to the ends of love, the power so released would have been merely destructive. The release of power was the opportunity for love, yet the opportunity could not have been taken unless there had been *both* the intervention of love-with-authority, from outside, *and* the good formation of each child that acted to ensure that the barriers to love were not insuperable.

Here are the two related but contradictory facts about the relation between formation and transformation. Formation, according to a law which is holy and just and good, is necessary if man is to live. Yet, in practice, if its influence is unbroken, it leads not to life but to death of love by asphyxiation. Transformation therefore can only occur when formation breaks down, and this often happens because people break the law, because they sin. Yet nobody could say that love is the result of sin, for sin is disorder and separation and nonsense, and love shows itself as peace and unity and lucid sense.

This is the paradox that St Paul wrestled with, and it is one whose elements we can observe any time we take the trouble to look at ourselves or other people, or read any kind of novel that is about real people. It is the paradox that has produced the division discussed in the introduction.

This paradox cannot be resolved in the sense that we can somehow discover it to be illusory, a result of misunderstanding the situation. The attempt to resolve it in this way is precisely what has led to the division in the Christian consciousness, which itself reflects a fundamental division in types of awareness of life. On the one hand there is the stress on formation, to such an extent that transformation (if admitted at all) can only seem an occurrence so entirely hidden and mysterious that there is nothing we can or need do about it except believe that it happens. On the other hand there is the stress on transformation, to an extent that makes consistency and continuity in formation seem irrelevant and even wicked, a sort of betrayal of the gospel of personal truth. Neither of these types of awareness is encountered 'pure', but both are strong enough in their own spheres to colour a whole culture. Two such cultures, side by side, can be seen in Europe of the nineteenth century, for instance, when respectability and civilized behaviour seemed absolute as ideals of the good life to some, while others saw value only in the anarchy of the artist, the autonomous romantic hero. In our time the former view is giving way to the latter, as I suggested in my introduction, and the Christian trend reflects in more precise form the change of awareness in Western culture as a whole.

But Catholicism, if it is to be true to itself, cannot simply swing with the pendulum, but must also struggle to see both ends of the arc, and the point of suspension. A feeling that this is important is responsible for a great deal of agonized tension among Catholics, and makes many people pull hard against the trend of existentialist thinking. For Catholicism is a tradition, it is a continuing thing embodied in an organization, it has a history. And to deny the tradition, the continuity, the history, would be to deny the very thing that has made it possible for the unique personal decision, the timeless act of love, to occur at all. In practice it is next to impossible to hold the two parts of the paradox in balance, and give both their due. In practice, that is, for the individual. But the Christian thing is precisely not a happening to an individual, but a sharing, by each individual, in something which is bigger than himself and which yet makes him, in his decision, most himself. Therefore the body in which this sharing is done must be able to contain the paradox and constantly try to express it, knowing that the attempt can never be more than partially successful.

If the pathetically familiar little example of human behaviour that I have described has some validity as typical, then it must not only display the paradox in intelligible personal terms. It should also be able in analysis to display those elements of the whole human situation which are involved in this divisive paradox, and so perhaps make possible a synthesis which respects the total separateness of formation and transformation, and yet devalues neither.

In order to discover more deeply and precisely the elements displayed in the conflict-situation I have described they need to be isolated, and re-presented in the form of some human event which is shaped more particularly by one element, although the others, I hope to show, are also present. But before describing what I think are broadly the human constituents of the situation as a whole I want to notice something about the psychological *results* of the solution of the conflict in the way I have described.

I have described the final result as peace, and it is the Christian notion of peace—a dynamic participation, a life, rather than a mere absence of strife. But in the traffic of love as it is given and received in the peace of Christ, human beings are affected in two ways that seem to be contradictory, and are oddly parallel to (but not the same as) the contradiction between formation and transformation. The two children in my example emerge from conflict into peace, and both come thereby to a greater knowledge of themselves. They are more aware of their true nature, and of what separates them from each other—the difference, the selfness from within which they approach the outside world. It is not in the conflict itself that they come to this knowledge, for as long as they are actually quarrelling they are refusing to know either themselves or each other, but are only defending themselves and attacking each other. Their energies and desires are contained within the terms of their limited aim. (A fencer's attention is totally involved in covering himself and in looking for a weakened guard in his opponent through which he may break. He does not think of himself except as a thing, to be defended, and of his opponent, also as a thing, to be pierced.) It is only when they have been drawn into repentance and reconciliation that they can achieve the self-awareness of humility. Real knowledge of oneself is something that people can only dare to accept when love has broken through. Without love, self-knowledge must be rejected because it weakens the defences against the outside world. When it cannot be so rejected it is contained, held, encapsulated in a stoic despair, or gloated over in its containment like some repulsive but fascinating animal. If the boy in my example were to know and acknowledge his fears and his secret longings, when he was still shut off by resentment, it would be too painful, too disarming a knowledge. He could not bear it. But in the light of love self-knowledge is bearable, even welcome. So one of the effects of reconciliation is greater individuation, a more complete awareness of oneself as distinct, yet not cut off.

But the other effect is a greater degree of communication, and it occurs in the same movement, for the same reasons, as the increased self-knowledge. The distinguished self is able to give itself. Its defences are lowered, there is a meeting, and this meeting could not have occurred without the awareness of being distinct. But it is a particular kind of distinctness, an unafraid and clearsighted self-awareness; it is not the withdrawal of pride that defends the beleaguered citadel but the confidence of being valued that makes openness possible without fear. This paradox, that love grows with growing individuation, and that self-awareness as separate is the prerequisite of self-giving in love, is related to the other paradox which has yet to be resolved, that of formation and transformation.

The typical human conflict-situation with which I began contains all the elements that make up the ideas that come to us labelled sin, law, grace, flesh, spirit. In order to discover how they are related to actual experience, and to each other, I shall draw out of this theologically charged situation four ideas that can be further studied and perhaps illuminate better the notions of formation and transformation. These four are contained in the whole event, not merely in its solution, and they are: encounter, self-discovery, the release of power, and community.

In my example, the idea of encounter is obvious. The complex psychological interplay of events and people and characters that has formed the minds and hearts of the two children is like a sort of undifferentiated, half-cooked emotional soup. They don't know what it all means, they aren't using most of it at all. The encounter between them helps to 'cook' the ingredients. The children aren't consciously aware, any more than they were before, of the separate influences that have made them feel like this, but somehow an integrating process occurs, and it does so because two different temperaments clash—and it is the difference that matters. It is the otherness, the irritant effect, the alien and even threatening nature of the temperamental and physical being that is not known, is not one's own, that produces the integrating and self-discovering effect. Violent emotions are brought into play and are *felt*. All these felt things are felt in relation to the alien qualities and emotions in the other, and this is what clarifies them. So encounter seems to contain the idea of conflict, with which I began, though exactly how remains to be seen. And encounter leads to self-discovery.

The element in the conflict situation which I have called the release of power is not so much another part of the whole process as another way of thinking of the development as a whole. Something is let loose, and this something is in fact the agent of self-discovery, but that is only part of the movement. The movement is continued in the other result of resolving the situation, which is community. But the release of power works throughout the situation, not just in its result, and indeed it does not operate in the same way in the result. In fact it structures the whole situation, though it is not the only factor determining the outcome.

All these four elements are to be found in some measure in all the endless permutations of human relationships, from the most fleeting and ordinary to the most permanent, far-reaching or exotic. But in order to find out more about them I have chosen particular kinds of experience which show each one especially clearly. The idea of encounter seems likely to be discovered most fully in that dangerous and potentially life-changing encounter, the sexual one. Self-discovery is seen in its most dramatic and typical form in the experience of conversion. The less easily grasped but essential notion of the release of power in human relationship can be seen by studying prophetic inspiration, when a man is seized by some power that seems to him to be greater than himself.

The vaguest, most difficult, most familiar and most important idea of all is that of community. It contains all the others, and if it doesn't it is a sham. It is in this experience, if it is a valid one, that the solution of the paradox must lie if it is to be found at all. And yet the community experience I have chosen as my example is the most ordinary and un-exciting of all—it is a family, an ordinary family, gathered to discuss some common problem. We certainly have a problem. Perhaps the family can point out the way in which its solution may be possible.

ENCOUNTER

THE example of encounter I have chosen for description and analysis is that most intimate and far-reaching of all human encounters, the sexual one. There is, of course, no such thing as a purely sexual relationship, for the desires and hopes and fears that shape it are as various and apparently irrelevant as those that, in my first example, influenced the course of the children's quarrel. It might even seem that the most complete and typical of sexual relationships, the married one, showed the sexual encounter in its least 'pure' form, just because it is a whole way of life and not just a series of sexual incidents. It is partly because of a vague notion that marriage is, in some way, an adulteration of sex, or simply an optional extra to go with it, that the climate of moral feeling in this generation makes it hard even for Christians to see marriage as the fulfilment of something that extra-marital sex can only grope for. Marriage appears rather as the legalization of a situation that could exist just as well without it, other things being equal.

It is because of this climate of feeling about marriage that I have chosen to describe a relationship that has such an attitude as its background. I have tried to describe the way two people, in a non-Christian situation which involves this negative view of marriage, work out their encounter, and it is a saving one, although one limited in its effects insofar as it is *not* married in the full and Christian sense. This seems to offer a better chance of seeing why in fact *marriage* has to do with salvation, and provides for a sexual encounter which is salvific. The sexual encounter, though thoroughly mixed in with other elements, is most

fully itself, therefore most fully salvific, when it is made in this
setting, but only if *marriage* is understood as salvific. And usually
it is not. It is by seeing the sexual encounter striving to achieve
its full stature that we may be able to see that it *can* be a saving
encounter, and that this is most likely to be so in marriage, properly understood.

The two people concerned in my imaginary example are not
young people in the throes of their first experience of sex. The
woman is twenty-five, and is still living in her parents' home.
Her father is dead, but her mother is still comparatively young,
and does not make demands on her as a nurse or housekeeper.
But there are a younger brother and sister, still at school, and as
often happens these children have assumed an importance in the
family that the elder daughter never had. For one thing this
elder daughter is not pretty, whereas the younger one is, and for
another the elder daughter was born at a time when the parents
were separated by war service, and the mother had a struggle to
carry on alone, tied by the baby when her energetic nature drove
her to carry on a career. She resented the rather sickly baby (and
anyway wanted it to be a boy) and her resentment grew, later,
into a tolerant contempt for a girl less attractive, less intelligent
and less vital than herself. The birth, ten years later, of a son
confirmed the daughter's lowly status in the family. Finally a
pretty bright little girl with unlimited health and energy deprived
the older sister of what family prestige she had so far retained
as the only daughter.

A few years later the death of the father left the family short of
money, and the small income provided by a pension and insurance had to be supplemented in any way possible. It was taken
for granted by everyone, including herself, that the elder
daughter, just starting work in the offices of a big store, should
devote her wages to supporting her family. She has done so ever
since. Since she shares her mother's estimate of the value and
needs of her brother and sister there is very little left to spend on

herself. Indeed she has no desire to do so, for she is devoted to her family and never questions her own status within it. If other girls in the office sympathize because her clothes are dull but serviceable and she scarcely ever goes out, she smiles vaguely and replies that she is very happy, and that she isn't the gay sort. Both of which remarks are perfectly true, as long as she has a rather limited notion of happiness. She has never thought much about getting married—not, that is, as a real personal option. She has thought cloudily that she might, sometime, and her mother has often told her loudly that she ought to 'marry and have a home of your own', but she has sufficient shrewdness, under her surface of stupidity, to know very well that remarks like this are merely meant to quiet her mother's own occasionally unquiet conscience by assuring it that she is not *really* keeping her daughter from having a home of her own. But since the daughter has no desire for a home of her own she can afford to understand and good-humouredly ignore these remarks. She has, up to the time I am describing, so completely accepted her position as the despised yet necessary elder daughter that she has no resentment whatever. Her own estimate of herself agrees with her mother's.

She does not notice, any more than her mother does, the contradiction between this notion of herself and the facts of her career. For she has been promoted to an important job in the buying department, a position where judgment and flair are necessary, and an ability to take risks and make decisions without too many hesitations or post-mortem doubts. Her job takes her to other towns now, and she meets more people, wears better clothes. But when she comes home she slips into her usual position there, and finds no difficulty in doing so.

It is because of her rise in the firm she works for that she is present at an office party at which the doctor employed by the store is also present. He is the other part of my couple.

He is not married and doesn't want to be, since his medical career is deeply satisfying to him and absorbs most of his emotional and spiritual energies. He is doing well at it and is trusted

and relied on by his patients. His intelligence and gifts have taken
him right out of his home background, which was narrow and conventional, but really and humanly good and loving—a fact which
he recognizes, and which (though he does not know this) makes
it much more difficult for him to realize the extent to which he is
in revolt against it. For the need to get away from it and the need
not to deny it—because of its essential human soundness—are at
war in him, and remain unresolved because unacknowledged and
unacknowledgable. Domesticity secretly revolts him, while he
consciously respects and admires it; consequently he devotes himself to his work, finding in it a great measure of emotional satisfaction. But since he cannot recognize fully the roots of his devotion to his patients, neither can he fully release into his work the
passionate dedication that is part of his nature. It never quite
happens, and he is used to this, and to his reflex withdrawals from
certain kinds of emotional challenge. The unused passion makes
itself evident only in a childish tendency to show off, and in epi-
sodes of violent and irrational anger when someone flicks a sensitive
spot—when another's weakness, need for love, or good-natured
physical 'bonhomie' somehow touches the surface of the suppressed emotions connected with sex and family life, which he
feels as one all-too-cosy, stifling and deadening whole.

It is therefore not as surprising as it seems that he is attracted,
at the party, to a girl who is totally uninterested in men, and has
made no attempt to charm him. She is not shy, because she has
accepted her position, and she is interested in his work because
she has no particular desire to draw attention to her own. But
her comments are quick and shrewd, and as their conversation develops he discovers that she is both intelligent and sensitive, though ill-educated. And when his questions draw from her
a brief but honest picture of her home background his interest
is quickened by a compassion she would be surprised to know
about.

A week or so later he calls in at her office and asks her to go
out with him. She accepts, and before long it has become a habit

for them to go out occasionally, to a film, or into the country on a Saturday, or just out to supper together. The girl's mother is slightly caustic, but she cannot admit even to herself that she does not want her daughter to have any·real friendship lest her subjection should begin to seem unjust. So she confines herself to teasing and mildly malicious comments.

It is this reaction that first makes the girl realize how much she values her new friendship, for she finds herself resentful of her mother's remarks and inclined for the first time to compare the way her mother treats her with the way someone else does. Next time she goes out with him she is much more aware of her enjoyment of his company, is taking it less for granted. She is beginning to see him as more than an interesting person, for now she sees him as a person in relation to herself. She watches him as he watches her, listens to his reaction to what she says, is suddenly aware, now, of herself in a new way.

And he sees this new awareness in her, sees it as a sort of melting and flowering, both at once. She is both intensely conscious of him in relation to herself, yet quite unconscious of herself except as responsive to him, and the combination is entrancing. She has made it clear, often, that she regards herself as totally committed to her family, at least until the children are grown up, and this is the reason why he has been able to go so far in the relationship. His mind never puts her in the area labelled 'marriage', but since this exclusion is quite unconscious he has never had to face the fact that she is not, objectively, unmarriagable. Indeed he is not aware of the reason for his own unwillingness to marry, and still attributes it to his devotion to his work. So this girl is no threat to his rejection of domesticity, and he can respond to her as he has never responded to a woman before.

The outcome of this relationship is entirely foreseeable to anyone observing it from outside, but the two concerned in it are unaware of what is happening. They both have settled ideas about what they are and what they will be. Both are completely committed to their responsibilities, and the strength of this commitment is the strength of a deep need for some sense of meaning and purpose in life. So these commitments seem to them unshakable and eternal. Both have rejected marriage as a real possibility, without quite facing the fact, and both, also, have definite though not much considered moral principles about sex outside marriage. These are not so much due to specifically religious notions, though both are vaguely Christian, as to a need to consolidate their chosen position as a meaningful one by rejecting anything that might undermine their self-respect.

But the relationship is developing, and inevitably becoming more consciously thought about by both. One evening the girl is kept at home when her mother has 'flu, and they miss an evening together. The degree of disappointment this causes them surprises them both, and makes them begin seriously to question their feelings.

Then begins a period of curious semi-estrangement. Both are more and more aware of the strength of their own feelings, but neither is sure what the other's feelings are. They are wary of each other, and afraid that a false move may destroy the fabric of mutual understanding that they have created. Both of them now realize its enormous importance to themselves, but the degree of importance each has in the other's life is still obscure. So they both are very anxious not to do anything that might let the other suppose that more was expected than was intended, or that more significance is attached to a particular action than appears on the most superficial assessment. So, for instance, when he asks her to have supper in his exceedingly shabby and spartan bachelor flat, after a film, she says 'yes' because to say 'no' might make him think that she thought he might make love to her. And he accepts her 'yes', and in fact does no more than make supper and conversation with her, but he wonders whether she might think that he thought she had said 'yes' with the hope of being made love to. He wonders whether she is offended or relieved. And in fact he does know, now, that he wants her sexually, but he has no intention of saying so or of doing anything about it, in fact he is fed up with himself for feeling like this, and rather angry with her.

She hasn't thought seriously about the possibility that it might turn into a love-affair. She has thought of it as an objective possibility, not being totally ignorant, but the idea isn't real to her. Her devotion to him is a whole thing that she has not analysed at all, but she still does not know how he feels. Once she did consider the relationship as a sexual one she would have to face a totally new situation.

Sooner or later, however, the nature of their feeling for each other is bound to become more apparent, for no relationship stands still and the only way to avoid a clearer definition would be to withdraw from each other, a course which neither can bear even to consider.

The whole future of the relationship turns on what happens after their feelings are first allowed to become explicit.

But it can happen that they never do. A truly moral act is a personal, conscious decision. If the moral formation of either has been of the kind that produces strong reflex reactions to certain stimuli, rather than a personal decision, the challenge of the situation may bring these reactions into play. If either of the two poses to himself or herself the conscious question: shall I commit this *sin*? then the question must be answered in the terms which the word sin demands and implies. But if the 'moral' reflexes are so strong as to make personal decision scarcely necessary then the answer will be implicit in asking the question at all, and it will be 'no'. This answer is dictated by early training and is not, therefore, a fully moral act. But if the reflexes are not strong, or if some previous crisis of personal development has destroyed the power of suggestion inherent in the form of the question, then the question will provoke a conflict and a need for decision. A decision taken at this stage, and in this form, is a fully moral decision, but it is one whose material is incomplete. Neither the man nor the woman knows, at this moment, what is involved in their desire for each other, why, that is, they have this strong need for each other. Therefore if one or other, realizing that they are on the brink of an immoral act, decides to bring the relationship to an end at this point, they are doing what is right, from one point of view, but they are also foregoing (of course without knowing it) the chance of discovering that in themselves which drew them together. The area of the personality of each that is still unused and demanding to be used will remain unused and potentially explosive. There is always the possibility that it may be brought into play at some other time, by some other means, but this is in fact a little less likely now, because of the moral effort involved in deciding to terminate the relationship. The pain and humiliation involved may make them cautious of any emotional involvement. On the other hand, a challenge to decision that does succeed will probably be more violent and go deeper because of the greater resistance that had to be overcome. If the situation is simply arrested something remains undeveloped, unused. It may often be right and necessary to arrest it, but this is what happens.

In this imaginary case, as I have described it so far, the termination of the relationship in this way is equivalent to the ending of the children's quarrel by the simple assertion of parental authority, so that the conflict is stopped but not resolved. The intervention in the case of the grown-up situation is an interior one, as the moral formation of one or other asserts its influence. The same effect could come about through the direct influence of a third person, at the time, but this does not alter the character of the intervention. It acts from outside the situation itself although, as in the case of the quarrel, it is to some extent involved in the sense that the moral formation of these two people is part of them, and therefore part of the material of which the situation is made.

But there is a difference in the two cases. In the case of the children the fully explosive encounter had already taken place when the intervention occurred. If it had not there would have been no occasion for intervention of any kind, for the children were totally unaware of the hidden energies waiting to be released. The two grown-ups, however, do know to some extent what is involved, and are able to be afraid of it, and therefore to stop it before an actual explosion occurs. Therefore in their case there is a possibility (in practice a rather remote one) that they will be sufficiently aware of what is at stake to realize that it is not enough to arrest the relationship, but that the potentialities which it offered to release must, somehow, be used. The situation, in fact, is one requiring marriage as its full resolution, in the normal way. But in these two there is a strong tendency against marriage, because they don't see it as the resolution of their encounter, a way to freedom in love, but rather—at least for the man—as a restriction, an end to love. The girl would probably learn more easily to see the kind of relationship that is needed, and even that marriage is this kind of relationship, though she has not before seen marriage, as a fact, in this light. But she is at this time learning her life through the man, so she does not see it like this. So they go on, groping for the relationship they need, not severing it, since no clear moral issue presents itself, and not able to resolve the mounting conflict because they can't see clearly enough. But the nature of their need for each other has a dynamism of its own, and carries them on, as if, without their knowing it, the self of each were forcing them to provide for the discovery of that self. Something has to break through, eventually.

The flashpoint occurs during the next stage of the relationship. If the couple's moral ideas are either fairly vague to begin with, or rendered shaky by the emotion which they are suffering, it is most likely that they will continue to see each other and to do so alone, whenever possible. This will be made easier for them by a certain intellectual confusion that commonly accompanies the awakening of any strong emotion. This seems to happen because the emotion, which is not fully understood, contains implicitly many new challenges with which the usual intellectual apprehension of moral issues has not been accustomed to deal. Therefore the consequence of seeing each other often is not really faced.

So it happens that after a few weeks an evening comes when the two have had supper together in his flat, and have been talking about a novel he had given her to read. (The way she responds to ideas that he tries out on her is an increasing delight to him because her reactions are never stereotyped, but compounded of ignorance, sensibility and a surprised and entranced interest in so many new mental experiences.) As she answers a question she looks up from where she is half-kneeling, by the fire, and her rather plain face is lit by her enthusiasm, so that its features are invisible, but he is only aware of a whole person gathered to a point and, at that point, totally unguarded. And he bends down and kisses her, putting one hand under her head in a gesture that is both tender and tentative.

The effect of this slight physical contact is to alter the whole colour of the relationship. They are dazed by their discovery, wrapped in a numinous mist that makes it almost impossible to be aware of the particular significance of anything they do or say, because self-consciousness is drowned in a self-awareness which is acute but undifferentiated. The man knows, with a part of his mind, the full implication of what he is doing and where it might lead, but it is a purely intellectual knowledge. Not only does it not occupy his attention but it is so detached from his emotions that the threat to his peace of mind which it involves is not even recognized by his feelings at this stage. The experience is so direct and immediately personal that it rings none of the bells in him that have usually chimed warningly at any risk of involvement with a woman. This is 'different'—the cliché of lovers, which is in fact sober truth, even if it happens more than once in a lifetime. It is 'different' in that it is an experience of another person that by-passes all the usual thoughts about and reactions to other people, even sexual reactions. It is a total awareness of another whole, there are no parts to be examined or assessed or compared with other experiences. It is this wholeness of the experience that gives it its special character, the character which *can* make it a saving one.

But this, that makes real 'falling-in-love' important, also makes it dangerous. The very wholeness of the experience makes it impossible, for the time, to relate it to anything else. It is this that makes it so hard for those who are not in love to understand the lover's indifference to morality or public opinion or even personal safety. It is this that makes lovers so impatient of any attempts to judge their action by any other standard than that of service to their love, or to defend any course of action that seems to conflict with the needs of love. The degree to which people in love are thus indifferent to external values varies enormously with temperament and education and age. The 'area' of personality which is engaged by the relationship may not be as great in those bound by older loyalties, habits and standards, and in that case the new love will give way, or adapt itself, to the requirements of the existing situation fairly soon.

But in my example the two are people who have a great deal of unused personality. There is more to both of them than they or anyone else suspects. Therefore the new experience is for them quite overwhelming. They are almost afraid to say anything or do anything that would define what is happening. They have a sense that to ask and answer questions might be to lose what they have found, as Psyche lost Cupid.

For although the language of a relationship expresses it, and is therefore necessary if it is to know itself and grow, it also limits it, ties it down. Something essential is gained by the use of a language to express the nature of what has happened, the salvation event, but something also is lost. So in the days that follow each of them is almost, but not quite, consciously keeping out of mind the likely progression of a relationship that is now recognizably sexual. There is indeed enough to live on, and in, without looking forward.

For the time being the luminous though undifferentiated knowledge which they share blots out every other consideration. The sense of freedom, of exaltation, of having almost discovered the secret of the universe, is so intense that ordinary concerns and loyalties seem drained of colour, without definition or meaning, irritating interruptions to the one vital concern, which is to know, to discover, to enter the new world to which each is the other's gateway. This remains true even though both continue to carry out their duties with the greatest devotion, indeed with an increased devotion, because of the release of spiritual energy that has occurred.

But the relationship is now going forward under the momentum of the sexual feelings they have released. The man is much more aware of exactly what he is about, but even for him the specifically sexual is so completely mixed-up with the whole personal discovery that he can ignore all his usual reluctances. The overcoming of them even adds an extra punch to his pursuit of love. Formerly his relations with women kept a fair balance between curiosity and fear, so that nothing much happened at all. This time the fear merely makes it necessary to keep facing forward and refusing to look out of the corner of one's eye.

When a relationship reaches this stage it is normal for the couple to realize that what they want is marriage. It is what they really do want even if they don't know it, because they need something whole, something that satisfies the need to give entirely. The desire to get married when there is real understanding of what marriage is about is not, for people who are really in love, just a way of tidying up the relationship socially. It answers to the need for a certain recklessness in giving which is characteristic of people in love. And even though the long working-out of marriage may show little that is obviously adventurous, the desire to enter into a relationship which is total and legal and (at least in intention) permanent certainly does have a recklessness about it that is practically lunatic, seeing how much is being taken on trust. But it is just this risking of oneself, with no safety clauses inserted, that is satisfying to people in the grip of passion. It is only when marriage has come to appear to be the safe thing, the self-protecting thing, that it becomes repugnant, and this is presumably one reason why marriage was regarded with distaste by the tradition of chivalry.

Marriage has had a bad press, romantically—using the word to refer to that same ancient tradition. Without delving into the historical reason for this state of affairs it is clear that nowadays there is, side by side with a new realization of marriage as indeed the answer to the need for risk, a habit of regarding it as a watering-down of passion. And indeed for many it is, just because that is how they think about it.

The marriages of parents naturally have a great influence on the children's notion of what marriage is like, and the couple I have described are not uncommon in this respect. A disillusion about marriage as an institution, based on one's parents' marriages, can and does modify or even cancel out the 'natural' tendency to look to marriage for the most complete form of mutual self-giving available. The marriages of the older generation always, anyway, look rather staid and stuffy, but in *this* generation there is among younger people a strong and *conscious* desire for risk and reckless commitment that is much more than the normal contempt for the caution of older people. And in a world that seems likely to have no future to speak of there is a need to feel one is facing facts by refusing to bank on the future. This means that the need for recklessness requires an explicitly short-term commitment, not because that gives one a way out, but because to look further seems like the cultivation of a comforting illusion of security. For this reason marriage as an institution does not appear to have much to offer to this need. It becomes simply a legal convenience, not morally meaningful.

In the case of this imaginary couple, the influences against marriage as the desirable way ahead are very great, both from their family background and the general ethos of the time, so it would be strange if they found their solution in it in any clear or obvious way. It is far more likely that, in their happy but bewildered and rather apprehensive state of mind, their need for reassurance and continuity in the relationship will lead them to consummate it without seriously considering the possibility of marriage. But this step, which they take without really facing up to the issues involved, inevitably changes the character of the relationship.

Once they have taken the steps of consummating their love there is an immediate need, for both of them, to make it appear to themselves that this is quite normal. For the main need of both is to *continue* the relationship, and both are vaguely aware that they are now facing far more complex problems than before. But a determined assumption of the normality of sexual relations between them makes it possible to go on, for a while, ignoring these. Experience makes their love-making easier and more satisfactory physically. If this makes it even more important to them to continue the relationship, it also lets them see, by removing one problem, where the real problem lies, and it makes them wary.

So both of them are now to some extent pretending. Both try to appear less anxious, more determined, than they really are. The implications of their deep and fierce attachment are beginning to be worked out at other levels than at that of whole, undifferentiated meeting. The encounter that seemed a perfect at-one-ment has to reckon with those areas of life in which they are not at one, not least that of their bodies. And the very fact of physical union makes this lack of oneness painfully apparent. Indeed this stage of the relationship is one at which the sexual encounter is more like a head-on collision.

Each is to the other an immensely powerful symbol of unused spiritual resources. Once they have surrendered to the magnetic pull of this symbol (and by not opposing it they did surrender, whether they knew it or not) it draws them together with great violence, and without giving them the opportunity to modify on each other's behalf the particular shape of their own emotional personality. So the encounter is uncomfortable and even painful, for each is, almost literally, 'up against' the other's qualities of mind and heart, expressed in physical and verbal gesture in a proximity that allows little room for manoeuvre. But these qualities are still largely unknown even to their possessors, and they

begin to discover them only in relation to each other. This discovery occurs also in the early stages of a marriage, but it is less
frightening because there is more room for trust.

But in any case there is a real conflict going on, a close and
watchful sparring, a searching for weaknesses in the other, and an
attempt to cover up his or her own. One reason for this is that
by allowing themselves to experience each other physically they
have each lost some claim both to self-respect and to the other's
respect. This is naturally most acute because they are not
married, but it happens in marriage too, and is one reason why in
some cases the ardent suitor becomes rapidly a careless and even
contemptuous husband.

Part of this experience is the result of the deep personal significance of nakedness, which makes people feel exposed in more
than one way. Aspects of themselves that they dare not uncover
are demanding to be set free, and this is the reason for the com-
pulsive excitement of discovery and the panic fear of being discovered, which are so interjoined that they form one single emotional complex, and one which is characteristic of the early stages
of a sexual relationship. The feeling we call modesty, or shame,
or self-respect, according to its context, is there to protect the
personality from exposure. Exposure is also what it deeply desires,
and its accomplishment brings a huge sense of achievement and
release, often followed by a reaction of fear, because the person
is now committed, but is not sure to what. The other is to a great
extent still unknown, still an enemy, an enemy to whom the hos-
tage of self-respect has now been given. And with this fear that
the disclosure of self will be abused goes a corresponding sense
of power over the other. Nakedness, both physical and psychological, in the sexual encounter at the stage of collision strips both
partners of some of their illusions, both about themselves and
about each other. Whether there is more of fear or more of contempt, and how much each is outweighed by generosity and compassion and concern is a matter of individual temperament, as well
as of the marital status of the couple. The contempt is likely to

be shown in the man and the fear in the woman, but this is not invariably so and there is probably a bit of both in both, anyway.

The couple I have been describing experience this crisis of exposure very acutely, because of their previous heavily defended condition. They are both, secretly, a little contemptuous of each other, and afraid of being themselves despised. In reaction they try, in undercover ways of which neither is aware at the time, to hurt each other and to expose each other's weaknesses and hidden motives. The need to do this is not simply vengeful, it is also part of the need to discover each other in a more defined way, but it is a dangerous game, and it is at this stage that many relationships come unstuck, before they have really had a chance to discover what the relationship is for.

In some cases the need to defend oneself and hurt the other becomes so intense that it breaks into open conflict and blows up the whole relationship at least for the time being. Whether this happens or not will depend on the kind of formation the person has experienced. It could happen if, for instance, the woman had been previously married to an indifferent or selfish husband who treated her, physically, as little more than a private prostitute. In that case her need to preserve her self-respect would make her cover up her sexual emotions jealously, and she might find it impossible to cease her defensive tactics in her new relationship, because the man's need to discover himself in her could only be felt as an attack, and her very existence would seem to depend on repelling it. This could happen even when the attraction between them was one growing from a genuine complementarity in their needs, such as I have imagined, which *could* form the basis of a good marriage.

The same stormy conclusion to the affair could happen in the case of a man whose formation had made him sexually selfish. The same kind of background as I have imagined can make a man escape the repulsive domestic aspects of sex not by finding an emotional substitute but by treating sex as a purely physical routine, with women to whom he is emotionally indifferent. In that case he would find himself treating this woman whom he really needs, emotionally, with that lack of consideration or tenderness that has become habitual. She would not understand the reasons, and would not know that in time he might do what he most needs to do, which is to make his sexual behaviour express his real desire to give himself. Without this understanding she could only interpret his behaviour as a betrayal of what he had seemed to promise, and withdraw, embittered and humiliated. In either case this would destroy the relationship, and leave the two to rationalize and cover up their outraged feelings as best they may. The chances of further emotional development are remote, and this is a common enough reason for divorce.

It is clear enough that the positive development of the affair as a *love* relationship, of the kind which is properly a married one, depends to a very great extent, perhaps entirely, on the previous formation of both partners. As in the case of the two children, the release of spiritual power comes about through transgressing (going *beyond,* not *disobeying*) the Law, yet if there has been no formation by a Law directed to the service of love this power can only lead, left to itself, to bitterness and frustration. But the children are not capable of guiding themselves into the fruitful resolution of their conflict, because they are not yet sufficiently formed to act purposefully in moral matters without guidance. The two grown-ups have acquired, through some experience in the *practising* of the moral values in which they were formed, an inner sense of direction, a real though unformulated notion of the needs of love. This is equivalent to the children's mother, who gives them this guidance at the point when they need it. The lovers' guidance comes not (necessarily) from intervention by a third person but from their understanding of what love means. It operates within them, yet it is, in a sense, exterior to the situation as such and in so far as it is *not simply* a formative influence but a definite 'voice', offering guidance which can be accepted or refused.

This is why the working out of a sexual relationship can only

be fully successful when the couple are married, provided they
have learned to regard marriage as something more than a legal
convenience. (When legal marriage has become humanly de-
based, in a particular culture, then there may be *illegal* unions
which are nearer to the real character of marriage than those made
according to the official ethos. This is true to *some* extent at the
moment, at least within a certain stratum of our culture, as I suggested earlier.) An understanding of the obligations of love is inherent in the notion of what *real* marriage involves of loyalty, service, and devotion. The influence of this understanding, however unreflectively it be adhered to, helps to form the kind of
attitude to the individual occurrences of life that can make them
fruitful of love, but besides providing this formation it also became the 'voice' which is the couple's own personal understanding of and deliberate adherence to the values it teaches. Therefore during the acute conflict stage of their relationship this interior intervention in favour of love, and at the expense of personal pride or malice, is the thing that can save a relationship
and allow it to develop. And it is only in the degree to which this
happens that the transformation by passion becomes possible.
The encounter has ceased to be a collision; at some points at
least each personality has surrendered its protection of egoism.

The two lovers with whom I am concerned have reached this
point without actually making what could be called a clear decision. An actual, recordable decision need not always occur, because if the couple are very fully 'in tune' from the beginning
they do not recognize a possibility of refusal, so that in practice
the decision was made beforehand. The results of decision follow,
but the 'turning point' character of the moment is unrecognized.
I have not chosen to describe here a situation in which this conversion to love precedes and is the *setting* of the love affair, but
rather one in which the love affair is the *occasion* of conversion.
This is because when a love affair (leading to marriage or not)
occurs in people already 'converted' the sexual encounter does
not have the same decisive character. It still uncovers, reveals,

creates communication, it opens up, and therefore it continues the process of conversion. But the particular significance of sexual feeling as the agent of conversion is more clearly seen when the sexual emotion itself is the means whereby the collision occurs, the barriers are broken down and communication becomes possible.

This is what the ritual exchange of promises, the *ceremony* of marriage, is intended to make clear. It has not, in the past, been regarded as necessarily connected with sexual *feeling*, but it is clearly a commitment to a sexual *encounter*, and in the Christian ethos it is a commitment to an encounter that should, in some way, 'convert' the couple in relation to each other. Since the commitment is explicitly to a sexual relationship it is clear that in some way (*how*, has exercised theologians for two thousand years) the sexual encounter is a saving one. So the modern (and often suspect) notion that sex is a means to salvation is not so odd after all. It is so because it is the most intimate possible human encounter, the one that demands, of its nature, the most complete self-giving, even though the actual giving in any one case may not amount to much. But marriage as a Christian institution is designed to ensure the maximum gift.

The opportunity for this self-giving comes about because there is conflict, as I suggested in the first chapter. Conflict in some sense seems to be not only an inevitable part of the whole progress of a love affair, however smooth. It is present also in each individual 'meeting' of lovers, so that each one enacts in miniature the psychological pattern of the whole relationship, but with a shift of balance, a variation of emphasis, and progress towards greater unity, or regression towards estrangement. In even the most peaceful and joyful relationships it is there, because however serene, tender and accustomed the couple are there is always an undiscovered area of personality which needs to be discovered, and therefore a challenge that can provoke the formation of personality in response. This can be so even in would-be purely physical intercourse, simply for fun, but in that case

c

the formation will probably be automatically blocked as soon as it begins to reach the conscious level. This continuing need to know and be known is also the thing that can make a long-established sexual relationship still new and challenging. The relationship does need to go further, does not seem to achieve final satisfaction even when the couple are deeply devoted and at one in heart and mind, because the need and desire to be known is still coupled with a fear of being known, a fear of the emergence into daylight of what has been safely hidden—or, rather, safely not existing as a human fact at all. Coming to birth is painful, the shadowy womb-life is attractive, and it is only the continued challenge of love that can constantly provoke into life new areas of being.

This element of challenge and response can properly be called conflict, but it is conflict in a very different sense from the clear antagonism that underlies the first stage of a love affair, especially one outside or preceding marriage.

This imaginary couple have so far experienced conflict in a real sense, and have suffered a good deal under it, but their fears have not daunted them, and just because they have not allowed themselves to be panicked their real tending to each other has, in overcoming fear, become sharper and more definite. But the situation has carried them along to a great extent by its own momentum. They could have turned away from each other, but since they have not wanted to do that they have had little to do but give in to this pull that draws them together. Yet the very continuance of their relationship is making it clearer and clearer that they cannot continue to drift. They are becoming accustomed to each other, and they know each other better as ordinary people. They are beginning, reluctantly, to be aware of all that threatens their relationship, in themselves and in each other, and in their circumstances. A decision has to be made, though they do not realize this, and will not realize when it has, in fact, been made. For this decision is not so much a choice, in the sense of looking at two alternatives and picking one, as an assent to an invitation.

The invitation is contained in the relationship itself. It does not present itself as a decision for or against love, from the outside, but as the demand to surrender to love *as already known,* but in a much fuller and more decisive way. They have, in fact, though not consciously, taken on what can only be called a quasi-marriage.

To decide in detail the successive stages that show this decision in its making and its extension is not necessary, but in order to make clear the way it happens it helps to watch it happening, on one particular occasion, just as I watched the occurrence and resolution of one particular quarrel out of the dozens that punctuate a normal childhood and form it, and express it. And if the particular meeting that I want to describe cannot be isolated as *the* decisive one it is certainly *a* decisive one. For it does seem that any relationship progresses not in steady ascent or descent but in jumps, followed by periods when the new stage reached is further experienced and assimilated and exploited. So my couple passed a crisis when they began to go out together, and another, greater, one when they first made love, and another when their love-making was first consummated. And while in theory they could have 'changed course' at any time, in practice this does not seem to happen; rather, gradually developing emotions and ideas remain below the level of conscious thought and decision until something happens to make it possible to express them. This 'happening' is of a kind that makes clear the dependence of sexual feeling on marriage as its way to fulfilment.

This particular evening the man is very tired, and it is not merely a load of extra work that is weighing on him but also the growing tension of his preoccupation with this woman. He has come back from a weekend with his parents, and is therefore feeling resentful and guilty and reckless. He feels the need of a decision, a break, though he does not know this. More than ever he wants the woman who has come to occupy a place in his life which he now knows to be much larger than he had ever intended. And so more than ever he resents her, too, and tries to drown this resentment in concentration on her physical desirableness.

But even in this simplifying fog of sensuality he has not stopped reaching out towards the 'real' which this woman represents to him.

The woman has missed him intensely during the few days of his absence, for lately they have been seeing each other nearly every day, if only for a few minutes in a café. And she has, during those days, had time to become much more aware than she had recently been of her mother's suspicion and barely disguised jealousy. She knows, now, that her mother has almost deliberately distorted and suppressed her elder daughter's life. She sees her mother as the possessive, vain, selfish woman she is, yet she also sees, with eyes opened by the experience of love, the loneliness and frustration and fear that made her so. So moments of hatred give way to moments of agonised compassion. But the realism of her new vision makes it impossible for her any longer to take it for granted that her family's claims must override all her personal needs, or that this would even be good for her family.

On the other hand she now knows that the man she loves does not represent any kind of haven in which she can seek refuge. To a great extent his feelings are beyond her understanding, but she knows, and fears, an uncommittedness in him, a reserve which keeps her out, a need for her and yet a suspicion of her. And, feeling that he might yet reject her, she has not been able to trust herself to him entirely. But this feeling she does not want to face. He is all the reality she knows and she will not let it go.

In the brief separation, therefore, both have been forced to recognize that they have, insensibly, separated themselves from the safety and normality of their daily lives. They have been drawn out of their setting, and are in a sort of no man's land. And both of them are still firmly facing towards each other, they have ignored or pushed aside the excuses that have presented themselves for turning away.

So she comes to his flat, as they had arranged, on the evening of his return, and the sight of each other blots out all their half-hearted protective little plans for cooking supper or 'talking things over'. Physical desire is both an escape from decision and a push towards it. They cling together in a sudden frenzy of need, and their love-making is suddenly more violent, less tender than ever before. In their haste, their need not to see each other but rather to be buried in each other, they are scarcely aware of each other as people.

It is this that brings things to a crisis. The man knows, with curious detachment, that he is evading some kind of knowledge, and he knows that if he could look at it he might, horribly, recognize it. This he cannot bear to do, but the very fact of his avoidance makes him aware of what his inability to face something in himself is bound to cost this woman. He feels himself in some way permanently cut off from her, and he knows, therefore, that his love-making is to that extent a sham. And it is her self-giving that forces him to recognize this. And because of this sham quality which he cannot help and deeply does not want to help, he is accepting the knowledge of his love for her, and her need, more fully than ever before. The violence of his sexual behaviour becomes an expression of his decision (which he does not know he has made) to make all he can of the relationship, no matter what it costs him. The fact that he cannot commit himself in a totality which is in practice not available to him makes his actual commitment sharply compassionate and real and also painfully humiliating, as he sees himself in relation to her. But it is the humility of real love, and therefore its illuminating is not merely painful but also peaceful.

The woman is bewildered and even shocked at this display of unbridled sensuality. It makes her acutely aware of that undiscovered region in her lover which she fears, and which she senses as the source of this panic violence, though she could not tell why it should have this effect, any more than he can. But because she has always kept herself, in spite of her fear, entirely open towards him, she experiences his demanding, childish greediness as a strong demand for love, a cry of need. She is repelled, yet the repulsion only adds strength to her own response of compassion. In overcoming her own fears, which have been intensified by the direct challenge of 'neat' untender sex, she has, without knowing it, made her decision for love. In her agony of desire to comfort and console and strengthen she is quite unaware, at the moment, that anything has happened to *her*, for her whole attention is on him. She is not even aware of humiliation, because for the time she is really 'beside herself' and wholly given.

(The fact that the overcoming of a revulsion may actually bring about the decision is clear from a real-life example of conversion quoted by Thouless in his *Introduction to the Psychology of Religion*.[1] A gambler, suddenly ill and fearing death and damnation, wanted to cry for mercy—mainly from fear—but the presence of a maid, lighting the fire in his room, made him reluctant to look foolish by falling on his knees to pray for forgiveness. In overcoming this reluctance he actually made his decision. 'By the grace of God I did put myself on my knees before that girl, and I believe it was the turning point with me.' But the assurance of being saved came later, through study of scripture—he did not, at the time, realize that the salvation event had already happened. He was too much absorbed in the event itself, he was wholly, and therefore not self-consciously, given.)

This is the moment of decision for both, yet they are not aware of it at first, and each assent to love is made alone. But what follows is something that they share, for the solitary battle that each fought has broken down the defences in each one. And through these broken dams the power of the spirit is released.

This description of a sexual encounter between two people who have not gone through a ceremony of marriage—for a mixture of reasons, some of which they can't help—shows that the couple have reached a point where their refusal to turn away from love has forced them to commit themselves to a relationship which can only realistically be described as a married one. In other words *insofar as they really love* they find themselves involved in a marriage, though they may not yet be able to recognize it as

[1] Cambridge, 1923.

such, and make it explicit. And insofar as their love is handi-capped it is so because they lack the conscious commitment that marriage requires. There is a really saving encounter, but it is limited by sin—the fearful refusal of love. Yet this sort of situation arises in marriage, as often as not, and it is this fact that has made it hard to see that there is anything essential about what seems to be an arbitrary social and legal convention. Perhaps this analysis of what it is that can make a sexual encounter a saving one, in spite of restricting fears and prejudices and selfishness, helps to show what it is in a relationship that makes it a real marriage, and what is extra to that, though customary.

The particular relationship I have described has spread out a little the stages of conflict and resolution, in a way which is likely to occur in such circumstances. They are often greatly telescoped, and may appear to coincide, or even change places, when the 'decision' is almost immediate, and the personal difficulties involved have to be worked out afterwards. The couple described here had such formidable obstacles to overcome that only the conflict-nature of their encounter (preserved by their desperate need for each other from forcing them apart) could break them down enough to release the power of true passion.

Passion in this sense is not simply unbridled sexuality or a sort of romantic cancer (though it can express itself as both these) but primarily the power of the deepest springs of personality, which St Paul calls the spirit, when it is released. It is the same power which was released in the two quarrelling children, and was 'channelled' when they recognized each other, and momentarily forgot themselves. In their case the power was 'shaped' by their mother, in this case by the adult response to an inner, but clear, demand for the gift of love.

When the decision has been made, whenever and however it comes—in one huge crisis, or in small scarcely felt progression over several weeks, or months, the relationship is transformed. The lovers enter a new world. Having overcome, by love, the antagonism and fears that kept them apart, their relationship slips into one of pure passion. It is quite amoral, in the sense that it seeks no justification from any Law or external standard, but contains its own assurance of absolute value. It is almost unbearably happy, and manages to be so even when it is threatened by imminent parting, or aware that the future will demand decisions that can only destroy it. Real passion is timeless, and deliberately so, thrusting away with reckless courage any consideration but that of the eternal now in which lies the transcendent experience of love. This is the kind of vision of life that makes it possible for quite sane people to consider getting married.

Not all sexual relationships show passion in this 'pure' form. Even quite satisfactory ones can miss it out, in a sense. In a long-term relationship it is possible for people who are sufficiently love-directed and patient to work out their temperamental encounter, in terms of formation and transformation, so gradually that no great explosion occurs at all. It would be possible to suppose, then, that no change, no decision, had occurred. Indeed it might not, for there can be a cold war, a fairly comfortable, workable truce, in a marriage. But there can be a true decision, a real transformation, that makes no fireworks, yet produces the same dynamic peace. The process is the same, nothing in fact is left out, but there is no stage which can be characterized as that of pure passion because the stream of spiritual energy flows, less violently but just as effectively, between the banks prepared for it by the demands of ordinary married life. This is the reason why passion is usually regarded as characteristic of extra-marital relationships, whose circumstances force the power of the spirit to break through in one huge explosion. It is possible, once the experience of passion has been analysed, to discover the same elements in the less compact development. So long as passion was looked at, as it were, 'across' the idea of marriage it looked so alien and peculiar that it seemed to have nothing to do with the serene unfolding of love later on in marriage. Hence the deep suspicion of passion that has characterized traditional moral teaching. But when passion is put in the foreground—not because it is more important than marriage but because it is simple and total as an experience, and can be looked at in one glance—then the light that glitters in the prism of passion can be seen refracted in the rainbow of the whole of a happy marriage. And not only in marriage, for (as I have discussed in another book) sexual passion is a 'typical' experience and shows the nature of the breakthrough of the spirit in relation to many kinds of living. And it is perhaps by seeing what passion is like—the uncovering of personality, the definition through conflict, the need for decision—that it is possible to see why marriage is in fact the right setting for sexual passion if it is not to lose itself in compromise and despair. The things that threaten my imaginary couple threaten them because, for one reason or another, they have not been able to trust each other enough to commit themselves entirely to each other. At every turn it is this lack of trust, the *absence* of the recklessness that passion demands, that has come near to wrecking the real achievement. All that they truly want of each other and for each other can only truly be developed in an unlimited relationship, and it is an obscure sense of *this* that makes the decisions that *do* occur, decisions of love. In other words it is the desire to achieve what marriage is intended to achieve that makes something real and valuable out of the relationship. And the extent to which it lacks what makes a marriage, it lacks what makes it the thing they really want. But, in marriage or in a 'pseudo-marriage' of the kind described, what does this breakdown mean? What has actually happened? This release through conflict into passion shows very clearly the interaction of formation and transformation. The description of the event makes it clear that the opportunity for a transforming breakthrough, the chance to make a decision for love, only occurs because the previous formation has shaped a personality that is inclined to love. Love cannot be taught, but the ideals that express the needs of love can be learned, and so can the kinds of behaviour appropriate to love. In childhood it can be helped, given channels to run in, though not created. In adult life also the daily decisions express a 'direction' of love, or deny it. Without this formation—as it were fitting the person to the needs of a power it can in no way order—the spiritual energy released by conflict of some kind has nothing to give it meaning as *love*, no human 'shape' to inhabit. It can only dissipate itself in futile striving and aimless desire that does not know what object to seek. This 'shaping' is the function of marriage as an *institution*, a formative one.

But if the moment of transforming decision depends on formation, in another sense formation depends on transformation. This is difficult to express, but important. The human spirit seeks to know itself, for example in the couple I have imagined, who find in each other the symbol of their 'lost' selves. But they do not know what it is they want, they are simply aware of a huge need. (' . . . for we do not know how to pray as we ought, but the spirit himself intercedes for us, with sighs too deep for words.' Paul to the Romans, Chapter 8). The action to which this agony of prayer impels a human being is one which leads up to the moment of decision, but it is the actual movement towards decision that gives *form* to certain aspects of personality that had been inchoate, meaningless, before. It would not be quite true to say that the transformation is what actually *forms* these previously formless aspects, but it does seem to be true that the conflict aspect of the encounter gives form. Certain feelings and ideas that had no conscious existence before are brought into existence by the challenge of opposition. Just as acute danger may develop, on the instant, physical and mental powers that their owner had never dreamt he possessed (indeed *had not* possessed before, in any meaningful sense) so the attack on the personality which is implicit in the conflict situation actually brings into being, *forms*, personal qualities that are needed in the making of the decision that transforms. But this in itself depends on previous formation, for it is only because they have the courage and 'sense of direction' to keep turned towards each other that the lovers can experience their conflict as both forming and transforming. If they are too much afraid they will withdraw, and the conflict will end in the quiescence of restored chaos, not of achieved peace. In this case unmarried lovers will probably part, but married ones may be kept going by the sheer momentum of routine—that dreaded ghost who is so often a benevolent spirit. For it keeps people *going on,* it gives them time to think, and recover, and renew their courage for a further encounter which perhaps will not fail. The openness to each other, which can persist in spite of failure, or finally make a resolution possible, is not itself the transforming decision, or at least it is not the final point of it, but it may be considered to be a part of it in the sense that it is at least a semi-decision, a deliberate tending towards a decision, though leaving a way out. It is the assertion, from the depths of human life, of the obscure knowledge that this way lies salvation. But it is not itself salvation, it is not the decision of love, only its preparation—one without which no transformation can take place.

This psychological fact is not a new idea for theology. Gerhard Ebeling, discussing the resurrection appearances of Christ, says: 'Those to whom they occurred became believers. There is no account of anyone to whom the Risen One appeared who did *not* become a witness to the resurrection. It is true that in every case knowledge of Jesus is presupposed, and that means that *the question of faith has already been raised* (my italics). This is also true of St Paul. To this extent, therefore, knowing the Risen One meant knowing him *again.* This was not a communication or special additional revelation, but solely the revelation of Jesus himself. He appeared as what he really was, namely, the witness of faith. But the witness of faith is recognized only when one accepts his witness in faith. The appearing of Jesus, and the coming to faith of him to whom the appearance is imparted, are therefore one and the same.' What appears, and to which assent is given, is that *towards* which love already tended, but lacked the final, exterior challenge that is the occasion of actual decision.

This double effect of encounter in its movement towards decision is the delicate and hardly-seen root of the double effect of the truly peaceful resolution of conflict which I noticed in the first chapter. There is both greater individuation and greater communication, not one after the other but as aspects of one movement of growth. But in sexual relationship this can be seen more clearly because the event is not only the one single encounter, whose parts are so tightly compressed as to be hard to distinguish, it is *also* the whole series of separate events which have each the same conflict-resolution pattern, but which are also, together, one movement of growth, though with 'turning points', as I have suggested. This growth can be stopped at any time, but if it is not stopped it develops according to its own nature, though in any number of different shapes, depending always on the type of formation that went before.

This continuous formation-transformation cycle is suggested and therefore helped by the structure of marriage as a way of life. So, once the decision of love has been made, once the power of the spirit has broken through and produced the passionate experience, this transforming event has to work itself out in a life that goes on. It has to transform, in fact, the whole person, and in order to do this the person has to be brought into existence, has to be *formed*. Just as the children's mother in the first example was able, by her real love, to provide the conditions for a decision of love in her children, so, in the lives of the lovers, their own realized love can provide the conditions for formation towards their own further decisions. They have opened the doors to those hidden needs whose reflection in each other draw them together.

If this imaginary couple had been more selfish and tougher they might have managed to keep the doors shut, and merely amuse themselves, or find escape from the frustration and tedium of the continuing cycles of living. But there is in these two a real desire for life, and the courage to risk something in searching for it, and this means that what was hidden comes to the surface, and becomes a motive power for action, even though its roots are not recognized. The woman becomes aware of the degree of self-deception that had been involved in making herself think that her home responsibilities were providing her with the kind of life she wanted. She had always vaguely supposed that circumstances only were preventing the full experience of life that some other people had and that therefore time and change of exterior influences could bring about a transformation. But this hope was so unformed and distant that she had never thought of a fuller life as something she really *wanted* The new experience shows her that she *had* been wanting it. Her experience is a surprisingly mature one because she has in fact grown up to a great extent through the patient exercise of her accepted responsibilities, but this she does not realize. Therefore one of the things in her that is given existence, is 'formed' by her assent to love, is the realization of her new experience as something that both completes and opens her in a quite new way. She is too young to see her experience in any kind of perspective, she cannot compare it with anything else, she does not know (though she might *say* she knows) that there is a future going on beyond, one in which she will not be able to live by the single reality of this encounter. Therefore, at this stage, her reckless assent to the demand of her new love produces a kind of double standard. A new realism shows up her former contentment as based on illusion, for only the new thing is real. But a tender heart and a sense of loyalty are still refusing to let her consider betraying her former allegiance. She thinks the two are compatible, indeed she is determined to force them to be compatible. Her formation had not been able to give her more than a superficial security, but she has learned a good deal about love. The new experience of it makes her doubt whether the word 'love' could ever be applied to any other, but the same 'sense of direction' that makes her able to respond with love to the demand for decision also prevents her from rejecting her other responsibilities, even though her refusal to do so endangers her new love. This is the result of a particular kind of formation, the kind that makes possible (as in the case of the two children) a positive use of spiritual energy. To some extent it checks and controls the power that is released, and this controlling is painful because it seems to be a struggle against the transforming power of passion, and in this situation passion alone has a convincing personal value. Yet passion uncontrolled cannot produce the results that the emotion indicates.

Supposing this woman had received a formation which made her more deeply selfish, or that her home life had been actively unhappy? In that case she would not have had a very deep motive for checking and guiding the impulse of passion. Therefore she would feel that nothing could prevent the continuance of this state of total experience, a shared transcendence of normal limitations. But the fact of living a human life is itself such a limitation. There may be no previous emotional or domestic ties to be considered, but there is the need to go on living. As soon as passion comes up against the need to have money and somewhere to live it is no longer 'uncontrolled', and it suffers accordingly. The emotional situation I have described only shows in a fairly acute form the unavoidable interaction of formation and transformation values, at a point where they seem to be contradictory. Yet, as I have tried to show, they are not really contradictory in the only place where we can know anything about them—that is, in particular human situations. Neither has any meaning without the other. So the woman in my example feels as if she were contradicting the nature of her passion by her determination not to reject old loyalties. Yet these loyalties have actually been given their new definition and reality *as* binding loyalties only in the act of decision in relation to her new love; her decision is therefore a decision involving them, though it is one simple act of self-giving, in which there is no analysis, no rationalization. So she can feel that she is casting off the old completely, and she needs to do so, she needs the concrete undertaking of marriage, in fact, to define the decision. She does not know that although she has cast off the old she has in fact found it again because its reality is not the external facts of her home life but their significance in herself, and this significance has now been transformed in her own single act of decision. For when transformation occurs it transforms the whole personality in so far as it is aware of itself—that is, in so far as it has reached full definition as personal.

This statement is not immediately convincing, since it is clear that there are still operative many aspects of the woman's nature which may act against the direction of love which she has taken. There is also the fact that because she is not intellectually aware of the new formality of her relation to her mother and brother and sister she can probably be persuaded out of carrying through its implications, and to the extent to which she does so she will be obscuring and betraying her decision for love. But these qualifications only serve to make clearer the nature of transformation. It is not an intellectual process, but in order to be effective in continued living it needs to express itself in terms of realized moral obligation. It is a simple act, but one involving the whole person, and the person, as involved in the decision, cannot include those obscure motives and hidden needs, with their resulting behaviour, which are likely in practice to modify the continued full effect of the spiritual power then released. These obscure aspects of a person are not fully formed, have no existence as personal, therefore they are not involved in the saving decision.

In the case of this woman there are many resentments against her life of which she is quite unaware, and these are likely to prove troublesome in future because the release of a great deal of spiritual energy has 'created' much in her that was not available before, and with this upheaval much else has come nearer the surface, though not yet defined. There are also fears of her new love, of many unexplained negative reactions in her lover, doubts of his real feelings, and with this an increased sense of risk, for the childhood insecurity that made adult relationships difficult is still there, though covered up by custom and external stability of life. In the discovery of a wholly new self, not only the home relationships but this false security suffer a disillusioning process, and the new self is horribly at risk. But this sense of danger is not sufficiently realized to be defined and included by the act of decision. It remains, therefore, outside the fully personal, and is a threat to it. So the saving decision is already threatened, both by influences from the former life and by reactions to the new situation in which the decision has occurred. This threat is present in many marriage relationships, but in marriage the deliberate and conscious commitment involved is a considerable help. To get married means to be forced to consider as far as possible the implications of what one is doing, and also to define the nature of the relationship by the words and gestures of the ritual that brings it into being as a public fact. Marriage does not eliminate fears of each other and doubts about the feelings of the other, but it does, as any external self-committing act does, bring into play as many as possible of the motives and needs that lie below the surface, so that they are involved in the decision and hence become fully personal. The place of public act and ritual, making concrete a conscious decision as part of the process of transformation, is important. If passion is a word for the breakthrough of power that makes true decision possible, marriage is the word for the 'language' in which, and only in which, the decision can be understood and worked out. And the definition stands: transformation affects the whole personality.

How does this work out in the case of the man? In him, the obstacles to transformation are greater, because his personal incompleteness is not simply a retarding, due to insecurity, of the development of the ability to surrender to love. His incompleteness is due to an actual, though unconscious, rejection of an important part of life. The very fact of the sexual setting of his decision threatens to uncover what he has hidden, and it is only the fact that the woman seems inaccessible, tied by existing responsibilities, that makes it possible for him to respond at all. If she had appeared to be free to marry him, his interior resistance would have been unlikely to let him get as far as this in the relationship. The same kind of revulsion from a whole area of life, represented by a sexual relationship, leads to homosexuality in a different type of person. It is not sex but marriage, and its stifling associations of motherhood, that repel him. So the fact of his surrender to love is a constant threat to his precarious personal direction. His response was real, his decision does transform, but that in him which is fully personal, and comes to defined existence in the act of decision, is more circumscribed than in the case of the woman. Part of what is defined in the movement towards decision is a realization of himself as vulnerable and untidy, as less clearly directed in relation to his whole pattern of living than he had imagined. Impulses and desires, some of them discreditable, which he had formerly known as real but peripheral ills (to be overcome, perhaps, or to be lived with patiently), are fused into self-consciousness in the act of decision. This is because the collision aspect of the encounter made their personal reality unavoidable, as he saw them in relation to the woman. So here, too, the conflict *forms* the personality, in one and the same movement of which the saving decision is the climax. Yet the preparation is formative, and the decision transformative. They are not confused, although formation is the prerequisite of transformation, and transformation has a kind of 'backwards' action in enormously speeding up, or perhaps crystallizing into sudden perfection, the slow formation that has been going on since babyhood.

This description (with digressions) of the progress of a sexual relationship is not complete. But it should have made clear the relationship of passion to marriage, of formation by the values of a daily life to the moments of decision in which they are both broken down and opened out. Marriage as a way of life is both formative and apt for transformation. But this account should have shown also the kinds of obstacles to love that create the conflict element in the encounter, and this view of marriage via a relationship that lacks such completeness may have shown up more clearly why marriage is, after all, not the running down of passion but its development. And this development is one of a continually greater degree of openness, of givenness. That being so, it requires, psychologically and theologically, the normal result of the sexual encounter, which is a child. The child is both the symbol of what the relationship is doing to the couple—increasing and releasing life in them—and the means whereby this should come about. There is no limit to the givenness required of people who love, but the child is the sign of it, and also a sort of warning and challenge to a relationship that, by its very nature, runs the risk of developing a selfish and in-turned character that could destroy its reality, its potential as the setting for conversion.

The main purpose of this description has been to make clear what actually happens to people under theological headings which we have heard so often that they have ceased to mean much, if they ever meant anything. For meaning is a personal act, it is both a summing up of experience in a total emotional-intellectual grasp, and in the same act an intention towards the future, onto which the meaning is projected. If theological concepts are meaningless they are not even theological, because theology is about man's encounter with God. It is about a happening to and in man. If something happens to a person of which he is not aware and cannot be aware—in other words that *means nothing* to him —then in fact nothing has happened that can possibly be of any real significance in his life as human. In that case God has no meaning, and there *is no* theology. We reflect on theology, and our reflections assist the consequences of the happening, and encourage further happening. In other words theology is formative, in the sense used here, and, as I hope is apparent by now, formation finds its meaning and definition in transformation.

The human situation described here was offered as an example of the idea of encounter, as theology, and the setting of the whole affair, its condition of being, its very existence, is *sin*. But sin, too, is historical. The way people sin is part of their particular culture, and so is the way they are saved. In describing a situation of this kind it is possible to see how sin is not simply individual action which is recognized as morally wrong, though that is how it hits us, how we experience it. It is the whole messy, frightening condition in which people live: the man in a state of unresolved rebellion against his background, with a suppressed spiritual energy that he tries, only partly successfully, to canalize in his work; the woman accepting a wholly unjust state of affairs because she has been conditioned to do so by a mother who is herself the victim of fear and uncertainty and resentment; the whole set-up kept in being by a rigid suppression of spiritual potential.' This world, in a state of sinfulness, is full of people knocking up against each other in a haphazard way. These encounters release the power that is in people, they react on each other and form each other in startling and unpredictable ways. Some encounters are bound to be unplanned and unplannable, and to produce uncontrollable results. People can't altogether direct or organize their lives because they don't understand either themselves or other people well enough to do so; therefore the relations between them are likely to be a series of destructive clashes.

So there is separation of one kind of activity from another kind of activity, arranging of categories of living, planning of relationships. This is the Law. The disorganized bashing about of human beings is to some extent prevented, and people assume a pattern and a meaning in relation to each other. When they meet, they meet in these planned relations and their encounters are preformed, or at least that's the idea. In this way the violent power that underlies human life and is sparked off by encounters is controlled. But it is still there, and if it is to be used it must be acknowledged. So the *Law* should make provision for people to touch the sources of power, but with care and under strict precautions. This power is outside the Law, but also makes the Law necessary. *God*, as a formative idea connected with Law and order, also suggests the idea that there is something more in human nature than Law and order, and that we had better be in some awe of it. When this is understood it is kept in special areas, either geographical or psychological, and both are approached with ritual words and gestures that are planned, yet not merely planned. They express a realization of power as unpredictable, yet not inimical but on the contrary essential to a man's life. This is *liturgy*, which protects man from the direct experience of the sacred, but also keeps him in touch with it—which is necessary since it is the source of life. This double function of keeping in touch and yet protecting has already been touched on as part of the value of marriage as an institution.

This use of liturgy is an awareness that, for good or ill, our culture has lost. Not only non-Christians like the couple in my story have lost it, but Christians too. There is no dangerous power, no sacred, in people's consciousness, therefore no liturgy that can bring about a meeting without an explosion. Religious liturgy is not now, on the whole, a contact with the sacred but an external expression of a highly idealistic secular concern. It is a matter of good formation, not of transformation. That is a useful thing to have, for forming religiously well-shaped people, but it doesn't deal with the problem of what is underneath, except by regarding it as alien and outlawing it.

This is what the couple in my account tried to do in the days before they met. They didn't think of the vague, untamed area of life as belonging to the devil, because they had never learned to think like that, but both in their different ways disallowed it, because it would threaten their peace. They lived by the Law, in some contentment. And they did not consider any other kind of life worth living. They did not 'boast' of their way of life in the sense of thinking it worthy of special honour, but fundamentally they were 'boasting' in the Pauline sense, as did the Jews, who did indeed have a Law—cultural and ritual and ethical—which was 'holy and just and good'. The Law which has been the security of this modern couple is also all these things, though their cult is more strictly cultural, and their ritual domestic or political rather than religious. To them also it could have been said, 'you rely upon the Law and boast of your relation to God (though they wouldn't call it God, but "life" or "society" or "my responsibilities") and know his will and approve what is excellent, because you are instructed in the Law' (Romans 2:17). They are both good, even loving, people.

But their encounter challenges this goodness, from the beginning. It makes them discontented, it makes them aware that something is wrong with themselves and with their circumstances —but the two are really one. They now see, even dimly, a life beyond anything they had imagined, they are, to each other, prophets or preachers of a new kingdom. They are the 'intervention' in the deadlock of the Law or of conflict uncontrolled even by Law. There has to be an announcement, a 'preaching', for 'how are they to learn without a preacher? And how can men preach unless they are sent?' But the 'sending' is of one to the other, in response to an obscure invitation each senses in the other. This 'preaching' makes them look with acute distaste on much that they hitherto accepted as good. It seems stifling, a threat to life itself. 'Did that which is good, then, bring death to me? By no means. It was sin, working death in me *through what is good,* in order that sin might be shown to be sin.'

But what they are announcing to each other is something that neither has, as a possession. It is something they can give each other, but only when each becomes aware of a demand 'outside' him or herself, and responds. They give each other access, therefore, to something which is beyond the control of either, and in order to do this they need a 'liturgy' which both brings them into contact with the thing, the power, that brought them together, and also protects them from destruction by it. This is what the physical gestures of love are for, and this is why the first effect of making love is to make them aware of separateness, rather than of greater unity. They are impelled to these actions, which belong to their love, express it and strengthen it, yet they were, in a way, more totally immersed in it in the brief time when they met it in each other, yet had not yet 'put it into practice'. But all liturgies are also connected with the Law, which has to continue as a continuously formative influence. So this liturgy is properly related to marriage as Law.

This 'liturgy' is a putting into practice of a new life, in a way which makes clear the nature of the new life. It relates it to the structures of the Law, and pins it down in time and space as a fact of physical-emotional 'thereness'. And the ritual that initiates the relationship, that of the ceremony of marriage—however simple—states this relation clearly.

But it is not itself the new life, and in the example I have described it is noticeable that the 'liturgy' of love was used *before* the moment of complete conversion, as well as providing a setting for it. So our modern tendency to use liturgy as mainly formative contains the possibility of a renewed awareness of it as transformative and, paradoxically, a renewed understanding of the formative value of marriage makes possible a much clearer view of how it is the setting in which sexual love can become most fully transforming.

The transformation occurs in the moment of self-surrender to love. Each is responding to an invitation that comes to him or her through the other, and could not do so otherwise. The response of each is a total gift of the whole person as it then exists, it is unconditional and unreflective. It is of their own deeper self, yet it is not possessed but only exists in its givenness. This is *faith*, which is personal, yet cannot arise from the person without some intervention. For each one, alone, is helpless, and only the knowledge of *being loved* has the power to set free into faith. This being loved happened when each was still in our usual state of muddle and alienation—sin—but made workable and more or less comfortable by the Law: 'While we were yet helpless, at the right time Christ died for the ungodly. Why, one will hardly die for a righteous man—though perhaps for a good man one will dare even to die. But God shows his love for us in that while we were yet sinners Christ died for us' (Romans 5:6). This conviction of being sinful comes into being as part of the new awareness of being loved, and so the love that responds comes out of an awareness of sin. Sin, it must be said again, means *both* the messy human condition—an environment that we are soaked in—and *also* the shabby and unloving behaviour that we indulge in, as indeed appropriate to this condition, therefore not seeming to matter much. But awareness of being loved makes it seem to matter a lot, in fact it really seems to *be* sin, though most people never use that word to describe their feelings.

This *giving* of love is so hard precisely because of this background of sin. So giving love finally involves a sort of death, for this giving is a giving without hope of return—not because there is likely to be no return but because the act of giving excludes this kind of consideration of results. It is timeless, unreflective, total. It is a giving, then, to someone who is a 'sinner', a gift thrown into a void. So the lover dies in giving his love.

But the response to this love is also a dying, for it is a surrender without any knowledge of what may come of it. It is a response to love, but it is a response to a love which is set against an unknowable future. It is extremely painful because it means leaving behind all that seemed certain and comforting before, risking them—in fact it means dying to them. And this is a real dying, a real leaving behind, without conditions, or it does not work. Faith is total abandonment, a jump into a void. The security of the Law, which made it possible, is left behind. It is irrelevant to what is happening, even when the Law provides an essential part of the framework that makes the nature of the event recognizable, as in marriage.

So both in giving and receiving love there is *obedience*, a surrender to the command to love of which each is aware through the other. *Each* is both a giver of love, which involves a dying, and a receiver of love, to which the response is also a dying. It is a death 'outside the city', beyond the Law—*even though the love is completely lawful.* (The fact that in my example it is not lawful, serves to highlight the fact that this is a decision not *according* to the Law but right outside it, even though it may and should *use* it.)

And out of this death a *new life* is born, one which is shared. That which is shared is of both: it is not possessed by either but only exists in this sharing. It is not an emotion, though the revolution it accomplishes makes its existence felt emotionally. It is a life, the life of faith, the life which is proper to the spirit, the real self, in man, and because it is a life it demands to be stated as such in the public aspect as well as in the private one.

One of its effects is to make it possible to be aware of sinfulness very acutely, but to accept this without despair. The sinfulness is painful, because it is so obviously contradictory to the meaning of the new life. Lapses of temper, acts of self-indulgence or mean-ness that formerly seemed unimportant now stand out in con-trast to the love that is the centre of life. But they are only to be expected in a person who has so recently been totally in his sins. They are to be overcome, but they are not so terrible as they seemed in the movement *towards* the decision of faith, when sin-fulness was in process of being an experienced and painful fact. Now the lovers are *free* (and their freedom is in proportion to the completeness of their self-giving)—not in the sense that they will never again do anything mean or shabby but in the sense that they do not feel inescapably *stuck* in the state in which such actions are appropriate. All the same, they will passionately want to avoid such actions. 'How can we who have died to sin still live in it? Do you not know that all of us who have been baptized into Christ Jesus were baptized into his death? . . . For if we have been united with him in a death like his we shall certainly be united with him in a resurrection like this. We know that our old self was crucified with him so that the sinful body might be des-troyed, and we might no longer be enslaved to sin. For he who has died is freed from sin. But if we have died with Christ we believe that we shall also live with him.'

This strange and yet perfectly familiar complex of events whose centre is the moment of the decision of faith comes about in the encounter between two human beings. The decision does not always occur, for lack of love-directed formation may make one or other turn away before the point of decision is reached. Or the invitation may be refused, for in the comfort of the Law as forma-tive, and in the immature happiness it protects and offers, we have 'great possessions' which are hard to leave. The decision depends to a great extent on the type of formation that has gone before, but the decision is free and is personal. If the answer to the invitation is 'yes' the result is life.

This love affair is redemption at work. For to this woman, this man *is* Christ, and she finds life through him as far as she is able to at the moment, which may not be very far. What they have announced to each other *is* the good news of salvation, and their response to the invitation that each proffers *is* the salvation occurrence, *is* faith, though it is hampered and incomplete, because—for the reasons described—they are still to a great extent bound by sin, in both senses. And this surrounding and threatening sin shows up clearly what is the nature of the event that transcends it, and draws them onwards, by its very nature.

To say that the mixed-up, tragic and possibly ill-fated love affair I have described is redemption at work is not to say this is all there is to redemption. In a sense, it is true to say, this is all there is to it, because the work of redemption in any human being can only act in the setting available. In this case the setting precludes at first a real understanding of marriage as a potential resolution of the encounter, though it seems that the very momentum of the relationship may end by bringing them to this understanding. This 'setting' is not peculiar to these lovers, but affects most of our contemporaries. Yet *still* the *nature* of sexual encounter works towards this resolution, though blind and chained. In the next chapter I shall be describing salvation in a context in which the Christian labels can normally be used to describe what is happening, but the salvation event is still an event determined in its structure by formation.

But in another sense it is not true that this is all, for salvation is not just the sum of its endless, peculiar and pathetic individual manifestations. This is evident from the fact that the 'new life' that occurs is a *shared* thing. The implication of this will be examined later on, but for the time being it is enough to say that when St Paul uses the huge Christian words—Law, sin, Christ, faith, death, life—he is being *more* realistic than I am, not less. He is referring to the facts in their nakedness. I am presenting them in their costume of particularity, so that we can approach them without fear, and without the fear-begotten fog with which we surround the demands of love, and which protects us from the encounter with Christ. So, paradoxically, the dressing-up can bring us face to face with the naked truth.

CHAPTER III

SELF-DISCOVERY

In the last chapter the idea of encounter, dug out of the incident in the first chapter, was spread out and analyzed so as to make clear its theological structure. I looked at the relation between the formation that determines the nature and scope of the encounter, and the transformation that can break through it and revolutionize the whole set-up.

This chapter takes the process a little further, and tries to see more clearly how such a transformation affects the personality, how it works itself out, how it extends its reach—or loses it. And I shall do this in terms of the conversion experience which it is natural to describe in Christian terms. Indeed one part of it takes place in a specifically Christian context, one whose theological meaning is therefore already prepared.

This has its dangers, as can be seen from reading biographical or autobiographical accounts of conversion. In these, past events are obscured because, first of all, they are given (without other description) the proper and relevant Christian labels, and then these labels, taken out of the particular setting that gives them personal meaning, are dipped in a prepared stock of luminous paint and stuck back on. So that, in retrospect, nothing is seen but a kind of religious phosphorescence that effectively hides what really happened. It is only in rare cases that a man of singular honesty as well as singular intelligence can recreate the experience in all its personal vividness and in a totally unreligious way. Augustine did it. Yet even he did a bit of unconscious falsifying, but in a way that helps to clarify the actual nature of the experience, as we shall see.

But I hope that it may be possible by now to use the Christian terminology in describing an imaginary conversion, and to use it as descriptive in a precise way, rather than as simply a useful summing up. It was in order to make this possible that the setting of a particular salvation event described in the last chapter was made totally non-religious. In the same way it is possible to describe, quite authentically, an event occurring in a completely religious context, and do so in terms of psychology or sociology or, conceivably, chemistry, provided one uses the words as *descriptive*, according to the particular point of view adopted, of what is happening, not as *containing* the happening. The use of perfectly good jargon to wrap up and then throw away perfectly good human experience is unfortunately quite usual, so much so that people who value their experience are afraid of exposing it to description lest they be deprived of its meaning. But real description simply describes, and it should assist meaning, not emasculate it. So to describe conversion as 'an outbreak into consciousness of a new mental construction which appears to introspection to have had no period of development in the mind' (Thouless, *Psychology of Religion*), is helpful, though limited. Yet it can appear to be an attempt to deny that 'anything has really happened', and will be resisted as such by people to whom conversion has 'happened'.

But similarly it sometimes seems as if to describe a human event in Christian terms were an attempt to dehumanize it, to make it unreal. The person concerned may feel he or she is being deprived of what they know as specially *theirs*, and is being offered instead a sort of publicly-owned religious 'thing'. Something of this reaction seems to have been behind the indignation of a well-known atheist who was accused by a Christian of being 'really' a believer. The tactless Christian was describing in Christian terms something which he saw in the atheist's reaction to life. It was a true description of an event, or rather of what such an event does to the personality. But the atheist's experience had probably been expressed to herself as one of deliberate and conscious rejection of Christianity and its God. This also was a true description, not of the nature of the event but of the material of it, the way the choice or decision presented itself to her. St Thérèse of Lisieux, as a child, was cured of a painful neurotic illness when her statue of our Lady seemed to 'come alive' and smile at her. She was acutely distressed when the stereotyped piety of the nuns who heard her story seemed to be depriving her of the immediacy and truth of the experience of 'Our Lady's smile'. To her, it was the most 'real' thing that had ever happened. It was too close to be describable, and when she was pressed to do so and her childishly clumsy description taken up by others, the experience was made an object, she was deprived of it.

In what follows I hope to avoid the wrapping-up process. My intention is to describe—but it is inevitable that an account of conversion will produce emotional reaction of some kind, for we are not neutral about this. Indeed it would be pointless to write this account if I did not want emotional reaction. This is a moral tale, and it describes a type of event that most people are strongly tempted to reject with loathing or to dismiss as nothing but emotion.

Part of the moral crisis through which this generation is passing is precisely a difficulty in recognizing that conversion can happen at all. Intervention in the normal structures of comfortable illusion is a possibility we doubt, or even feel morally bound to repudiate. Most writers and dramatists are saying either, 'no intervention is possible', as in *The Caretaker*, or, more poignantly, 'an intervention is possible, and we want it but it doesn't happen'. *Waiting for Godot* is about the desire for a conversion that doesn't occur. The two tramps never quite give up hoping for the encounter that will save them, but we never find out whether their patient half-hope is an illusion or not. Will Godot ever come? The usual answer is, no.

And when a dramatist does admit that an intervention can occur, does occur, he is sure that the opportunity will be missed. In *Look back in Anger*, Jimmy Porter hears that the old woman he really cares for is dying and wants him. He is softened, compassionate—and afraid, because of the vulnerability he feels in this invasion by compassion. So he wants his wife Alison to go with him. He is admitting his need of her—something he never does otherwise. He is open to her, and his need is an invitation to her to respond by lowering the defensive barriers, surrendering to love. She nearly does—but the humiliation involved is too great. She has kept her integrity so far only by resisting all Jimmy's attacks; if she surrenders to his need she will be abandoning her only security, she will be at his mercy. So she refuses, and goes to church instead—a frightful ironic comment on the role that religion so often plays in people's lives. The dramatist is saying, 'conversion could occur, but it doesn't'. In fact it does occur, but the obstacles are formidable and we need to be reminded of them. The excruciating experience of being dramatically involved in the rejection of the possibility of salvation is in itself a kind of offer of salvation. Shall we surrender to the feeling that the situation is hopeless, or shall we—as our angry sense of frustration seems to indicate that we deeply want to do—refuse to give in, and go on waiting for Godot?

Yet even when we do continue to hope that Godot will come tomorrow we feel rather shamefaced about it. We can offer no reason for expecting him. So when someone says, loudly, he has come, we are inclined to be suspicious. We've been had too often. This is perhaps the reason why an account of conversion may seem phoney. I hope it won't, because it follows an account of a love affair, which few are inclined to regard as a phoney sort of event, and the parallels are clear, which is why I have presented these two kinds of conversion situation in this rather illogical order. Both of them are about the need to love.

My subject is a man in his early forties, married and with a family of four, the eldest of whom is sixteen. He works in the research laboratories of a huge firm of manufacturing chemists, and he is good at his job, which is interesting and seldom altogether boring, but is not very taxing and often monotonous. He gets on well with his colleagues, who find him pleasant to be with because he is both interested and undemanding.

He comes from a formidably intellectual family, and his mother is a strong-minded woman who has carved out a political career for herself, with the encouragement of her husband, an idealistic and rather donnish person, who was never sufficiently involved with his wife to mind very much what she did with the part of her life she didn't spend in bed with him. This part he enjoyed; consequently they were a happy and united couple, noticably easy-going in their attitude to their shared life, and not at all dependant either on each other or on their child. They shared a strong sense of the importance of high intellectual and ethical standards, and imposed these as a matter of course on their only son, without ever supposing that they were doing this, because they 'never interfered'. Consequently a lot was tacitly expected of him, but he was never given the support of a sense of belonging to the group in which these standards prevailed, and the superficial 'take-it-or-leave it' permissiveness of his upbringing made it impossible for him to realize that he was in fact striving to fill a role for which he was quite unfitted. But he was able to devise a comfortable sort of adjustment to life and to being a failure without feeling one, opting out without rejection of his parents' affection, because of the solid groundwork of security given him in early childhood by a mother's help. She was a kind and simple woman who belonged to a fundamentalist Christian sect. She left when he was almost four.

His parents would have been very surprised if they had known that their son felt himself to be a failure in relation to them. Even when he failed in his exams, did not reach university, and scraped into a job that would never bring him any great opportunities or distinction, they suppressed their disappointment so successfully that they convinced themselves they had never felt any. And the son himself was not aware of his state of mind as one of having failed. He used to say he was an ordinary sort of chap, and didn't want anything more from life than a decent job and a happy, comfortable home. Which was true. He married, in his twenties, a girl who worked in the same firm. She is a Christian of a regular, Church-going, sincere and taking-for-granted kind. She is gentle and undemanding and cheerful, and scarcely ever opens a book.

So in early middle age he is content, easy-going, undemonstrative. He suffers from chronic slight fatigue, but then so do many men of his age. His home life is placid on the whole, though his eldest daughter irritates him and worries him and they have frequent rows. She is an intelligent, forceful girl, full of fierce anti-nuclear idealism at the moment, and contemptuous of her parents' easy acceptance of their modest but comfortable life. He finds her aggressiveness revolting, and her friends unbearable. He thinks of all this as inevitable teenage craziness, but is worried by his own strong reaction to it, because he is really fond of his daughter and would like to help her; yet every time she opens her mouth she says something that makes him lash out with ill-aimed, panicky violence.

It is probably in an effort to atone for his inability to get on with this girl that he begins to read the pacifist and communist pamphlets that she is always leaving about. He has to overcome a certain revulsion in order to do so, and he reads them, at first, in a wary and contemptuous way, minimizing to himself and others the importance of his action. 'It's only fair to know what they say', and 'After all, they've got to work it out for themselves', are two ways in which he explains his attitude. With similar devices he covers up the fact that he is to some extent influenced by what he reads. He would call it 'seeing both sides', but the fact is that he is beginning to question his previous assumptions about the necessity for nuclear weapons, or the complete adequacy of the Welfare State as a means of dealing with social injustice. There is a conflict going on in his mind between the unexamined and unconnected principles of his moral and social philosophy (if something so inchoate can be so called) and the attraction of a crude but coherent statement of a totally different attitude to life—one which makes demands, which disrupts. The conflict remains at the intellectual level, or at least appears to, for to allow its emotional roots to appear would be too destructive of the only kind of peace he knows—the peace of the Law, in full and manifestly successful control of human waywardness. Since the conflict appears at this stage to be purely intellectual it can safely be allowed to continue. There is no very strong temptation to avoid it; rather, when the original revulsion has been overcome, the study of left-wing literature becomes more and more absorbing, and the resulting dialectic gains momentum. But he is still convinced that this is merely an interesting theoretical study, he is simply 'trying to see the other point of view' and being fair to the young people's visionary idealism.

One day he actually asks his daughter about her political opinions, and since she is generous as well as enthusiastic she conquers a desire to crow over this apparently sudden change in his attitude, and answers his questions with sense and an unaccustomed humility. It is in this way that he gets to hear about the practical work being done by a group of people—mostly young—in the town where they live. They have organized an unofficial and easy-going kind of club for anyone who has nowhere in particular to go in the evenings. The place is the basement flat of a young man who deliberately bought it for that purpose. He moved to this squalid and over-crowded part of the town, leaving his parents' comfortable home in the 'best' part. He himself sleeps on a camp-bed in the tiny 'kitchen' at the back, while the main room is entirely devoted to the club. Since it is warm and the atmosphere unofficial and undemanding it is quite popular, and its frequenters include quite a few old people, as well as teenagers. Most of these latter are politically minded, but others come because they have been invited, and once there, they find it homely and comforting and (though they wouldn't admit it) a relief from the complications and passions of the groups they

D

fall into usually, as well as from the tensions and squalor of over-crowded homes.

All this the respectable father hears from his daughter, and he is moved by what he hears. The effort it cost him to abandon his pride and talk to his daughter about her ideas has in fact made him more open to the appeal of what she tells him, and her im-mediate response, the unexpected confidence she shows in him, creates a new relationship between them. The achievement of this relationship has made him more aware of himself, especially of a certain smugness in his attitude to life. The act of reconcili-ation makes him feel that he has been both unjust and stupid in the past, and he then offers himself to the future in repudiation of that past, which only appears worthy of repudiation in the light of a new love. If his resentment of his daughter had been stronger, because, for instance, she represented a mother to whom he was definitely hostile, he would have found it very much harder to sacrifice his pride, which protected him from all that she signified. In that case he would not humiliate himself by ask-ing her questions 'on the level', and in order to excuse himself from doing this he would need to repudiate *intellectually* the opinions she professed, and then justify his emotional intransig-ence in terms of the intellectual position which he dare not aban-don. Whether one regards his old or his new political stance as objectively sensible is irrelevant. The change presents itself as rational, but it is seldom or never *merely* that, and this applies to all cases of so-called intellectual conversion.

This man is not by any means yet 'converted' in the ordinary sense, but there has been one turning point, and it lays him open to new influences. He would not say that he has changed, only that his relations with his daughter have improved, and he can now understand her feelings better and *share* them, to some extent. So in fact there has been a conversion of a real but limited kind. In the movement towards it he was defined in relation to his daughter and in this self-discovery becomes aware of that in him which was inimical to the new relationship—he knows it as sin, and *repents*.

This new self-knowledge is very limited. It has transformed only that part of him which is related to his daughter but, as in the case of the couple in the last chapter, this new awareness of self in one relation casts its light on the rest.

The effect that such 'lighting up' has on other relationships depends on why they exist. If this man's wife had been a second powerful mum, instead of a retreat from one, the reaction to her might have been one of revulsion and rejection, as he finally began to be able to get rid of the flattening home influence. But in this case it makes him feel more warmly towards her. After all, she is the girl's mother, she is an extension of himself, therefore, in relation to their daughter. His behaviour to his colleagues, however, remains virtually unaffected. This part of his life has few links with the small but important area in which he has been changed.

A few weeks later he goes with his daughter to see the club and meet the young man who runs it. In the meanwhile he has insensibly slipped from regarding his daughter's opinions as hers, with which he sympathizes, to feeling them as to some extent his own. But if questioned he would probably explain his position rather in terms of an increased sense of social responsibility, of sharing the girl's conviction that 'something needs to be done', than of altered political conviction. He feels in terms of people in need, she in terms of principles to be put into practice.

So he is in a receptive though embarrassed frame of mind when he is confronted with the people who run the club, and those who frequent it. He has known, even seen, this sort of thing before, but not with eyes open to what it means. He is deeply disturbed, the very foundations are moved, by this confrontation, and especially by the young man who runs the place. He is an ugly and intense person who concentrates his whole attention on the one to whom he is talking, as if to communicate his own passionate conviction by sheer force. But when he is talking to a suspicious old tramp brought in by one of his young disciples he is suddenly gentle, infinitely adaptable and undemanding, with an apparently infallible sense of when to speak and when to be silent. When he talks to the people who help him, however, he is brusque, almost fierce, and expects absolute obedience quite as a matter of course.

The reluctant visitor finds himself told off to listen to the troubles of a shabby young couple who come to the club because their home is a room in a lodging house and if they turn on the radio the old woman in the next room complains to the landlady. The flood of worry and complaint flows over him, he tries to be sympathetic but hardly hears, because every inch of sensibility is being assaulted by varying impressions, and he is dazed with it all. Hours later it is his daughter who says 'It's time to go home', and he rises, and says goodbye to the zealot whose room this is, and the man looks at him, smiles at him, and says 'Come back. We need you.'

In the situation following this excursion there is still room, theoretically, to think of the visit to the club as simply a gesture of friendship and understanding towards his daughter and the other young people. They have these enthusiasms which one must admit are praiseworthy and valuable, and they should be encouraged, but one's own life is already arranged, it has its own pattern of usefulness—less dramatic, perhaps, but necessary.

This is the line that might be taken by a man whose unused self seemed too greatly threatened by the challenge of need, to whom the unused areas were a real danger. (This is the position of Alison in *Look Back in Anger*.) The man I have chosen to describe is a man only partially awake, but that in him which is still unaware is not so frightening that it needs to be violently resisted. It is therefore comparatively easy for him to realize the encounter with enthusiasm and with need as a personal challenge. The 'intervention' that gives a definite form to the response he makes, when the encounter releases his power to respond, is in this case probably a mixture of the ideas picked up in his recent reading and the reflection on his life which a closer relationship

with his daughter made possible. This idea of 'intervention' may
seem too vague and varied to be helpful, yet it does seem to be
present in some form or other, and its distinguishing characteristic
is that although it is, inevitably, partly mixed up in the whole
formation of the person concerned it appears, in the encounter
that demands faith, as a third element. It provides a symbol and
a moral direction that focuses and defines the need to expend,
to break out.

Although he does not know it, this man's decision was taken
while he was in the club that evening. He saw his life, in the face
of this challenge, as a futile succession of evasions of reality. He
realized that he had never tried to take hold of life but had
drifted, always avoiding the sharp edges of decision. He was able
to see all this, and not run away from the knowledge of it, because
of the young man who ran the place. He recognized a power and
a will that surpassed anything he had ever known, and this—
even before the man spoke to him—was a communication of love.
Love *exists*, it *works*, I *know* it. And he was able to accept this
communication because he had already established a narrow but
real communication with his daughter and was therefore open,
able to hear. The young man did not make a very great effort,
apparently, to get to know him, or to convince him that he was
needed or valued. His mere existence, being what he evidently
was, was enough. It was, in itself, a summons, and would have
been, even if he had not spoken a word to his visitor.

What if such a man had not been there, if this particular in-
carnation of a vital concern for human beings had been absent?
It may be that the fact of the enthusiasm of the others, or even
the fact of human need with which he was confronted, would
have been enough, in his already receptive state of mind, aware
as he was of his own failure in relation to his daughter, to make
a deep and lasting and action-provoking change. The chances are
that in this case the challenge would have been accepted anyway,
but the nature of the response would have been different. It is a
matter, once more, of the coming-into-being of a person in the

movement towards decision. It is only what actually *is*, as personal, at that moment that can be transformed. If the new visitor to the club had been simply impressed by the young people's enthusiasm and good will, and moved by the need of those they tried to help, he would almost certainly have decided to try to help them himself. There would have been a genuine change of heart, a turning away from cosy indifference, a repentance of former inactivity. But he would have made the decision as, still, a person with values and standards and achievements of proved, if very modest, worth. He would think of himself as bringing these to the service of others, in a way which he had been too lazy and indifferent to do before. He would have been, in fact, like the rich young man who was genuinely touched and fired by the preaching of Christ, and assumed that, with his good education and virtuous life, he had something worth giving, and could use his great possessions, material and spiritual, in the service of this new ideal that he now perceived. There is a genuine intention to give, and it is valuable because (if it is not too heavily challenged) the putting into practice of the ideal thus perceived may well continue to form the person in a way that will make it easier to see and respond to a further and more crucial demand. But the self-assessment involved in the decision is not a real self-knowledge but merely an unexamined assumption about oneself. And it is still unexamined in any real sense when it is expressed —as it often is—in lengthy self-justification.

But the danger of this is that the genuine goodness of what is done as a result of this kind of idealistic decision may make it appear to be sufficient. This expenditure of talent and energy, this sacrifice of time and money and comfort, and all the measurable success achieved in whatever undertaking absorbs the 'convert's' will to serve—all this is manifestly worthwhile. What more could be asked? But this is not enough, this is not faith, not a leap in the dark but a purposeful movement in full daylight. There is no real dying and therefore no new life. And the real invitation is always an invitation to death.

So in this case it was the encounter with another man who was himself given that made the demand a much more searching and complete one. It could, all the same, have been dodged in the way described, but this man is fundamentally too honest and also too naturally warm-hearted to do this. Having once been dug out of his refuge of I'm-not-the-sort-of-chap-that-can-do-anything-much he is prepared to face the full extent of his own real inadequacy and failure, as opposed to the rationalization of it which his whole life represents—his cult of being ordinary and nothing special.

In the movement towards decision which is his response to the invitation proffered he discovers himself as not only lazy and indifferent but smug, conceited, vain and hard-hearted. His apparent humility, in asking little of life, he realizes as simply cowardice and pride, that would not expose itself to failure. He sees that he has failed in all sorts of ways—in relation to his wife, of whom he required that she should be simply a cushion to protect him from any self-knowledge; in relation to his children whom he has seen as pleasant extensions of himself, blameable when they were unappreciative of the security and comfort he gave them; in relation to his colleagues whom he now sees he has encouraged to find in himself a justification for their own personal attempts at evasion of difficult decisions—just because he *is* so kind and easy and utterly harmless.

All this is not, of course, realized fully in the moment of encounter and challenge and response. The kind of self that he has discovered is realized gradually, later on, but it is at this moment that he actually sees, and seeing, repents, and repenting, is reconciled. He is reconciled to *himself*, to this newly stripped and worthless and unlovely self, for it is in realizing the complete worthlessness of all that he had thought worthwhile, in the rejection of all this as loathsome and futile, that he discovers his real value. And this value is not something he *has*, not a possession —great or little—but precisely something that is given, and is only realized in being given.

So far all the events that have been described can be compared quite easily with those that occurred in the progress of the lovers in the last chapter. But in the case of the lovers the putting-into-practice of their new life was to some extent built into the situation in which conversion occurred. Theirs was a sexual relation and it was natural to work it out sexually, though the way in which they reconciled this with the rest of their lives remained problematic. But at least to a great extent they did not need to ask themselves what they wanted to do about their love.

In the case of this man the working out is not so simple. Certainly he begins to come regularly to help at the club, certainly he tries to see his wife and children more as people and less as furniture. Certainly he tries to be more than a feather-bed to his colleagues when they discuss their personal problems. But how far should the change extend? What actions are demanded by his new life?

The answer to this will depend on the language in which his conversion is expressed. This means more than simply the words with which he explains, to himself and others, his new awareness of life, though this has a great deal to do with it. It means the whole mental 'picture' he has of the nature of the change. But at first this does not matter.

In the first days he does not reflect much, he is overwhelmed with the joy of his new awareness, with the relief as from the dropping of a huge burden. He seems to breathe more easily, he is surprised to find that he has far more physical energy than before. Sexually he is much more relaxed and even rather abandoned, a change which both shocks and, when she gets used to it, pleases his wife. He has none of the intensity and fire of the man who inspired him, he is still a quiet and easy-going person, warm and gentle by nature, rather than passionate or wild. But the change is deep and obvious, even though unspectacular. So in these early days he is carried on by the sheer power of his new experience of life. Everything seems easy and delightful, he does not ask himself what he ought to do but just does it.

But the language of his new life is a fairly narrow one. Part of it is vaguely political, but in his mind the political words are summed up in a sense of responsibility for people in need. His response was not to a particular ideal of reform or revolution but rather to the need that made *other* people want reform or revolution, and their enthusiasm in wanting it. Therefore his real and genuine commitment does not carry with it, as part of it, any obligation to pursue particular political ends. The language of his conversion experience is mainly one of personal responsibility and relationships. He knows that he has failed, and his failure is to people. He has not cared, either about his family and friends or about the appalling need that was under his nose every day, if he had cared to look. His repentance is for *this*, and it is deep and genuine, but the results of his repentance, the working out of his reconciliation, can therefore only be expressed in terms of such direct caring. What this caring might involve in the way of actually changing his way of life was not something of which he was aware in his experience of conversion, therefore it is not part of the transformed awareness of life. It is something he has to work out, from cold, as it were.

In this working out language is vital, and this means even actual words, because his transformation actually transforms the words which were involved in the conversion experience. He has used, all his life, words like 'working-class', 'poverty', 'self-sacrifice', 'responsibility', and many others that explain to himself the situation to which he responded. He has used them to describe, from the outside, in his usual easy-going and unattached way. But now these words carry the colour and power of his whole experience. When he uses them, or hears them used, they 'mean' for him the whole indivisible awareness of life as new-born. Their old meanings are still there, and still useful, but they are now capable of conveying even to other people who have not shared his experience, a little of the power of the spirit whose eruption in himself they define. And when he uses them among the other people with whom his new life has brought him in contact then the words carry an immense and almost intoxicating significance. They are a sign of a shared life, but, more than that, the use of them actually creates this sharing, renewing and strengthening the awareness of it among them.

This is the liturgy of this small assembly of people who have responded to a call. And just as the lovers felt that, although their physical love-making was essential and right, they had in it lost something nearer the heart of the love, so this group is probably most keenly aware of its nature in moments when each, perhaps separately, is engaged in actual work for the people who need them—for it was this that brought them together. Yet the act of expressing to each other, in words, what they are doing and why, and how they can do it better, is clearly essential, and gives them a renewed desire to go on. The words take them, in a sense, away from the heart of things, but without them they could not understand what they were doing, or go on doing it. And since they use their special words and phrases to recreate and further their experience of their togetherness-for-a-purpose the words not only express it, *they also limit it.* The meaning of the words, for them, is transformed and luminous, but this transformation cannot go beyond the reach of the ordinary, everyday connotation of the actual words. In this case, since the language of this liturgy is that of social consciousness and responsibility, that is the sphere in which it must operate, in practical terms. In the case of one—the leader—social consciousness took the form of abandoning everything else in order to serve the poor. But this is not built into the structure of the group as such, it is not part of the meaning which the whole group attaches to, for instance, the word 'self-sacrifice'. This action *preceded* the founding of the group, and is not a necessary condition of belonging to it, therefore the liturgy does not include this idea as a consequence of membership.

For some members of this loosely organized group, affiliation to a particular political party is their way of putting into practice the concern of the group as a whole. But again, the nature of the group's call is not distinctively party political. Therefore conversion in its context does not involve or transform political consciousness of this kind, and political words, while often used by the group, do not carry the current of shared life that makes words alive when they actually express, for these people, their experience of being called.

As for the man whose conversion I have described, he has not abandoned his livelihood, nor felt any need to join a political party, therefore his commitment, though real, is limited to personal and immediate relationships, at home and in the club. The need for any drastic external change of life, other than his evenings at the club, is not apparent, though he has a vague but strong feeling that something ought to be changed. It is difficult to know what, because there are no clear requirements involved in this conversion. At first he longs to clear his life of the clutter of inessentials that surround it—the social engagements, the little luxuries, the little comfortable routines of home that have for so long carried him along and prevented him from being aware of any other reality. But to alter these things would mean giving a reason for doing so, above all to his wife, who would be most affected. And he can't think of any convincing reason, even one that convinces himself. It is only a feeling, however strong. It lacks a language in which he could make sense of it. So, in the end, he does nothing, though of course when he spends evenings at the club he can't go out with his wife, and she has to explain that. She does so, with a mixture of pride and embarrassment, for although bewildered she has caught something of her husband's enthusiasm. Lacking a language, however, she finds it hard to convey this to him, and he is afraid that he may have upset her. Although he is determined to go on he also decides to do nothing that might worry her, and leaves his home life untouched as far as possible.

The same applies to his life at work. His attitude to his colleagues has changed, and they notice this, and of course rumours have reached them of his goings-on down the shabby end of the town. He puts up with teasing good-humouredly, but finds it is hard to explain what he feels about it. He doesn't feel obliged to persuade anyone of the value of what he is doing, in fact he dislikes talking about it, for the words that express it feel naked and crude and terribly vulnerable, when exposed to the attention of the unconvinced. In fact, his clumsy sincerity impresses people, but he does not know this, and retreats into half humorous self-concealment, so those who secretly longed to be given a share in the 'something' that they felt he had are disappointed, and revert to their old attitudes.

The result of all this is that, after a few months, the effect of this genuine conversion has dwindled to very little.

This does not happen through any deliberate turning away from whatever is clearly seen, but simply because no real attempt was made to bring the whole of life into relation to this new vision. No necessary course of action seemed to be involved, therefore old habits were allowed to keep their position. But the reason for their existence, as protective of a then 'unconverted' personality, has gone, therefore they are no longer harmless or even necessary devices for going on living in a dim and unpurposeful world, they are positive enemies. Yet if they are not clearly recognized as such the defence against them is disarmed.

So, some months later, there comes an invitation to the house of some old friends, not seen for years, who have done well and are now fairly rich. The wife wants very much to go, for she foresees more invitations, and an entry into a new and more luxurious world. Her husband does not want to disappoint her but he has, in fact, promised to take charge at the club on that night. In his confused condition this is a crucial decision. The others in the group are counting on him, he still regards himself as committed—but to what? His commitment is not even coherent enough for him to be able to explain to his wife why it matters so much, and why it is worth the sacrifice of a certainly pleasant evening, a possibly more exciting social future. He wants to do so, but finds it impossible, and the conflict merely makes him unusually irritable. On the other side is the obvious fact that to accept the invitation would please his wife, towards whom he has been feeling a little guilty for some time. He knows he is up against a real choice, and he is in some anguish of mind about it. He sees, clearly enough, that his whole new awareness of what life means is at stake. He sees this, and he knows, coldly and clearly, that beside this the rest is shabby and worthless. But he is tired of embarrassment and conflict, tired of trying to live two lives, tired of the endlessness of the work and the ungratefulness of the people one helps and the brashness of the younger, hot-headed, helpers. And, seeing all this, he chooses. He accepts the invitation to dinner and turns away from the invitation to death.

He does not know that, underneath, his wife is disappointed and depressed. He is busy covering up what he has done. He will go to the club on many other nights. His wife has first claim. One must have a sense of proportion. And so on.

But of course he gradually stops going to the club at all. He becomes more reserved, and instead of his former, unconverted friendliness there is a new irritability and surliness. His attachment to the comforts and routines of life is aggressive and demanding rather than simply accepting.

The reason for this is that the transforming effect of conversion is not simply undone. It cannot be, it is once for all. An area of personality has become aware, has come to existence in a crucial choice, and it cannot afterwards become non-existent. All that became known is still known. But there are still areas that have not reached definition as personal, are therefore still unconscious and exert their influence in unconscious but real ways. The habits and attitudes that are adjusted to these influences, that balance them and keep life going more or less evenly, are still there, and they stay there, unless something in the self-awareness of conversion demands that something be done about them. They can be attacked, they can be modified by the power of the new life which feels them as inconsistent. But it has to be a determined attack justifiable in terms of the purposes of conversion, or else the habits of the old man may well prove tougher than the wavering idealism of the new.

The old habits can simply smother the new life and hide it, gradually; no clear decision against the vision is made, there is only a gradual loss of clarity, as the adjustments to unconverted values become more far-reaching and leave less room for purposeful living. The transformation has not been undone, the defined, formed person is still there, but is not being used, is asleep or drugged. It can become a nostalgic memory of youthful enthusiam, safely wrapped in layers of accommodation to 'the world'. And the world isn't bad, except from the point of view of the new life in full operation. The world gets along alright, and has room for kindness and cheerfulness and good fellowship and even for helping the unfortunate.

Or, as in this case, the new self can simply be deprived of the power to act, by a single decision against it. In this case the old attitudes and habits have assumed a certain coherence as a way of life, with an obvious value, one which can offer itself as a valid alternative to a life that, in the light of it, appears as it does from *outside*, when it is unchanged by the inner vision of transformation. And, from the outside, the irritations and discomforts and failures are the things that stand out. But once they are allowed to appear like this the decision is almost taken—the decision *against* the new life. The transformed personality is still there, but it is a sort of corpse. It cannot be undone, but must be carried about, like the pitiful woman who was brought to entertain William of Normandy, a woman with two trunks—one alive, the other dead but still attached to her living body, and carried around wherever she went in all its putrefying horror. But, since nobody likes to carry a dead self around, the knowledge of its presence has to be blotted out by any means available. And since no means are infallible there is likely to be a strong reaction of defensive anger at anything that seems likely to uncover the knowledge of this horrible and inseparable companion. The intellectual dishonesty and moral recklessness characteristic of people who are suffering from what we revealingly call a 'bad conscience' is so well known as to need no description.

It seems important to realize that when the personality has been transformed it stays transformed. Whatever happens, the definition of personality thus achieved continues. It can be refused admittance, refused acknowledgment, but it is still there. And it can, sometimes, be used by the will that has refused to live by it. So the repentant awareness becomes a remorseful awareness, and the unbearable knowledge of what one is like is faced not in love, but in hatred and despair and rejection of what cannot be rejected because it is oneself.

In the convert I have described, the failure to live by his conversion is due at least partly to his lack of understanding of what is involved. He has no guide, other than his own repentant conscience, to assist him. The young man whose example acted as the agent of his conversion is no help because he is not really interested in anyone but the poor whom he serves. The others are so much material, only real to him in the context of their work. (This is the limit of the language of *his* conversion, which did not show him any ideal of sharing with, or service to, those who work with him.) The young people in the group are too young to understand the older man's difficulties, and an older man and woman who also belong come themselves from a very poor social background and cannot share his doubts and conflicts. And since this group is simply a spontaneous gathering, with no rules or established philosophy and no tradition, it has no *corporate* and explicit self-awareness as a group, which might serve to support the wavering member. Its liturgical language has a very poor vocabulary, for transformation does not only depend on formation beforehand—it depends on it afterwards. It depends on it in the way former habits assist or hinder the working out of the new life. It depends on it for the way the self-discovery of conversion expresses itself, and therefore commits itself. So it depends on it for the way the new awareness confronts the old.

The explicit self-awareness of the community in which conversion occurs limits the way the conversion works out in the individual convert. This applies, as I discussed earlier, to the language of liturgy—the sharing of the experience of the new life in outward words or gestures, or both—but also to the explicit aims and standards which the community sets itself. The community's ability to renew itself, by constantly extending the area of conversion in its members, and by involving new members, depends both liturgically and morally on this explicit self-awareness. Without such a language in which to share both its purposes and the norms that express those purposes, the group depends on the degree of enthusiasm and dedication of its individual members who are, each in their own way, themselves to some extent dependent on what they see in the others, because this is their only 'language'.

In order to see the kind of difference that it makes to be converted in a context that carries its own nature and purpose written clearly in its face I want to follow the dis-converted convert a little further.

For about a year he drifts along, not very different, apparently, from the man he was before his conversion, but a little harder, a little less pleasant. His relations with his daughter are naturally very bad, but she has left home and he seldom sees her. He is deeply resentful of his wife, who was the cause of his defection. He does not admit this reason, but he snaps at her for her timid and puzzled attempts to re-establish the kind of closeness they seemed to have after his conversion. But she, too, is disappointed and a little resentful, for something had begun to stir in her, until he killed it.

So he takes to staying out later in the evenings, sometimes. He goes out for a drink with one of his colleagues, finds congenial and pleasantly distracting company, and does not want to go back and face his conscience in the shape of his distressed and injured wife. One evening, going home late and rather the worse for wear, he staggers into the road too soon, is knocked down by a car and taken to hospital with fractured ribs and arm, a badly cut and scraped face and chest, and a pierced lung.

The effect of both these circumstances—the fact that he was drinking, not convivially, or as a normal part of life, but as an escape and a protest and a revenge, and the fact that he is ill and so cut off from ordinary life—is to put him into a state in which he seems separated from the safety of life as he knows it, from the soothing framework of customs and routine and accepted behaviour: from the Law, in fact. He is on his own, with nothing to hold onto, neither his rather defiant self-respect, nor the daily necessities of work, nor even the confidence of being in control. For he is in pain and cannot sleep, and is ordered about by other people. His wife visits him, and cries, and tries helplessly to comfort him, and the sight of her, just now, tears off many of the protective layers in which he has managed to dress himself. He is vulnerable and angry and afraid, fighting against memories he cannot bear to face.

This kind of condition can be produced by illness or catastrophic loss of fortune, or by moral collapse, or a mixture of these. The essential is that something happens that makes the normal structure of security, the life of the world, seem no longer safe or even very real. There is a loss of self-respect, a loss of a feeling of belonging to anything. It is the condition induced in the two lovers I described by their own actions, that separated them from their normal lives, and also from their normal vision of themselves. It is the condition of the two children whose anger had taken them frighteningly outside the confines of their ordinary feelings and types of behaviour. It is also the condition of the subject of this chapter when he was first confronted with the reality of poverty.

This condition of estrangement from normality is not in itself transformative. It has no particular value at all, indeed it is dangerous, it can lead to panicky efforts to find *any* kind of sense or refuge, or to withdrawal into a semi-animal life of minimum response. All it means is that the power of the formative influences

—good or bad—is decreased to an extent that makes the person vulnerable to intervention that could otherwise be ignored or repelled. If the two children in the first chapter had not lost their tempers they might have been too well pleased with themselves as they were to have any desire for a more intimate encounter with each other. If the two lovers had not experienced shame and anxiety and fear they might have been content to muddle through a fairly superficial love affair, never really giving each other anything. If the man had met the single-minded servant of the poor in his own house, or in a pub, he might have been interested or even moved but he would have been unlikely to have been so bowled over.

So in this later and more complete breakdown of the coherence of what St Paul calls the life of the flesh, he is vulnerable to a type of influence he would normally reject without difficulty even, probably, during the period of his first conversion. What happens in this case is that one of the night nurses, herself a young and enthusiastic evangelical Christian, gives him a 'tract' to read, a fairly crude and conventional account of a conversion. She gives it him when he is lying awake at night, in some physical distress and worse mental pain. The silence, broken by breathing and grunts and occasional clatter from the sluice, the dim light, the sense of isolation, the prospect of empty hours to be endured before daylight restores a minimal sense of belonging somewhere— these things belong to night in a hospital. In this setting he reads the little story, for lack of anything better to do, and because the kind little nurse so obviously wanted him to.

So he meets love expressed in Christian words, and the words stir the memories of his childhood, when he was loved, and loved by a woman to whom the words of Christian faith were a natural way of expressing love and concern. He encounters Christ as the one who cares, and who wants him.

The Christian idea of conversion is that whatever the circumstances and people concerned a real conversion is a conversion to Christ and in Christ. I shall discuss in more detail in a later

chapter exactly why one can say this, and not mean the statement as merely a metaphor. At this point, however, it is already
possible to see how the vision of overwhelming and sacrificial love
can transform. An idea of Christ may come over with extraordinary vividness, either because he is eloquently described, or
because even a trite description, as in this case, is encountered in
circumstances producing sensitivity. If the vision that is conveyed
does have this impact, the reaction is as great as that to any encounter with great love. It is greater than most because any account of Christ must show him as *above all loving*. His is a
heroic self-giving, without condition or limit. If people can respond to real love even from a comparatively selfish person, it is
not surprising that they respond to the love of Christ, once the
idea of his love ceases to be a phrase in a sermon and becomes a
personal reality. For this to happen the normal resistance to
awareness of love must be broken down. In situations between
human beings the relationship itself can produce the conditions that break down the resistance, as in the two cases already
discussed. In this present case the resistance has been broken
down by suffering and loneliness, so that there is a felt need for
love, and it is recognized when it is offered. The immensity of
the love recognized is overwhelming, it makes all other ideas or
experiences of love seem dim and even ridiculous. Once this is
fully realized the response is implicit in the knowledge. There
could be a refusal, but the man I have described has already lost
so much that the fear of self-loss that makes people reject love as
an appalling threat is brushed aside. It is there—it always is—but
it scarcely counts. He has, through suffering and helplessness, become 'as a little child' and his response to the invitation to enter
the kingdom of heaven is as swift and complete as that of the
child who was once loved in the name of Christ. There is little
struggle, the stage of conflict, of breaking down, is already over.
And the self-awareness with which he responds to this invitation
is so total and so peaceful that the agony often indicated by the
word 'repentance' is almost unnoticed. He knows himself, in the

face of this tremendous love, as not only futile and cowardly and proud but also cruel, ungrateful and mean. He knows himself as more profoundly worthless than his former conversion was capable of showing him, for then he still thought of himself as a decent, if not very generous, husband and father and a hard-working sober citizen. Now he knows that his marriage was a refuge from love, not a giving of it, his work an escape from commitment, his respectability a blanket to protect himself from other people's needs and his own nature. This realization of himself is not terrible but an enormous relief. He finds no pleasure in contemplating his own sordidness, as if to make himself realize all the more the value of forgiveness. This kind of self-indulgence, sometimes needed to bolster up a defective conviction of being loved, is not necessary for him. His self-discovery is primarily a discovery of himself as loved, and the clear knowledge of his worthlessness in the light of that love is a pain that is not so much blotted out by as totally involved in the peace of reconciliation.

The results of a self-discovery in this kind of setting differ in two ways from the previous, less complete one. The first difference is that this time there is no human community within which conversion takes place. There is no fellowship, no obvious human aim or work of a practical kind to which conversion commits him, as in the first case. And since both his childhood experience of Christianity and this new one are divorced from any kind of Christian community the transformation in this case does not include an awareness of Christianity as a community, in any form. He knows it only as a relationship with God in Christ, who loves him. This is his conversion context, and no other.

But the other difference is that the faith to which he is converted, however individual his conversion experience may be, contains in itself definite moral directives. A Christian, of any kind whatever, regards himself as bound to obey the commands of Christ. He may interpret them in any number of different ways, but obedience to Christ in some form is the way in which he puts his faith into practice. And it is clear from even the very simple little tract that caused the upheaval that obedience to Christ means loving other people—*any* other people—with something as near as possible to Christ's totally given love. So this time he does not have to wonder what he is committed to, or rely on a vague feeling that he ought to change more than his evening occupations. In the light of his new self-discovery he knows where his failures have been and therefore what he—not anyone else at all but just he himself—needs to do about it. His practical decisions follow quite readily and peacefully from his realization of himself as loved, and therefore able to love. In the silence he re-plans his life, quietly and without any great sense of upheaval. There is none of the sense of achievement that he felt before, because there is now nothing (or very little, since there can never be *nothing*) to achieve *against*. Since he is totally given, or as totally as he can be, he has not to reassure himself that all is well. It just is. It is true that when he is better, and in the ordinary world must put into practice his far-from-ordinary plans, he will find it much more difficult than it seems at the time, but he has a kind of quiet conviction that will probably carry him through.

The weakness of his position is his isolation. He has only himself with whom to work out, through the years, the meaning and purpose of his calling. This means that he may lack the renewed conflict and resolution pattern, the dialectic of a community of common aims but differing temperament and interpretation. He will lack the power of some kind of liturgy to express the meaning and purpose of his life, and so extend it towards the future —a liturgy which is not purely self-devised and therefore capable of providing the stimulus of conflict as an aid to *continued* self-discovery. He is in some danger of becoming narrow, perhaps smug, and attached to his own ideas.

But these are dangers, not certainties. He may have reached so deep a humility and so clear-sighted a charity that he runs no risk of betraying his conversion. The community he needs he may well create, by the power of his love, and he will know

Christ as its centre and source. Or he may join an existing one, and bring to it this same awareness of the meaning of love.

But even without a community, and without a liturgy, he may go forward, because he does have a language. His faith knows itself in words whose *ordinary*, outside meaning conveys a scope that is co-extensive with human life itself, not one confined to a particular sphere of concern. Therefore when their meaning is also the meaning of the personal self, the transformed self, the transformation involves, at least potentially, *every* aspect of life. So in a real sense his faith does exist in the context of a community, because in Christ every man is his brother, and this community does have a liturgy, because so many of the words he uses in ordinary talk with ordinary people are words that, for him, carry the power of the spirit. Therefore even for those who do not see with his vision the words he speaks have a power they recognize, though they cannot name it.

It is interesting that when a convert looks back on his conversion, and the life that went before, he tends to describe it in ways that appear ludicrous to other people who remember him as he was before conversion. A way of life that was virtuous and respectable, even very good by ordinary standards, can be described without conscious exaggeration by the convert as steeped in sin, given over to loathsome excesses. In the case of young converts this is often due at least partly to the fact that awakening sexual feelings were regarded as horrible signs of depravity, because of an education suspicious of sexuality. When the suppressed feelings break through they often take a religious form, quite naturally, because the thing suppressed is not simple physical sexuality but the ability to love, the whole spiritual energy of the person. When a focus is provided for all this spiritual power in the idea of Christ who loves and redeems, then all of it is directed towards him. In the light of this new freedom of love the old, muddled, furtive and fearful traffic with sexual feeling, however slight, seems really repulsive. This is often true of grown-up converts also, in whom sexuality, with the power to love

which is bound up with it, has been suppressed. But even to
people who have had a normal sexual life the pre-conversion life
seems monstrous. The fact is that what was, at the time, a necessary and normal adjustment to the demands of living now
appears as an evasion of love, and it is in comparison with what
love clearly demands that it appears so horrible. But at the time
there was nothing with which to compare it, and indeed no desire to make any comparison. The life of the flesh, and the Law
which controls it and guides and educates it, seems perfectly good
and indeed is perfectly good to those who live by it. It only looks
like a lunatic mess to those who have seen the real thing. That is
why St Paul talked about the former life of his converts as if they
had all been wild libertines—perhaps some of them had, but the
chances are that a lot of them were perfectly respectable shop-
keepers.

Augustine, looking back on his pre-conversion life, saw it as a
round of sensual indulgence alternating with arrogant intellectual
feats. In fact he spent fifteen years with one woman, with whom
it nearly broke his heart to part, and he was clearly a conscien-
tious and patient teacher, a devoted if domineering friend, and a
surprisingly long-suffering son. But he was right, all the same,
because he saw that his love for his mistress and his success at
his job had, in fact, kept him from surrendering entirely to God,
and had done so just because all these things *were* really good. He
described this hindrance in terms of loathsome pride and sensuality because that, in retrospect, was how it *felt* to him. His
revulsion from his past resistance to the demands of love was such
that he included the whole lot in one intense repudiation. He
never realized that it was, in all likelihood, the devotion of his
discarded mistress, through all those years, that made him sufficiently 'human' and secure to be able to listen to the word of
salvation, when he heard it. A child alternately spoiled and repressed, a brilliant boy flattered and indulged, would have had
little chance of becoming a passably pleasant man, let alone a
saint, without the formative influence of an enduring love.

The account of conversion given here is of a conversion so complete that it can only be called sanctity. This is not accidental. If conversion is the process of self-discovery it is a discovery of the self which is the spirit, and its complete discovery can only mean the complete freedom of the spirit. This is a state nobody attains on the plane of life as we know it, whose sphere is bounded by appearances (for we never know anything in itself). But self-discovery is the liberation of the spirit, even a little.

It comes about through some kind of conflict, in some kind of encounter, and the transformation that then overtakes some part of the human thing is what makes it a person: conscious, separate, and given. The separation in self-discovery comes about in the movement towards giving.

It can be arrested. Sometimes the vision of human baseness and powerlessness impels a man to reach out, knowing and creating himself over against the future, but the movement stops there. There is no assurance of being loved to give it the courage to take the final step, so this achievement of self is forever held in intense awareness of what one is, never flinching from the oncoming future but never surrendered to it in love. This existentialist moment of eternally arrested and eternally renewed distinction is the heroic predicament of the one who knows himself in need of love, and able to give it, but cannot see that there can be anyone to love him, or to whom he can give love, and therefore can only regard the surrender to love as a surrender to unreality and death. And of course he is right. Ultimately it is only the recognition of a love that is *itself* given to unreality and death that can create the power to make such a suicidal gift.

It appears, then, that the most important part of a human formation that can make way for the transformation of love is in fact the experience of being loved. And real love is, by definition something that only occurs in transformation.

Someone already transformed by love is needed, in order to convey an assurance of love sufficiently strong to penetrate the defences of the flesh in another and let loose the power of the spirit.

This is the work of the community of love, but the particular group of human beings cannot, in itself, do this unless it has within it the power of renewal, which cannot reside in any one individual, at the risk of foundering when he founders, and of endangering even his own ability to love. Sometimes one person, sometimes another, can find the courage to go on, and so renew the rest. It happens in a marriage, it happens in a group. But the source of this courage is not the person himself, or herself. It is recognized as coming from the thing *shared*. It may be one person who renews faith, but it is not faith in himself that he renews but just faith—the given-ness, the at-riskness, of love. Even when faith is renewed by one person providing support, for a while, for the other or others, it is still support for the sake of love, or it doesn't work. Support given out of self-confidence becomes possessive, and does not allow further growth. Support given for love is willing to see the support no longer needed. So whatever form the renewal of faith takes it is the renewal of something shared. The centre, the heart of it, is never possessed but always given.

But this thing that is given is immensely powerful. The accounts so far given of different aspects of transformation show this power at work, and the whole process of transformation can be thought of as the release of power. This is the power that transforms, and the next thing that needs to be asked is what sort of power this is, how it works, and what is its relation to formation, as well as transformation.

CHAPTER IV

THE RELEASE OF POWER

In the cases described so far something, some power, 'got out' and altered and shaped the situation. There is one kind of person in whose life this power does not simply break out, from time to time, but who seems to be possessed by it, almost to the exclusion of other, more ordinary, influences. This kind of person is a prophet, and as a prophet is not easy to identify with, and therefore might not carry conviction, it seems better to take examples of actual prophets and study them in the way so far used.

It is difficult to define a prophet. He evades categories, even his classification as 'prophet' is risky if it implies a recognizable, fixed type of person or vocation, with a definite place in relation to other types of person. A prophet is an oddity—a scandal or a nuisance or a bore or an outrage, according to the degree in which he interferes with the normal order of things. For he does interfere. He upsets things.

Jeremiah, son of Hilkiah, came of a priestly family, and was born at a time when the Kingdom of Judah was a more or less peaceful vassal of Assyria. He appears to have had influential connections, and he was intelligent and pious—that much is clear. He might have been expected to have become an influential member of the priestly group, and a useful adviser to the King, Josiah, who was concerned for the reform of religion. But something happened to Jeremiah when he was still in his teens (he describes himself as a 'boy', and was still too young to be married, an event that occurred fairly early at that time). This was an adolescent conversion, then, and although we have no information about the occasion of it, it seems clear from the plan of life that resulted, and also from the kind of language that Jeremiah used to describe the sins of his people, that his conversion was connected, as it so often is at this age, with sexual feelings.

This is so common as to seem scarcely worth saying, but it is perhaps rather more important in this case because the usual reason—the rejection of sexual feelings due to a puritanical upbringing—is unlikely to have been operative in a boy brought up in a culture that took sex so much for granted. To the young Jeremiah, his calling involved a resolve not to marry, and he explains that this is because the normal begetting and rearing of children is out of place in a community doomed to destruction. His own unmarried condition is a sign of God's wrath which hangs over the people. But when one sees how he describes Israel's and Judah's faithlessness to God in terms of marital unfaithfulness it becomes fairly clear that, to him, to be called by God, as God's people had been, involved a total self-giving, a surrender with which no other love, no other concern, must be allowed to interfere. Jeremiah's calling, then, demands that he have no other ties or concerns but the Lord's sending. He expresses this as a knowledge of himself as wholly known by God, and conditioned by his will:

'The word of the Lord came to me, saying: "Before I formed you in the womb I knew you, and before you were born I consecrated you; I appointed you a prophet to the nations." '

But the transforming effect of the decision to surrender to this call is not achieved without a struggle. If the response is to be a real death it cannot depend on any confidence in one's ability to carry out the task commanded. It must be a self-giving in the face of a future which is totally dark, just as in the case of the two lovers.

Two kinds of obstacles can oppose this leap in the dark. One is a consciousness of ability to cope with the situation by virtue of one's existing abilities. This was what the mother of the two children in the first chapter might have done, faced with the challenge of her children's quarrel. It was what the convert might have done at the time of his 'first' conversion, if he had not been robbed of self-confidence by the confrontation with a really dedicated man. The other is a consciousness of *in*ability to cope, a desire to seek refuge from an appalling demand by clinging to the (real) fact of one's lack of gifts or courage or opportunity or whatever. So Jeremiah, like Moses in a similar situation, says, 'Ah, Lord God, behold I do not know how to speak, for I am only a boy!' Both objections have the same root—the assumption that it is the virtues and qualities one possesses that are to be used in answer to the call.

It is at this point that the prophetic calling takes on a decisively different character from other kinds of conversion and salvation occurrence. The difference is in the kind of self which is discovered and realized in the transforming experience. The nature of this self-discovery is one of the marks that distinguish the prophet as opposed to the pseudo-prophets with whom the Old Testament abounds, and who are to be found in large numbers in every age. There is another decisive sign, as we shall see, but it grows out of this one.

This self-discovery is one in which the person realizes himself as totally without power—not only the power to do good actions but even the power to think worthwhile thoughts. All conversion involves repentance, a turning away from all that prevented the self-giving of love, a realization that, as preventing love, much in the past was incongruous and evil. But the prophetic calling involves repudiation of much more than unworthy and unloving behaviour. It sees that *everything* in the life of the flesh—the world as we know it—is futile and useless as a means of accomplishing the will of God. The truth of the world is so distant an approximation to the naked truth of the spirit, as perceived in the moment of revelation, that it can only be discarded. This is clearly only a greater degree of self-surrender than the 'ordinary' salvation occurrence, but the degree is what makes the difference.

Repentance on this scale means that the self with whom the convert is now reconciled is one in whom there is no support but in the will of the one who made the demand. Self-surrender of such a radical kind, all in one go, is naturally very rare, and the result of it is a 'take-over' by the power of the spirit. And it is partly the 'all in one go' character of the conversion that constitutes the prophet. It seems important to realize this, because an equal 'degree' of transformation can come about by slow, successive changes, a number of 'conversions', by which, each time, more and more of the whole man becomes real, defined and available as personal. This is the process that the lives of saints describe, and it is familiar at the much more ordinary level of people who are struggling to live a life of real love, and managing it, bit by bit.

This does not mean that people are converted in bits, that conversion is not, after all, once for all, or that baptism (when it is a realized self-giving to Christ) or any other kind of decision for love is 'only a beginning'. The person is one whole, and is saved as one whole, not in bits—but the once-for-all salvation in Christ can only reach a man as a person, that is, as a conscious being capable of love. Therefore his response can only come from him as personal, that is, as defined and aware, one who has come into conscious being under the touch of love. And this person is one whose existence is conditional on the formation that is provided by the Law, applied to the unformed and chaotic state which is the life of the flesh or—in the light of conversion—of sin. And this life of the flesh is a time-conditioned one. Time is its medium of existence, the thing out of which the Law shapes a human being. So formation can only give way to transformation *in time*, that is, in stages, as the formation of the life of the flesh allows. So although the response is the response of a whole person it is incomplete at any given stage of life. And, as the stages succeed each other, the unconverted area of life must still live and be formed by the Law, but under the guidance of the new and 'real' awareness of life which has been achieved in the single movement of repentence-conversion-reconciliation. If there is no serious backsliding this life-long process should end up as a condition very near to the complete conversion, in which all personal gifts and virtues are swallowed up, transformed, in a love which is not one's own, yet is most surely one's real self. 'Now I live, yet not I, but Christ lives in me.'

But this is not the prophetic character. This is sanctity, and a saint is not the same as a prophet, though a prophet may be a saint and many saints were prophets. You can become a saint without being a prophet, and you can be a prophet without being a saint, though it might be difficult to keep this up for long without ceasing to be a prophet. The point about being a prophet is first of all that the conversion doesn't happen slowly, it happens all at once, though there may be successive revelations that deepen and extend the original calling. And also, that the area of transformation is chiefly concerned with intellectual and emotional awareness, not first of all with the moral sphere. It is when one's own inability to know and to love truly is recognized that the kind of transformation occurs which can be called prophetic. This is why the prophet afterwards knows himself as speaking or writing not his own words, but God's, and bringing to the people not his own care and advice and support but only God's. This is what gives a prophet a kind of wild tactlessness, and an often infuriatingly placid acceptance of the fact that what he says doesn't persuade, doesn't 'get through'. Jonah, in that extraordinary morality novel about conversion, actually took this attitude to a false extreme, and far from wanting the people of Niniveh to repent at his word was highly offended when they listened, repented and were forgiven. He wanted his word of doom to be vindicated by the divine anger in action and this shows that he had been false to his mission by appropriating God's word to himself.

Jeremiah did not make this mistake:

'But the Lord said to me, "Do not say, 'I am only a boy', for to all to whom I send you you shall go, and whatever I command you you shall speak. Be not afraid of them, for I am with you to deliver you," says the Lord.

'Then the Lord put forth his hand and touched my mouth, and the Lord said to me, "Behold, I have put my words in your mouth ... and behold, I make you this day a fortified city, an iron pillar, and bronze walls, against the whole land. ... They will fight against you, but they shall not prevail against you, for I am with you, says the Lord, to deliver you".'

That was Jeremiah, voicing his conviction that not he, but only the Lord, spoke to the people. The prophet Ezekiel's sense of powerlessness seems to have reached the point where he was actually unable to speak except at moments when the Lord told him to, while Isaiah, in the famous account of his calling, expresses the self-discovery of personal worthlessness, and the conviction that this void has been filled by the power of God, and the worthless one is indeed chosen:

'In the year that King Uzziah died I saw the Lord sitting upon a throne, high and lifted up, and his train filled the temple. Above him stood the seraphim; each had six wings, with two he covered his face and with two he covered his feet and with two he flew.'

The self-imposed blindness of the seraphim who were emissaries of divine vengeance, and their covering of their sexual organs—'feet' is a euphemism—are an indication of the kind of abnegation which the prophet feels to be appropriate in the encounter with, and service of the divine power.

'And one called to another and said, "Holy, holy, holy is the Lord of hosts, the whole earth is full of his glory." And the

foundations of the threshold shook at the voice of him who
called, and the house was filled with smoke.'

The seraphim and other 'spirits' who are described in the Old
Testament are manifestations of God's power in particular
ways. So here the seraphim, spirits of fire, are the overwhelming
and searing knowledge of God's concern for his sinful people. In
the face of this revelation Isaiah discovers what he is:

'And I said, "Woe is me, for I am lost! For I am a man of
unclean lips, and I dwell in the midst of a people of unclean lips;
for my eyes have seen the King, the Lord of hosts".'

But the painful repentance, the knowledge of oneself as outcast,
is transformed into reconciliation and union. The same love that
is burning and terrifying is also healing and peace-bringing. And
afterwards there is the consciousness that a working out of the
conversion is to follow, and how.

'Then flew one of the seraphim to me, having in his hand a
burning coal which he had taken from the altar. And he
touched my mouth, and said, "Behold, this has touched your
lips, your guilt is taken away, and your sin is forgiven." And
I heard the voice of the Lord saying, "Whom shall I send, and
who will go for us?" Then I said, "Here am I, send me." And
he said "Go, and say to this people. . . ." '

So the personal gifts are seen as irrelevant, it is only by the
purification of agonized penitence that the prophet becomes fit
to speak the word that is not his own.

The peasant girl from Domrémy took longer to convince.
When her voices first told her that she was to rescue her people
from their enemies she cried and trembled, protesting that she
was 'a poor maid, knowing nothing of riding and fighting'. But in

the end she obeyed, and her bearing throughout her strange
career was characterized by a combination of simplicity, humility
and utter confidence that was only briefly shaken by threats, illness, fatigue, bewilderment and the fear of death. But before the
crucial demand on her was made Joan had heard her voices several
times, telling her to pray, to 'be a good girl'. She was, by all normal standards, already 'a good girl', but she interpreted the command as a call to devote herself to God, and she did so, withdrawing to some extent from the games and conversations of the
other children. In this separated condition she heard clearly the
call to 'go into France' and eventually obeyed, with staggering
results.

Bernadette Soubirous is not normally thought of as a prophet,
but she fits the definition of one as a person who is sent, and
whose message is not his own. So far from wanting to take 'the
Lady's' messages to others, Bernadette only did so because to refuse would have been to forfeit her communion with the presence
which had become, for her, the whole meaning of life. In the
light of this presence she became acutely conscious of sin—not
so much her personal sinful actions, though these worried her,
too, as the *state* of sin, the sickness in which the whole world was
soaked and, in it, herself. And she repented, she did penance for
sin, in a reaction whose directness and simplicity had none of the
tortuous self-directedness detectable in some hagiographical records of asceticism. Hers was a gesture of pure love, totally converted love. So when she was sent with a message she went,
terrified but obedient, and as steadfast as her predecessor, Joan.

John the Baptist spent a lot of time explaining that he was not
the Messiah. He only brought a message. 'The one who bade me
preach' is the authority to whom the crowds who came to him
should listen.

So a prophet is one wholly taken over by a power which he is
convinced is not his own, and it is a power with a purpose, a
message which must be conveyed to others. What kind of person
is used for this message, and what kind of a message is it?

E

There are two ways of thinking of the answer to the question, What kind of person? and both of them help to show the relation of formation to the release of the power that transforms. First of all we can mean the kind of relation in which a person stands to other people, in the class or religious or domestic structure. Educated or uneducated? Agricultural or industrial? In authority or under it? Stable or roaming? Married or single?

And the odd thing about people who have suffered a prophetic vocation is that they don't fit into any social pattern, either positively or negatively. They don't belong, nor are they part of an organized opposition, nor even an individual one. They seem to erupt through the cracks of a society, or even create cracks to erupt through.

As I suggested in the chapter about encounter, human beings cannot just bump around anyhow. This is too destructive, it prevents all growth or self-discovery, it makes the development of stable relationships impossible. So the chaotic and unformed life of the flesh must submit to the governance of the Law, and it produces what we call a civilization, whose self-knowledge is its culture. Every community organizes itself into groups and layers and patterns, which help to give all its members a feeling of stability, of belonging in a special place. People have their functions in the society, and they recognize themselves by these, and order is maintained by a system of conditioned rejections that prevent people wanting very strongly to get out of their place in the pattern. Particular types of behaviour, or particular kinds of clothes, help to keep people to their own places. The culture of a society expresses the kind of pattern of living within which it is possible for these human beings to live and grow and (often ritually) change from one area of living to another within the larger framework.

Mary Douglas's book on pollution and tabu, *Purity and Danger*,[1] examines this interestingly. Talking about ritual, she refers to 'secular rites', and explains:

[1] London, 1966.

'For us, individually, everyday symbolic enactment does several things. It provides a focusing mechanism, a method of mnemonics and a control for experience . . . a ritual provides a frame. The marked off time or place alerts a special kind of expectancy. . . . Framing and boxing limit experience, shut in desired themes or shut out intruding ones. How many times is it necessary to fill a weekend case to exclude successfully all tokens of unwanted office life? One official file, packed in a weak moment, can spoil the whole effect of the holiday.'

Later she says,

'Our experiences take place in separate compartments, and our rituals too. So we must treat the spring millinery and spring cleaning in our towns as renewal rites which focus and control experience as much as Swazi first fruit rituals. When we honestly reflect on our scrubbings and cleanings in this light we know we are not mainly trying to avoid disease. We are separating, placing boundaries, making visible statements about the home that we are intending to create out of the material house. If we keep the bathroom cleaning materials away from the kitchen cleaning materials and send the men to the downstairs lavatory and the women upstairs, we are essentially doing the same thing as a Bushman wife when she arrives at a new camp. She chooses where she will place her fire and then sticks a rod in the ground. This orientates the fire and gives it a right and left side. Thus the home is divided between the male and female quarters.'

And again,

'Culture, in the sense of the public, standardized values of a community, mediates the experience of individuals. It provides in advance some basic categories, a positive pattern in which ideas and values are tidily ordered. And above all it has authority, since each individual is induced to assent because of the assent of others.'

Power, in a society, is exercised for the preservation of this order, in ways that are themselves ordered. The articulation of power is the articulation of the society itself and although it has to be adaptable it must also be predictable, if possible. This is the peace which the world can give, and which we need, in order to go on living. It is ordered by the Law, which, if it is a good Law, provides a formation which is as far as possible according to the needs of loving. But no Law can fully satisfy the need to love, the restless spirit seeking a way to transform. And the more settled and orderly the society, the less adaptable it grows, above all when organization has become the end and not the means of life. In that case the power that a young and idealistic community can mobilize within the articulation of its own structure is repressed and denied. Then, when it breaks through it does so in the cracks, the spaces between the outlines that contain the parts of a society.

Mary Douglas discusses at length the fear, shown by many cultures, of people who are in a 'marginal state' and are held to be open to the power that belongs to 'formlessness'. There are people who have been left out in the patterning of society, who are placeless. 'He [van Gennep] saw society as a house with rooms and corridors in which passage from one to another is dangerous. Danger lies in transitional states, simply because transition is neither one state nor another, it is undefinable'—therefore it is outside the Law, which can only work by clarifying and arranging.

Prophets tend to occur outside the normal articulation of power. Either they come from people who are socially powerless, like Joan of Arc and Bernadette, or if they are born in potentially influential positions within the power structure they opt out of it, and exercise their calling outside it, often in opposition to it, like

Isaiah and Jeremiah and John the Baptist. Prophets will not be put in any category, they are strictly outlaws, and the reason for this is that they represent, in a sense *are*, the power which transcends and transforms the Law. This does not mean they necessarily break the Law. They may do so if they see that a particular formulation of it is in fact acting contrary to the purpose which Law should serve—the preparation of man for the freedom of the spirit. In practice prophets do usually end up breaking the Law, precisely because of the tendency of Law to become rigid and prevent what it is intended to serve. Jeremiah was flogged and put in the stocks, tried for blasphemy, and narrowly escaped death more than once. John the Baptist and Joan of Arc were 'removed' because they seemed to be a menace to Law and order, as understood by those in power, and Bernadette was subjected to police interrogation and even imprisonment as a troublemaker and a cause of social unrest. But the prophet's business is to make people see that the purpose of Law is to prepare the way for the Lord, that it is only a means, never an end, and that its fulfilment is only achieved in transcending it.

John the Baptist, who was 'more than a prophet', opted out of the useful and pious life to which his priestly birth entitled him and exiled himself in the desert. He was odd. He dressed oddly, he ate oddly and he talked extremely oddly. The representatives of the Law feared and hated him, but found it difficult to discover grounds for suppressing him because he spoke in the name of the Lawgiver and pointed to the failures of these guardians of the Law in relation to the Law itself. The common people adored him, because they had lost the security of the Law, and knew it only as a burden. They were humiliated both by the Romans and by their own leaders. They came to him in the desert, not just geographically but psychologically, for they were afraid, unprotected and full of half-expressed and ill-understood longings.

Joan of Arc was a peasant girl from a respectable family. She put on man's dress and engaged in war. She went totally out of her normal sphere and as a result her 'own' people rejected her.

But the people who belonged in the sphere she invaded also resented her, even while they used her, and finally they had their revenge. The poor people loved her, for they had lost their security already. The structures of society were no use to them; between the English invaders and the French nobility, they stood to lose, whatever happened.

Bernadette Soubirous came from a family that was neither one thing nor the other, the child of an impoverished miller who was not quite shorn of respectability. She was terrified by her commission to prophesy, which took her among prelates and police and government officials, a world of Law in every sense. Oblivious of what anyone thought, she continued to deliver the message of repentance and to deny all the accretions and elaborations of her message that other people devised in order to soften its impact. Nobody wanted her, not even her own people, who could not understand the simplicity of her message. She was outcast altogether, and lived out a lonely life as a nun, content with the knowledge that she had obeyed, while other people turned her message into a structure, and tamed it to conform with the Law.

This is what always happens, and this is why there have to be always more prophets, to tell people that there is a power that is greater than the Law.

What kind of person is a prophet? He is an outcast, a hybrid, an unclubbable individualist. The central example is Christ, the prophet of the kingdom, who was called 'Rabbi' but was not a scribe; who was a workman, but taught as if he had been a Rabbi; who was not a priest, or a politician, who was in fact quite unclassifiable, and for that reason a menace to anyone interested in maintaining Law and order. Even his origin is presented as uncertain, as if to emphasize his out-law condition.

What kind of person *is* a prophet, in himself? Just as the position of the prophet in the social order is impossible to pin down, so also prophets as people don't conform to type. There are clever ones and very simple ones, rugged types like Amos, poets like

Isaiah, gentle, gay ones like Francis of Assisi and stern, ruthless ones like John the Baptist. The only thing prophets have in common is that they have been sent, and the mission on which they are sent is not theirs, nor is the power theirs that gives them strength and patience and courage and makes them indifferent to the opinions of other people—not because they are sure they are right, but because only the message matters, and rightness and wrongness, as the world judges these things, are irrelevant. They do not require the vindication of being heard or of visible results. The success of the mission, even, is less important than carrying it out, though they grieve because men cannot hear the voice that they hear, as Christ wept for his beloved City, doomed because she would not hear his word.

Yet to say that a prophet is possessed by the power that transforms him is not enough. False prophets seem to be possessed, they speak with a voice other than their own, there is a power in them, they can do wonders. How can one tell which is which, and isn't the judgment really hindsight, because some prophets have said things that later generations have accepted as true, or at least beautiful, though their contemporaries didn't, and others have been convicted by history as imposters?

The test of the true prophet, the proof that he has been transformed, converted, reconciled and sent—that he is not drunk with the certitude of his own cleverness but with the spirit—is that the prophetic word is a *converting word*. It does not necessarily convert, but it is capable of converting those whose formation has been such as will enable them to listen. The prophetic word calls people into the wilderness, the in-between state, and there utters to them the demand for self-surrender—surrender not to the prophet but to the power that sent him. The false prophet is extremely impressive, too, he also moves men's hearts, he takes them out of themselves and transports them. But their emotion is one of self-affirmation, not self-surrender. The German crowds who listened to Hitler and were raised to near-ecstasy by the vision he offered them were not converted, they did not repent.

Quite the contrary, they became intoxicated with the conviction that they had no need to repent, that they already were the chosen, in virtue of their innate superiority. The true prophet calls to repentance and reconciliation. Those who hear him realize what they are, in their response to the unconditional demand, and so enter the new life of love. The false prophet tells people that they need no repentance, they are righteous. So, since this is what we all like to hear when we are afraid and humiliated, they easily 'deceive even the elect'. Anti-Christ is so very like Christ.

The false prophets at the time of Isaiah did the same as Hitler. They assured the King that if he rebelled against Assyria—which was what he was itching to do—he would be a great hero and win freedom and renown for his people. Of course everyone was delighted—no need to repent, no need to suffer humiliation, only the assurance of God's favour and a triumphant future for his people. But Isaiah kept on telling them that God's call was not to battle and victory but to humiliation and a total surrender to God's will. *That* was what the people were chosen for. It is scarcely surprising that the response was not enthusiastic. But some did listen, and were converted. There was a 'remnant' to whom the suffering that came upon Israel was not a scandal but a means of repentance and conversion. They were the 'poor' to whom the good news came.

Joan of Arc was a successful military leader, but she was in a state of permanent cross-purposes with the commanders of the army and the civil authorities. She saw her enterprise as a call to France to repent and accept God's guidance, then he would save her. The English were to be driven out altogether, not simply prevented from being a nuisance to the nobility. The crowning of the Dauphin was not a move to gain a strategic advantage but a sign of obedience to God. The Dauphin and the other military and civil leaders were delighted to make use of Joan's influence over the common people, and this, plus a certain superstitious fear of her supernatural powers, made them willing, sometimes, to listen to her plans. She had an absolute conviction (and one forcibly expressed—she once called her page a 'bloody brat' for failing to wake her when a battle had begun) of the God-sent nature of her plans, and it convinced others even when they feared and disliked her. But they had no intention whatever of letting her lead them into expensive and unnecessary campaigns when treaties—first of all the longed-for one with Burgundy—might do the job without risking either one's skin or one's possessions.

The prophetic word is a word of conversion, and that is its sole purpose. Any other results are incidental. Bernadette was totally uninterested in the later history of the spring that had flowed where her hands dug the mud. 'The spring is not for me,' she said, and when she was a nun she listened to the glowing reports of cures and crowds with a mixture of politeness, revulsion and indifference. By that time she was so accustomed to people missing the point that it no longer surprised her, but in earlier days it had made her lose her temper. 'Good Lord, how stupid you are!' she cried, weeping with rage and frustration, when people crowded round to touch her and ask her prayers. Her mission was a call to repentance and conversion and her own conversion had been to that purpose. The rest was a puzzle and a distraction.

The characteristics of a true prophet, then, are that he is sent —he does not choose to go; and that his mission is with power —the impact he makes is such that no one can avoid a decision, for or against; and that his message is a call to repentance, conversion and reconciliation.

The release of power in the prophet cannot be simply a matter of a powerful personality acting on people, for if it were he would be unlikely to run the risk of spoiling the cause he has at heart by unseasonable repetition of an unpalatable message. Prophets are usually tactless and rude to an unpardonable degree, and *lèse-majesté* might almost be described as prophetic etiquette. The power the prophet shows is solely a power to provoke faith, to convert—in other words he is the agent of transformation. But one does not have to live in the desert and eat insects in order to be the agent of transformation. The mother of the two quarrelling children was the agent of transformation, so were the two lovers for each other, so were, in my third chapter, the man's daughter, the club organizer, and finally the awful little tract and its well-meaning lender. In that case all these agents were doing what the prophet does, they were *prophetic*—but part-time prophets. And if this is really so, the power that is released when a man is seized with the spirit of prophecy is the same power that works in the little, unnoticed prophetic utterances by which human beings bring salvation to each other. To gather repentant crowds for baptism in the waters of Jordan, to lead an army to victory against all sensible predictions—these are works of power that anyone can see. But their power is no stranger to us, it is familiar, even domestic—though never really domesticated. The power that the prophet wields—or that wields him—is the transforming, self-discovering power of love. This prophetic sending is a mission on which every man is sent to every other man, and this 'sending' is itself the 'intervention' that can shape the outbreak of power in another. A succession of tiny 'prophecies' can add up to such an intervention, by the infiltration method described in the first chapter, or the intervention—the prophecy—can be one decisive one, but acting on an accumulated awareness, too fragmented in its parts to be useful without this final cohesive prophecy.

The prophet's mission is with power—very impressive power. It is often accompanied by 'signs and wonders'. 'Works of power', miracles and mystical experience are not things we expect to encounter, and from one point of view it isn't important whether we believe they happen or not. The point is that the difference between magic and miracle—even if the event is exactly the same —is the same as the difference between the fake and the true prophet, and the same goes for mystical phenomena. Never mind 'how' they happen, or even *if* they do, their truth or falsehood lies in the fact that the 'real' power, the power of the spirit, provokes faith. Pseudo-power is used to satisfy curiosity, as Herod wanted to see some miracles done by Jesus, his prisoner. Or it is wanted in order to gain an ascendance over others, which was why Simon the sorceror wanted to buy the power of healing from Peter and John. Or it may be desired as reassurance, as Macbeth wanted supernatural reassurance of his future and Saul went to Endor for the same purpose, though neither got much good of it. Or it can be used to impress the gullible and earn a bit of money or fame, or both. The maid of Kent, Elizabeth Barton, seems to have been one of the great host of false mystics, many of whom were self-deceived as well as deceiving, who told people what they wanted to hear.

But the power of the spirit, which work in the 'real', transformed man, comes from faith and produces faith. It is no more spectacular than is strictly necessary, and wonder-workers often seem more embarrassed than pleased by the effects they produce. Some (like the Curé d'Ars, who practically invented St Philomena as an explanation of the wonders that occurred around him) have resorted to elaborate frauds and concealments to prevent people realizing who was the agent of power. For they do feel, as the true prophet must, that they are only agents.

Christ is presented by the evangelists as both prophet and wonder-worker, and in every case he is shown using the power that was in him primarily to convert. He tells those who ask if he is 'the one who is to come': 'The blind see, the deaf hear, the lame walk, the dead are raised, and the poor have the good news preached to them.' These are his credentials, and their common denominator is that all these things provoke the act of self-giving which is faith. But, he adds, 'blessed is he who is not scandalized in me'—does not find me a stumbling block to faith. Because a work which offers the chance of salvation through faith also provides an opportunity for the refusal of salvation—unbelief. The power that works wonders is dangerous as well as wonderful. It is a judgment. So Christ the wonder-worker offered these things as evidence of his salvation-bringing mission, but when he

realized that people were treating his healings as wonders in the
false sense—as mere prodigies—he reacted by telling the healed
to keep it quite. When the Jews asked for a 'sign' as a proof of
his mission he refused one: 'Unless you see signs and wonders
you will not believe', for works of power are signs only to those
who have already 'gone into the desert'. These Jews wanted the
power but they didn't like the desert.

In the Acts of the Apostles, the accounts of spectacular release
of power always occur in the context of conversion. Wonders do
not happen in order to force people to believe, but *when* they
believe then things start to happen. 'The spirit came upon them
all', in the house of Cornelius, when the household accepted
Christ—which they did on the word of Peter.

Paul, writing to the Corinthians about the gifts they had from
the Spirit, sets them down in order, and prophecy has a fairly
high place; yet it is not the spectacular that he ranks highest, not
even the gift of healing. The gift that is the greatest, the most
reliable proof of the presence of the Spirit in power is charity—
the activity of love.

But charity seems a cosy, companionable sort of thing. It is so
familiar that it is easy to ignore its real nature, just as the famili-
arity of married love seems to have nothing to do with the catastrophic power of the outbreak of sexual passion. And, just as
looking at marriage 'through' its initiation by a clear outbreak of
passion illuminates it and reveals its own proper nature, so the
spectacular phenomenon of the prophet reveals the kind of power
which is at work in much less noticeable ways.

It is the power that transforms, and the conditions for transformation are the same whatever the scale of the occurrence. But
if, as I have suggested, the effect and degree and kind of transformation depends on formation it should be revealing to see how
the prophet's formation affects his message and its result.

The very conditions of release of power show the importance
of the formation, the setting in which the power is released.

The release of power occurs only when people have been

drawn 'into the wilderness', into the 'in between' state where the structures of ordinary life are not operative.

In *Purity and Danger*, Mary Douglas[1] also explores the interplay of order and disorder. Dirt, or uncleanness, is something which is out of the order we have arranged, the structures of the Law which make sense of the chaotic life of the flesh. But:

'Granted that disorder spoils patterns, it also provides the materials of pattern. Order implies restriction; from all possible materials a limited selection has been made and from all possible relations a limited set has been used.'

This is the Law, an imposed patterning of reality, to make it intelligible and usable.

'So disorder by implication is unlimited, no pattern has been realized in it, but its potential for pattern is indefinite. This is why, though we seek to create order, we do not simply condemn disorder. We recognize that it is destructive to existing patterns; also that it has potentiality. It symbolizes both *danger* and *power*.'

The life of the flesh—the world of appearances which is after all the only one we can be sure of without faith—is regulated by the Law, or it would come to bits. But it is only when it *has*, in some sense, come to bits that the power that underlies it and gives it meaning can actually break through. As long as 'the world' is functioning efficiently, the word of power is unheard, or if it is heard it is a scandal, a threat, an offence, to be removed as quickly as possible. Hence the notion of danger, of pollution, from aspects of life that do not fit into the recognized frames of living. But 'the wilderness' as an idea presupposes the life of the man-ordered city and arable land. If all were wilderness there would be no word to distinguish it. And the idea of an 'in-between' implies that there is a firm and enduring structure of life on either side

[1] See above, p. 124.

of it, something for it to be 'between'. It is in the breaking down
of the Law that the Spirit's work becomes apparent, but there has
to be a Law to break down.

There are those who go into the wilderness on purpose, like
the two lovers who draw each other out from the world of every
day, and there are those who are driven there whether they like
it or not, like the man who ends up in hospital, in the desolation
of physical and mental pain and the loneliness of sin and of night.
Once there, they hear the prophetic word, and must choose. But
the way in which the word is understood depends on the formation which has preceded the invitation to be transformed.
Quite literally, it depends on the language in which the invitation
is presented. If the language is not a familiar one it will not be
understood at all. But even when it is in a language which is fully
understood *the conversion which follows can only take up in its
self-giving that part of life which the language expresses and
affects.*

Just as the 'word' in this context does not mean only spoken
words but also actions, which are just as much (in many cases
more) valid as signs, invitations, demands, expressions of the
transforming power, so 'language', here, does not mean only
spoken or written words but the whole range of possible communication in and concerning a particular area of living. So the
physical gestures of sexual love are the language of this conversion. The language of the reconciliation of the two children is
the mixture of words and actions that makes up family living-
together. The man whose 'first' conversion took place in contact
with a group of socially concerned people was made up of words
and actions and feelings that had a political-social reference. But
if a language expresses a certain area of life it thereby also excludes
other areas. The two children's conversion did not affect their
religious life, if any, or their relationship with, for instance, their
teachers at school, or their responsibilities to others outside the
family. The two lovers used a language which also, because of the
way they thought of themselves as related to others, included and

affected their other human relationships, not merely the all-important community between the two of them. They were both mature enough and unselfish enough to see that this was implied by a genuine understanding of what their love, which was a married kind of love, meant. But lovers often do not see this, and in that case their 'language' expresses only the narrow area of their mutual commitment. The man who was converted into a social-responsibility setting also used a language that did not link up his conversion to his work or his 'normal' friendships.

This does not mean that the transformation is not genuine. It simply means that the area of living affected by it depends *entirely* on the kind of personal language in which the converting encounter is expressed.

It follows that the effects of conversion are also dependant on the formation in which transformation occurs. My language expresses the kind of person I am, as well as the kind of conversion this is. And the kind of person I am is going to use the language of this conversion to work out—put into practice—the meaning of the conversion. So transformation is limited in two ways which are really one. It is limited by the type of formation a person has had, and in practice this means the kind of language in which he has learned to understand what he is and work out what he is. And it is limited by the kind of language in which the person he is understands the offer of salvation, and responds to it.

It should perhaps be said again, to avoid confusion, that this does not necessarily mean that a convert could explain in words what his conversion meant. On the contrary, he is most likely to use words which are, to him, signs of a much greater range of meaning than he could possibly express. Certainly the words he uses to express his conversion will be either meaningless, or of very limited meaning, to the unconverted, and he can only convey to them what *he* means by these words if they are prepared to respond to him, as a person, sufficiently to feel the power in him that is articulated by the words he uses. So, for instance, a convert will tell a questioner that he was 'a sinner', and that he has 'met Christ', and will be surprised and baffled by a request to explain what he 'really means' by these phrases. Their meaning is, to him, utterly clear, but it is expressed *only* in these words, and unless he is introspective and articulate and also able to realize that his words cannot carry their meaning for him on their ordinary, un-transformed, faces he will not be able to communicate anything of their meaning for him. They *are* what he means, there is no other meaning. What is required is translation, and that means knowing two languages. This becomes even more difficult, because even when the convert has in fact known both languages—that in which his conversion is expressed and that in which the unconverted speak of the same events—he has only known them as emotionally neutral communication, not as signs of the inexpressible. But the new and vivid significance of his converted language makes it harder and harder for him to detach himself, and use the words in their unconverted state, as he used to know them.

Real translation, in fact, is not possible, because a truly effective translation would mean that the unconverted began to 'hear' the meaning the word has for the converted—in other words he would already be hearing it as at least a potential convert, who would not require translation. It would be, for him, a prophetic word, something sounding in himself, as himself and not an object to be examined, appraised, and used, as are the words of a foreign language. So, oddly enough, it seems that it is the very impossibility of a true translation that makes it seem so urgent, to the prophet, that he should attempt a translation. This attempt is the prophet's attempt to convert, to get other people to share his language, to mean by his words what *he* means.

The prophet's mission is to draw others to share something with him, and this something is the power that sent him, that breaks out in him. And if this is what he is trying to do then that means that the prophet's mission is to create a community. If a group of people share a language (in the sense of a totality of signs, not just words) then they are a community. But the community brought into being by the prophetic word is not just any kind of community, it is a converted community, for it is the conversion that makes the community.

This notion of what the prophetic word is for clearly leads on to the consideration of that fourth element in the conflict situation which I described in the first chapter. The release of power that occurs in the conflict caused by a true encounter leads, or can lead, to reconciliation and communion, a sharing in a new community of life. But this community is one that is conditioned by its formation, just as the individual is, and can only work out its conversion in the context of its formation, by means of the language in which its conversion expresses itself—a language which, in its turn, depends on the formation of the community as a *worldly*, in-the-flesh, community, *which it still is*, in great part, for no conversion is complete. The problem is to live in a way which does express the reality of the conversion, and prepare for the extension of this conversion, and which yet makes use, as it must, of the Law as a means of regulating and forming the unconverted area of life, without letting the Law usurp the functions of the Spirit.

In the second part of the book I shall try to show more clearly how this is attempted, and how well various attempts work, but first of all it should be helpful to look again at particular prophets and see how they created, or tried to create, community, and how far they succeeded, and why they did or didn't.

The community that Jeremiah was trying to create was one that already existed, as a worldly community, but had forgotten its real nature and therefore did not exist as a converted community. Instead of being a community of the converted—Israel, God's chosen bride—it had become a community of Law, and of the flesh, choosing gods that fitted in with its own wishes, and listening to prophets who reassured it that all was well. So when the Lord threatens wrath against the people who have forsaken his covenant, Jeremiah replies:

'Then I said, "Ah, Lord God, behold, the prophets say to them, 'You shall not see the sword, nor shall you have famine, but I will give you assured peace in this place.' " And the Lord said to me, "The prophets are prophesying lies in my name; I did not send them, nor did I command them or speak to them. They are prophesying to you a lying vision, worthless divination, and the deceit of their own minds." '

The doom that is to come is intended to prove to the people the falsity of the community of the world. And their reaction to the prophecy of the wrath that lies on them is to try to get rid of the offence by getting rid of the prophet. They prefer the priests who proclaim their righteousness in the Law, and the counsellors who are full of good political know-how, and the prophets who confirm them in their own plans.

'Then they said, "Come, let us make plots against Jeremiah, for the Law shall not perish from the priest, nor counsel from the wise, nor the sword from the prophet. Come, let us smite him with the tongue, and let us not heed any of his words." '

The result of all his warnings was that Jeremiah was beaten and put in the stocks, yet he obviously made more impression than his embittered description of his people's 'stubbornness' would lead one to believe, though it was the wrong kind of impression. The power that was in him impressed people, so that they regarded him as an oracle, to be consulted, not as the bearer of God's word, to be obeyed.

'This is the word which came to Jeremiah from the Lord, when King Zedekiah sent to him Pashhur ... the priest ... saying, "Inquire of the Lord for us, for Nebuchadnezzar King of Babylon is making war against us; perhaps the Lord will deal with us according to all his wonderful deeds, and will make him withdraw from us." Then Jeremiah said to them,

"Thus shall you say to Zedekiah, 'Thus says the Lord, the God of Israel. Behold I will turn back the weapons of war which are in your hands and with which you are fighting against the King of Babylon, and against the Chaldeans who are besieging your walls and I will bring them together into the midst of this city. . . .

'Thus says the Lord: Behold I set before you the way of life and the way of death. He who stays in this city shall die, by the sword, and by famine, and by pestilence; but he who goes out and surrenders to the Chaldeans who are besieging you shall live, and shall have his life as a prize of war.' " '

This is the choice—the choice which the true prophet always offers. It is only through humiliation that life is found. The suffering will come—is it to be as an offence, to be fought and rejected, or as repentance? No wonder there were many to persuade the King to put Jeremiah in the empty cistern to starve. Yet Zedekiah was doing his best, as he saw it, to keep his nation together, to pull some sort of coherent community out of the mess, one that might survive and grow again. Jeremiah's ceaseless prophecies were undermining the morale of the defenders. Zedekiah was trying to save his people, one formed and protected by the Law which, after all, had come to them from God. But Jeremiah saw that this kind of community was not the kind that the Law of Moses had been designed to form. What Zedekiah was trying to do was to avoid the very purpose for which the Law had been given—that the people might be holy, a sign to the nations, just because they did *not* trust in their own righteousness. Because they had so trusted, the formation given by the Law must be broken down, and in that breakdown, if only they understood it, they would find salvation. But first they must realize their total powerlessness.

'For thus says the Lord, Your hurt is incurable,
and your wound is grievous.

> There is none to uphold your cause,
> no medicine for your wound,
> no healing for you.
> All your lovers have forgotten you,
> they care nothing for you,
> for I have dealt you the blow of an enemy,
> the punishment of a merciless foe,
> because your sins are flagrant.'

But when the lesson has been learned,

> 'At that time, says the Lord, I will be the God of all the
> families of Israel, and they shall be my people.'
>> Thus says the Lord,
>>> 'The people who have survived the sword found
>>> grace in the wilderness.
>>> I have loved you with an everlasting love;
>>> therefore I have continued my faithfulness to you.
>>> Again I will build you, and you shall be built,
>>> O Virgin Israel.
>>> Again you shall adorn yourself with timbrels,
>>> and shall go forth in the dance of the merrymakers.
>>> Say, He who scattered Israel will gather him,
>>> and will keep him as a shepherd keeps his flock!'

The state of Israel when she has been brought back is not to
be externally different from her state in past times of prosperity,
but the future community that Jeremiah describes is a converted
community, repentant, reconciled, and whose righteousness is
from God alone. This is the purpose of all prophecy—a people who
will be a new creation, fresh from God's hand, virgin in spite of
past adultery. Jeremiah had a language whose words he already
shared with the people, yet he could not get through to many of
them, the things he said remained a scandal and an offence, to
be rejected. There is a legend that he was finally stoned to death.

His legendary fate links him with another prophet, Stephen, who also shared a common language with his persecutors. But they were no longer using its words as signs for communication, but only as ornaments of their own comfort and greatness.

How many actually heard Jeremiah's message, and repented, is unknown. There must have been some, or his words would not have been recorded and kept and worked over and passed on to later generations. But it was mostly in retrospect that his people realized what he had been getting at, and that he was right. This is a fate that seems to attend most prophets, for they really are disturbers of the peace—the world's peace—and it is bound to seem a 'work for God' to get rid of them.

In a sense their offensiveness is the guarantee of their truth.

John the Baptist was offensive in the most literal way possible. He was extremely rude, even to people who came to listen to him with, apparently, every intention of reforming their lives. For they were impressed by his eloquence and his ascetic way of life. They were good, law-abiding men, quietly proud of their membership of the chosen people, and anxious to make their lives a proof of their worthiness of such an honour. But John stripped away from them the very reason why they felt it was right for them to come to him:

'Bear fruit that befits repentance, and do not begin to say to yourselves, "We have Abraham for our father", for I tell you, God is able from these stones to raise up children to Abraham.'

Yet what he tells his converts to do is not difficult, they have no great sufferings to endure, as the inhabitants of the doomed Jerusalem did, for the people who really listened to John were those who had already lost their self-confidence under the humiliation of the Roman occupation. The things he told them to do were things the Law had always told them to do—but now their righteousness was not their own, but came from God only. And

John's own right to command repentance did not come from any title that he could claim. The anxious priests and Levites asked him for his credentials. He hadn't any. He wasn't the Christ, nor Elijah come back to earth, nor even 'the prophet' who was expected to precede the coming of the Christ in the last days. What on earth *are* you, then, they wanted to know. 'Let us have our answer for those who sent us. What do you say about yourself?' But they got no answer. He had nothing to say about himself, he was only a voice: 'I am the voice of one crying in the wilderness, "Make straight the way of the Lord".' It was precisely because he was 'nobody' that he could call on other people to take a leap into nothing, because it is only in the embracing of nothingness that the real self can come to birth, the real community arise.

It is probably not merely a coincidence that the two examples of prophecy in the Christian era that I chose happened to be women. There are others I could have chosen, such as Francis of Assisi, or the ascetic desert Fathers, or Bernard of Clairvaux, or Luther or Wesley, but in these cases the sheer offensiveness of their prophetic character was minimized by the fact that they belonged, after a fashion, *within* the structure of the organized ecclesiastical body, or a new one formed around them. This does not mean that they were false prophets, though Bernard at least was telling people what they wanted to hear in preaching the crusade, and Luther appealed to people for political reasons as well as really converting ones. It may mean that the people who heard them were in fact better attuned to their message than most and were converted without much disruption of the established order. It may, however, have another meaning, which is connected with the nature of the community in which they spoke, and this is something that needs to be discussed later, for the Christian community is constituted as itself prophetic.

But the two examples I chose were both prophets in the traditionally offensive manner, and the fact that they were both women is part of that pre-condition of the prophetic eruption—the 'in between' or 'out-law' state of the prophet. Since women had no official status within the ecclesiastical structure they were in little danger of being 'tamed', and their message came, inevitably, from outside the city as a voice crying in the wilderness.

But they are interesting for another reason also. They show how completely the nature of the prophetic message depends on the formation of the prophet and of his setting. The message can only be delivered in the language available. The prophets of the Old Testament spoke a language which was concerned with the origin and constitution and purpose of a people, one single nation, the Jews. But because that language has been taken up and used as part of the Christian language which is still (though rather impoverished) culturally available to us, it doesn't sound in our ears as purely the language of nationalism. It has, even for us, the ring of power which is more fundamental than patriotic fervour, however spiritualized.

But Joan's message also concerned a people, it was expressed in terms of the vocation and destiny of France. This was the only way it could have been expressed. In that time and place, it was the language available. To us it seems a narrowing-down of a divine vocation to apply it to one nation only, and see it as a call to rid the country of foreigners. Yet that was exactly what the older Jewish prophets were saying, what John the Baptist said, what Paul said—purge out the old leaven, that you may be a new dough, the unleavened bread of sincerity and truth. At one period of Jewish history it meant driving out foreigners and having no dealings with them—even their houses and wealth were to be 'dedicated', utterly destroyed, lest they prevent the people from taking everything from God's hand. At a later period the people must submit to the foreigners—but the reason is the same: they must receive all that is good from God only, never from their own power. John told his converts to discard all confidence in their membership of the chosen people, for the Christ would 'purge his flour' and burn up the chaff, keeping only the good grain, the 'fruits worthy of repentance'.

Joan's message was the same one. To her, the English were the foreign element whose presence brought misery and prevented the people belonging to God. She was to *save* France. From what? From the English, but not because the English were evil in themselves. Only because they came between God and the French people, not merely by causing misery but also by enmeshing the Dauphin and the nobles in a non-stop game of political intrigue so that there was no sense of purpose, no justice or truth in all of 'fair France'.

And the Dauphin must be crowned, must be anointed as God's representative, because that would be a sign that France was obedient to God, receiving her welfare from him and not from the bounty of whatever arrangement of dubious alliances had managed to halt hostilities for a while. Joan's aims were very simple, but they became enmeshed in the politics of people who did not hear the message but saw only a possible tool for forwarding their own plans, just as Zedekiah thought Jeremiah might be useful, if only he would say the right things.

Joan's call to prophecy came to her as voices, whom she identified as those of two saints and an archangel. The magnificent confidence of 'Thus says the Lord', gives way to 'My voices tell me'. At one period, the theophany of Yahweh was presented in Jewish literature always under the form of angels, or other spiritual beings, who represented some aspect of God's relations with man. Thus the transcendence of Yahweh was safeguarded. So, in the middle ages, the mercy of God and his goodness to men presented itself to the imagination of Christians in the figures of saints, and of angels who were imaginatively scarcely different from these saints. So it was proper that God's command should come to Joan in the voices of saints. And it is noticeable that this never confused her. Her voices were 'from God' and what they told her was God's word, which she must announce. There was never any doubt in her mind about the origin of her mission, however it might be mediated to her.

It is possible to see very clearly, here, the way the language of formation conditions the language that expresses the call to transformation, and also provides for its working out. It also shows how, when the response of faith is lacking, translation is impossible. The courtiers heard Joan's words, and they were familiar ones, useful ones. But what they meant as expressions of a transformed consciousness they did not know and could not know, because they did not believe her. The community Joan tried to call into being was the community of God's people— God's French people, since that was her total language. She failed almost entirely, and she failed because the language had become, for most of her hearers, too completely secular to be capable of translation any longer into the sacred words of a divine call. The poor heard her, but nobody bothered about them.

The same sort of thing happened with Bernadette's 'Lady'. It seems doubtful how far Bernadette herself thought of the 'Lady' whose beauty ravished her as coming from God. The connection was implicit rather than explicit. Her love for the lady led her to pray, and to make greater attempts to 'be good'. There was certainly no division in her mind between the lady and the practices of her faith, but neither did she see any need to explain, to herself or others, the nature of the connection. To Catholics of her class and period the most tender and real and satisfying faith expressed itself naturally in Marian devotion, for official French Catholicism of that time was still heavily dyed in Jansenism. The idea of God, or even of Christ, would have evoked no response of love or faith, but rather one of fear and awkwardness. Later in life Bernadette seems to have transferred the whole-hearted love she gave to the Lady to her understanding of her faith as Christ-centred. But this was a slow and scarcely traceable development. In those early days it would have been unthinkable. It would have been unthinkable too, for her hearers, who were very, very poor, without political and social status and with little religious education. The rosary was their prayer, the mother of God their theophany. They would not have understood any other— but this language they *did* understand.

But Bernadette's message, hesitantly passed on from the cave

outside the city, in the wild country of Massabielle, is the same
one that John cried in the wilderness of Judea: 'Repent!' '*Pénit-
ance*, Repentance!' Bernadette heard the Lady repeat. John told
the Jews, 'Bring forth fruits worthy of repentance.' 'Let processions come here,' said the Lady, for processions were the normal
language of sincere devotion for these people, and a common act
of penance also.

The language of Bernadette was mostly sign language. She did
not call people to baptism, but she obeyed a command to dig in
the earth, and a spring flowed, and people washed in it and were
healed. The call to prayer and penance was not so much in the
words the child spoke as in her actions, as she obeyed humiliating
and painful orders, and prayed with an intensity of abandonment
that those who saw her never forgot. John was a voice crying in
the wilderness. Bernadette, who uttered her message scarcely
above a whisper, was also a voice, a loud cry in the wilderness,
a sign of poverty and penance and utter self-surrender to love.

The community that was called into being by Bernadette's prophetic message did not last long. For a while the valley of the
Gave was filled with thousands upon thousands of people who
had left their farms and their villages, flocking into the wilderness to find God. They did find what they were looking for—the
sense of power at work. They were people who had little to hope
for except the ability to go on scraping a living. Bernadette, who
was not a priest or at all 'churchy', gave meaning to their lives,
and all of a sudden it made sense to pray.

But *this* was not a converted community. The crowds were
depending on wonders to confirm their faith, and they didn't get
them. There were real conversions, but they were quiet ones,
and the community into which they were converted was the existing one, the structure of Catholic Christianity at its most rigid.
The language of these conversions, then, had to be the language
of traditional Catholicism. There was no other. And it was this
language—its words and its symbols—that made the sign of Bernadette's Lady into the sign of Lourdes. It was still a sign, it was

still—is still—a word of salvation, but expressed in a language that did quite a lot to soften its impact. In other words, the converting word was capable of converting, but only within the area covered by the language in which it was expressed, a purely religious language, and a fairly narrow religion at that. It was in fact a narrower one than a later generation can perceive in the same words, for the words that Bernadette used have recovered, for us, some of the significance that jumps the gap from Jeremiah to John and from John to Bernadette: 'Repentance! Repentance!' 'Pray for the sick world!' 'Wash!'

Bernadette's world was the language of her message. So was Joan's, and John's, and Jeremiah's, and all the others. The formation in which the outbreak of power occurs conditions the form of the outbreak and its effect. That means that the community created by the prophetic word can only be such as the language of the existing formation community allows. The limits of the language are the limits of the community's self awareness as converted.

Obviously, then, the kind of setting in which a Christian conversion takes place conditions the kind of Christianity that results, and it immediately becomes apparent that a large part of the function of what we call the Church must be concerned with creating a language community—in the world, of-the-flesh, under the Law—which can provide the right kind of setting for the explosion of the power that transforms. It isn't so easy. If you do organize and do it well it can get to seem as if there were no need for transformation after all. The language works very well, it does all the proper Christian things, why allow anything so untidy as transformation? But then the power *does* explode, in unexpected places, and usually with an inadequate language, so that people cry 'heresy' and try to screw down the lid even tighter.

But if you don't organize enough, but rely on the power of the spirit to work in whatever language happens to be around, the result is that the outbreaks are expressed in so many different languages that nobody understands what anyone else is saying, and the community-creating effect of conversion is fragmented. Also, because of the small vocabulary of these various languages, the effectiveness of conversion even on individuals is minimized.

In that case it seems that any kind of community aiming to be Christian must be an educational structure, teaching a rich and flexible language, but must also deliberately leave room for explosions which can never be entirely predictable. It sounds positively Anglican.

Part Two

CHAPTER V

CREATING COMMUNITY

In the first chapter I suggested that community was something that came into being as a result of the successful resolution of the conflict created by encounter. But of course most *communities* are not like that at all. They come into being because a group of people happen, for any number of different reasons, to be living together. Since they are living together they must either try to get on together, or exhaust themselves not doing so, or decide to separate. If they can't separate the choice is down to two alternatives, and since if they take the second course there soon isn't any community they really haven't much choice at all. So the problem of people who live in an accidental community is to try to make it an on-purpose community. In other words any community is occupied in trying (perhaps not very hard) to *create* community, and in surviving its failures to do so.

Even a group of people who have deliberately chosen to live together are there accidentally in the sense that no one of them chose all the others as his community. Each chose to live in this community and so did all the rest. Their being together is not accidental, but the make-up of the group is. This is true even if the leader or founder actually did pick out all the others to suit himself. He didn't have an indefinite choice, he could only choose from those available. And he didn't completely know what they were like when he chose them. So however deliberate the choice of a community may be its membership still has the quality of 'given-ness'. These people just are there. Now they have to create community.

And all communities have to become on-purpose. Even if each one is a violent individualist and has no desire at all to be part of a community he will have to safeguard his very eccentricities by agreed demarcation between his area of activity and that of the others. In order *not* to be communal he has to acknowledge the existence of a community, and arrange his life accordingly. And as soon as a group of people agree to do or not do certain things in relation to each other they are *a* community, though not necessarily creating *community*. There is a relationship, however tenuous.

There is one kind of community in which both the accidental character of its existence and the need to make it on-purpose are extremely apparent, and that is the family. People marry on purpose, but Cupid's inability to shoot straight is notorious, and cynics have never been lacking to echo the remark of John More, Thomas More's father, that marriage is like putting one's hand into a bag full of snakes and eels—two snakes to one eel. And even under the guidance of the oracles of family planning the advent of children into a family is wildly accidental. The time may be planned, but the type isn't (yet, anyway) and even if some day we can order our kids from a mail-order catalogue we still shall not be able to control the play of circumstance that effects their development. Nor can we be sure which ones will grow up and which ones perhaps won't. So a family is a random, and sometimes wildly unlikely, collection of people. There they are, and they have to create community, make their existence on-purpose.

This is more true for them than for most communities because that is what families are for. We can see how deeply rooted is the idea that this is what families are for in the attempts that are made to do without the community of the family as the basic community. The Israeli kibbutzim sometimes take children from their mothers at an early age and rear them in nurseries. Though they see their parents every day for some hours, they do not sleep with them but in a different house, with the other children. And this is done precisely in order that the loyalty of the whole community shall be *to* the whole community, though family affection has its place. This seems to be in fact what happens, though it is too soon to tell whether, in two or three generations, the idea will still be working out as it does now, at a time when the adults are convinced that it 'ought' to work. Whether this arrangement is a good idea in terms of human development remains to be seen, and is irrelevant here. I mention this example to show that a family is normally expected to be a community-creating community. If it were not there would be no need to separate children from their parents except in case of acute need for the labour of the women, and even then there would be no reason why the children should not sleep with their parents.

If the normal family is especially clearly a community-creating community, as well as a very common and observable one, it should help us to work out the iea of what community is, and how community in *this* sense—which is a transformed, converted relationship—is related to community in the world, as formative.

At the end of Part One, I suggested a working definition of a Christian community as an educational structure with room for explosions. I am going to suggest now that this is a useful starting point, but is inadequate as a description of the real relation between formation and transformation. And I want to see what the relation is really like by watching an imaginary family coping with the business of using its accidental existence to create community on-purpose.

This particular family is a fairly big one, because it includes not two but four generations. The parents have the wife's father living with them, and the eldest daughter of the family is married and has a baby, but she and her husband are at the moment still living in the family home. This home is an ugly, shabby but large house in a Victorian terrace. The father of the family is chief clerk in a local bank. His wife has never had a job since they married, she has been fully occupied with the big, dusty (it is on a main road) and inconvenient house, with its walled garden at the back, and in rearing four children, of whom the youngest (an afterthought, if 'thought' is the right word) is only three years old.

F

Her husband is fifty, she is forty-three. The elder daughter is twenty, married to a young man who works in a garage nearby, and their baby is six months old. These three have two rooms and a bathroom at the top of the house. The other children are a boy of seventeen, in the sixth form at Grammar school, and a girl of fourteen, whom her parents have sent to a local private day school, since they consider the secondary school too 'tough' for a girl from a decent family. The children's grandfather lives in a big front room looking on the road. He used to be an insurance clerk, and was once in the army. He is not an invalid, but he is naturally lazy and glad of his slight rheumatism as an excuse to do as little as he reasonably can.

The problem that confronts this family is a formidable one. Their home, with the rest of the terrace, is to be pulled down to make way for a new, wider road. They will have to move. But that is only the beginning of the upheaval, for in fact this move is threatening the way of living with which they have managed quite well for a long time. It has worked so well, in spite of discomforts, that it did not really seem possible that it could change. They grumbled and made plans, often, but they never really imagined that the plans were more than castles in Spain. Now it is true, they have to leave, and they find that they are facing not only a move to a new home, but a re-assessment of their entire way of life. For a while they had hoped that they could simply find another, perhaps similar, house, and carry on as before, but it hasn't worked out like that. They have been offered a house on a new estate not far away, but it would be too small to hold either the old man or the young couple and their baby. On the other hand there is another big house, even shabbier than their present one, which some friends want to sell. It is much further away, and because of increased prices it would cost them more than they could easily afford, in spite of its condition, for it is in a good neighbourhood. It would mean the father of the family would have to take another job, probably at a smaller salary, because he is too old to carve out a new career, and isn't likely, now, to get a manager's job. He is not that sort. On the other hand they would all be together and everyone (except possibly the elder daughter's husband, who is too fond of his wife to say so out loud) would prefer that. They're used to it, and they value it, for all kinds of reasons. And there's a 'good' school for the other daughter. The older schoolboy could stay with friends until he finishes, then he'll go to university, he hopes.

But if they go to the house on the new estate they'll be more comfortable, there will be less work for the mother—and that's a consideration at her age. (Not so many stairs.) But less privacy —no walls to the garden. And different kinds of neighbours, mostly people whose living comes from the new clothing factory for which the estate was really designed. People say they're lucky to get the chance of a house like that, and if they take it the job at the bank can go on, no worry about a new job as well as a new house.

In a situation like this there are several ways of deciding what is to be done, and the methods of deciding are as much an indication of what kind of people they are as the decision itself.

> The husband can decide, and tell the others afterwards.
>
> The husband and wife can decide, and tell the others afterwards.
>
> They can hold a family meeting, at which the father, or both parents, announce their wishes but ask for comments and suggestions.
>
> They can hold a family meeting and come to it with open minds, as far as possible, and thrash out the problem from there.

All of these ways of deciding can be carried out in a manner that is good for the whole family, or that is good for some and not for others, or that is bad for them all. Some of the theoretical possibilities can be eliminated by giving an idea of the kind of people these are—in other words, of the kind of formation which is the material of whatever decision is to be made. For the fact is that this kind of situation is the kind in which community is created, or destroyed, and one in which, therefore, the existence of community already created is tested. This is one of those 'in between' situations in which power is liable to erupt.

Here is Mary Douglas again, talking about the 'in between' state of people being initiated into a tribe:

> 'During the marginal period which separates ritual dying and ritual re-birth, the novices in initiation are temporarily outcast. For the duration of the rite they have no place in society ... we find them behaving like dangerous criminal characters. ... To behave anti-socially is the proper expression of their marginal condition. To have been in the margins is to have been in contact with danger, to have been at a source of power.'

I am not suggesting that this respectable family is likely to become suddenly anti-social, but that they feel themselves to be suddenly in danger. Their danger is not a physical one—whatever happens they are going to have a sound roof over their heads, and money coming in. Their danger is the loss of the sense of belonging within a particular kind of structure, or rather a particular arrangement of related structures. In this unprotected condition emotions that are normally kept out of sight are liable to erupt. It will become evident, now, what these people are *really* like.

The father in this family is a sensible, assured man who has never had any illusions about his own abilities but is not on that account sorry for himself. He has high standards, ethically and intellectually, he has sensibility and integrity. His wife is a woman of vitality and charm, not pretty, rather fat, but with considerable sex appeal. She is devoted to her husband but occasionally angry (with fate, not with him) because he is so content with a mediocre job. She would have liked more social life, more variety, more fun —and possibly more men—but she has made a good job of what she has. The elder daughter is rather overshadowed by her mother, and feels safe with her. She is quiet, like her father, and biddable, but just because she is so easily pushed around her husband is fiercely determined that he will not allow his own wishes to destroy her happiness by dragging her away from her family before she really wants to go. All the same, he does want to get away. He is highly intelligent and ambitious and is taking a degree course by correspondence.

The other daughter is a dreamy, imaginative child who sometimes thinks she would like to act, and sometimes that she would like to be a missionary nun. Her elder brother is rather spoilt, and inclined to think that the whole family exists as a background for him. He is quite clever, but not very original, and he is jealous of his brother in law. He is devoted to his mother, but despises his father.

The little boy is an outrageous and charming nuisance. He is just like his mother, but he is not spoilt, since she has learnt her lesson.

Grandfather is, as well as lazy, a man whom it is impossible to contradict because he is gently certain that he knows best about everything. He is never offended when people disagree, he just doesn't hear them.

It is a good formation, then, on the whole, that provides the setting for decision.

It seems unlikely, in this kind of family, that the father will make an independent decision, but he might well do so in consultation with his wife. They might hope, by doing so, and by explaining their decision as tactfully as possible, to avoid unnecessary tensions and emotional scenes in the family.

On the other hand this is a man of unusually sensitive conscience, who, just because he is not a strong personality, feels a great responsibility towards the others and also is anxious not to use his position as head of the family to demand as a matter of course conformity with his wishes. He knows they are fond of him, and would dislike the idea of fighting him. His authority is real, but it is not the authority of personality. He is head of the family because he knows he is, he occupies that position, and the others acknowledge it without thinking very much about it. If he brings the problem to a family discussion he will be up against much stronger personalities, and he may be overruled, and he will not have the power or wish to assert himself. Yet it may well be (and past experience confirms this) that, alone, he will have a clearer, more realistic, view of what is best for all the others. Can he impose this? Wouldn't that be a kind of blackmail since he would be putting them in the position of seeming to be lacking in affection for him if they refused to conform?

This, then, is the first decision that has to be made—a personal one. And all decisions are personal, in the end, though made in the setting of a community. The conflict that goes on in this man's mind draws him into a solitude where he can find no support. His wife's willingness to back up whatever decision is likely to content *him* (since she is the sort of self-confident person who doesn't much mind where she lives, or how) only makes his agony greater, for it is clear that, with her powerful backing, he could easily impose any decisions he wishes on the rest.

He is a weak man, in one sense, but he is in a situation where weakness can become strength, of a different kind. The surrender that is asked of him is very hard, it means not only relinquishing his own preferences—that is not very important to him—but also relinquishing the right to decide, even though this may mean that a wrong decision may be reached. He feels that this is what he should do, and perhaps he is right.

But he is only right if the other members of his family are really able to make a responsible decision of *some* kind. If they were all at loggerheads, or too demoralized to do more than let their emotions rule them, would he be right to let them decide? In that case a surrender of his right to decide would probably be an abdication of his authority, a flight from responsibility. In *this* case, as he sees it, it is not an abdication but a *use* of authority. He, as the head, has the right to hand over the decision, and in so

doing he retains his authority, because authority is a relationship
—that between the symbolic *source* of the community and its
members. So the person at the head of a community is both its
symbolic centre and source and *also* a member of it. As a member
of it he is responsible to the whole, and for the whole, and this
is why he finds himself faced with a decision that is very hard
indeed, because he can have no certainty that his choice will be,
objectively, the right one. He makes his decision, then, over
against a future which is dark, and in doing so discovers himself.

What sort of self? This conversion is concerned with the use
of authority, therefore it is in his role as head of the family that
he realizes himself in this decision. He has always known himself
as devoted to his family, and prepared to forgo much personal
pleasure and comfort for their sakes. Now he knows that he has,
in the past, taken a lot for granted. He has assumed that the way
of life he had drifted into was the only possible one. He has never
wondered about what might be called the vocation of the family
as a whole: its possible effect on other families, its sense of
direction, as a human community.

All this is summed up in his new awareness of himself as *given*,
to and for the members of his family. The language of his conversion is a slightly stilted one, concerned with responsibility and
mutual service and one's duty to the community at large. It probably sounds stuffy, and rather unreal.

His wife thinks so, anyway, and is definitely fed-up at his hesitantly expressed but firm decision to consult the whole family
about their future. 'They're sure to make a mess of it,' sums up
her attitude. But this is a challenge for her, too.

She can at least partly make her prophecy prove true, if she
likes, by putting the children's backs up by her assumption of
their incompetence. Or she can get her own way by playing on
their affection for their father, and so getting them to decide as
they think *he* would personally prefer, thus thwarting the real
purpose of his sacrifice, and if she does this she can persuade
herself that she is protecting both her husband as a person *and*

his authority in the family. This is one way of destroying the reality of authority—by making it an object of superstitious and sentimental concern, which must not be subjected to stress lest the whole edifice crumble. The kind of loyalty and devotion that does this cannot create a converted community because it is keeping in being the symbolic centre of the *formation* community, even at a point when it should be giving way to transformation.

In the end she manages to overcome her irritation at what she regards as her husband's weakness, and decides to do her best to help the others to arrive at a sane decision which shall be theirs, their own—and that includes their father's. This decision requires a real conversion because she cannot really see the sense of it. She foresees trouble and scenes, and wants to protect her husband. But she sees that his own integrity as a person is involved, and it is in relation to *this* that she makes her decision.

But suppose her husband's decision *had* really been one of weakness, because he could not face defending his own decision about the home against his family's possible objections? Would she still have been right to support him? Or should she try to force him to make up his own mind, for his own sake? In that case, what about the rights of the others? Could she get them to see that they must support him, for the sake of family unity? And is family unity so important? And what kind of unity?

The criterion is the ability of the decision to create community—not the community of the world, or even of the Law, but of the spirit: the converted community. The practical results are less important. Even family unity only matters in so far as it is unity in the spirit, or is preparing the ground for this. If she had to cajole and bully the children into accepting their father's decision—which was in itself an evasion of responsibility disguised as its exercise—theirs would not be the obedience of faith, the surrender to love, but an accommodation to the needs of the world, their world. They might well continue to exhibit all the signs of family togetherness, and if they were Christians they would probably pray together like mad, but it would be a togetherness for protection, both from outsiders and from each other—realized as an enemy but not so dangerous if under surveillance.

But the real decision of love creates a real community. It is in the knowledge of this that the family comes together to discuss the problem that affects them all. It is noticeable that the father's decision to let the whole family decide has not weakened his position as the symbolic centre. On the contrary, his assumption of equality with them in this matter has reinforced their feeling that he *is* the centre. They will not, on this account, give a sentimental deference to his opinions—that would be to insult the reality of what he has done—but the knowledge that the freedom they enjoy is not only their right but also his gift will make them exercise it with an increased sense of responsibility to the family *as a whole*, which he represents and in whose name he has surrendered the sole power of decision—in the making of which he still shares.

This means that those whose formation has made them open to a challenge of this kind will, by the fact of their father's sacrifice, already be tending towards a positive response to the demands the situation may make on them.

There are at least two people, however, on whom it seems likely to have the opposite effect. The elder son, who has always felt that the family exists for his benefit, is the person who will in fact be least affected by the move, whatever happens. He has been protected in advance from the need to face up to any real challenge, so he sees the family conference simply as a decision concerning the prestige of the family, as a background to his future life. A family living in a working-class housing estate is not likely to add to his consequence, and he also assumes (rightly) that his father's personal inclination would naturally be to a continuance of the kind of life he is used to, as far as possible. So he feels that the summoning of a family council is just another proof of his father's weakness, and is a betrayal of his, the son's, best interests for the sake of placating the others—who are, of course, terribly selfish and unlikely to consider the thing from the point of view of a young man aiming to get on in life. He is therefore in a hostile and suspicious mood, and this is so because of that same action of his father's that has opened the hearts of the others. Self-giving is a judgment, a very deadly sword of division, even before a decision is made, or perceived as having to be made.

The other person who is not pleased is the old man, who also knows that his son-in-law would really prefer that his life should not be drastically changed, and was counting on this to ensure the decision that would also suit *him* best. He is afraid that if the family chooses the small house he will have to make a new life for himself. He knows the family will not simply leave him out. Whatever happens he will be provided for, but he might find himself having to make all kinds of adjustments to new people and new ways, which might not fit in so well with his habits, and wishes. In his case too, therefore, a blanket of selfish fear is isolating him from the community created by the challenge of the future.

One person is also to some extent isolated, not from selfishness but from fear. The married daughter has always relied on the sense of permanence and continuity the family gives her, whose centre for her is her mother's dominating personality, and although she could not explain it she is terrified of the threat of exposure to unknown dangers, outside the protection of home. She loves and admires her husband, but she has thought of him as adding to, and being part of, the strong structure of her family life. If they move to a smaller house she and her husband will be on their own. On the other hand she is really fond of her parents, and sees the advantages to her mother of a smaller house, with less work attached. She is also aware of her husband's political opinions, and of the kind of world he wants for his son. It is not the world represented by a move to another stronghold of middle-class respectability and privacy, however impoverished. And she knows, though she doesn't really face it, that her husband would prefer a more independent life. As a result of all these confused fears, the faint stirrings of a need to face up to them, the poor girl is in a state of considerable psychological disarray as she sits on the sofa with her baby on her lap, and anxiously watches her father while he explains the situation. She, even more than the others, is in the wilderness.

The members of the family who sincerely want to discover what is best for everyone are at a disadvantage to begin with. They have, or are trying to have, open minds. The two who know which side their bread is buttered have a lot of excellent and altruistic arguments to put forward, in a disinterested effort to keep the buttered side up. The grandfather does it best because he talks in a kindly and understanding way of everyone's needs, and of the value of the kind of family tradition they have all created, how important it is to hand on to the next generation, in a world of shifting values, something so good and secure. Everything he says is perfectly true, so true and so convincing that it is clear from the start that if his wishes are not followed it will mean a division in the family. It seems unlikely he could ever be brought to change his mind. If he has to submit to a different decision he will always bear a grudge, and feel that he was the sane and truly loving person in a family that had been undermined by modern discontent and desire for novelty. His arguments are especially persuasive because it is clear that it is precisely the kind of family tradition and continuity that he describes that has made this group of people able to discuss their uncertain future with so much mutual affection and desire to do what is best for all. The formation they have received in this 'accidental' community has brought them to the point of being able to create community. It would take a lot of detachment to be able to see that the old man is trying, in the name of what is truly valuable, to prevent the very transforming effect for which the good formation is a preparation.

These people do not realize clearly—the grandfather because his own comfort is involved in not seeing it, and most of the others because they have never had to think that way—that to choose to continue the family tradition might well destroy that very unity that made it so good. If the decision not to change is taken out of a fear of the challenge of the new and demanding then the resulting community will be one held in being by fear of the outside, not by mutual need and mutual support.

On the other hand the decision not to make a drastic change *might* be motivated by a realization that some at least of the members of the family would not be able to cope with a new way of life, and would be driven in on themselves rather than helped to openness and spiritual growth. If the children had been younger, or the past history of the family one of insecurity and strife, the chief need for all their sakes would be continuity, stablity, the absence as far as possible of challenge from outside. In that case the decision to continue to protect and to preserve would be the one that would, in the long run, create community. This decision would most likely be taken by the parents, however, without consulting the rest, because in this way they would be relieving the children of a burden of responsibility they were not old enough to bear. If this decision were explained to the children, so that they realized it as part of a movement towards community, this would be the kind of formation which carries transformation as implicitly the reason for its structures of protection and direction. This is different from a formation structure that *can*, because of the way it works, prepare the way for transformation, but does not carry that intention clearly in its consciousness.

But in the case of this particular family, at this particular crisis of its communal existence, there is a sufficiently complete formation for a decision, now, which will be transforming. This does not mean that transformation is inevitable, but only that there is a *real* opportunity, whereas a challenge issued too soon might be an obstacle to transformation, rather than an opportunity for it, because the challenge could only appear as hostile. Which indeed it would be.

The eldest son is less persuasive than his grandfather because of the obvious self-centredness of his arguments, although they are presented as concern for the others. Their effect is not, as in the old man's case, to create a feeling of guilt and doubt, but rather to harden their feelings against whatever it is he seems to want. His hostility brings out more clearly in their minds the value of the things he is arguing *against*, because his angry demands are in themselves a challenge. As the others try to meet it without reducing it to simply a personal retaliation they find their consciousness becoming much clearer of what is implied for them, as people, in a *different* sort of life. This makes the prospect both more of a danger (if that is how they feel) and more clearly an opportunity.

But it is difficult to keep the reaction from being a merely negative one, and in the case of the younger daughter the attempt isn't made. She is usually fairly remote, living in a fantasy world of her own, but her brother's assumption that what he wants must be right infuriates her, and brings her right out of her dream world. She suddenly sees—partly because she is accustomed to dealing with imaginary and heroic roles for herself—that there are exciting possibilities in a new environment, among different people, a more exposed and (as she thinks of it, having read some of her brother in law's books) more 'real' life. The thing fires her imagination, and her sudden involvement in the family situation makes her able to put over to them a little of her vision. It is anger that lets loose the strength of her reaction, but it is her particular formation, as a dreamer whose dreams have been shaped by certain solid and enduring values and affections, that gives this particular form to the outburst of passionate conviction.

Her conversion is rather peculiar, in that it is her own vision, born of anger, that in its communication to the others takes shape, becomes a challenge to *her*. As she speaks she realizes to some extent the nature of the demand that a real, not an imaginary, decision of this kind would make on her, personally, and this realization shows up a great deal of her former dreams and hopes as mere self-indulgence and escape. She is up against a real demand for self-surrender, and panics slightly, for all this is not clear in her mind but is emotionally implicit in what she is doing. She falls silent, a little dismayed at what she has done, in a state of acute self-awareness yet not quite knowing what to do with that self. But her brother interprets her hesitation and obvious embarrassment as weakness. 'That's nothing but an adolescent dream,' he says contemptuously, and suddenly she knows that he's right, but that it's up to her to make a real decision out of her dream, because the dream is *about* something real, even though it isn't real. It doesn't matter to her, at this point, what the family actually decides. Her own conversion is accomplished, and in the light of her new vision she will be able to accept and build up whatever the future turns out to be. She isn't committing herself to a particular future, planned by herself. That was the dream. She is committing herself to *the* future, which is not hers to plan. She expresses this, clumsily, by saying, 'I think we should do what's best for everyone, not just us.' What she means is perfectly clear to her, but not much help to the others. Her brother dismisses it as meaningless optimism. Her grandfather considers it ought to mean what's best for him. Her father knows what she means, and appreciates the ambiguity of the 'us', which could mean the speaker, and others in the same position, or could mean the whole family, challenged by a wider need. For the first time the challenge of a new kind of life begins to have a positive significance for him.

Her elder sister is sympathetic, resenting her brother's attack. She is stirred by her sister's enthusiasm, and looks hesitantly at her husband, who smiles back with warmth and amusement. He is touched and surprised by his sister in law's outburst, but all the more determined not to force the issue by putting the weight of his personality, his knowledge, and his comparative detachment, behind the decision he wants. Just because it would be comparatively easy for him to take command he refrains from doing so.

The arrangement of roles at this point is interesting. The centre of the family, which is symbolically the father, now really is the family, without symbols, because in wrestling with a common problem it is the crucial nature of the choice that has become more and more apparent, always in relation to the family as a whole. And its wholeness as a living thing has become more apparent as the outlines of its previous structure come under question and are found to be inessential. Yet if the father were not present, and had not by his free action made possible this discovery, the awareness would lack the coherence that his symbolic headship gives. So his authority is both essential, and, at the same time, diffused through the whole organism and therefore not a focus of attention as such, at least at the point of potential transformation.

The focus of authority has shifted, not symbolically but really, to the younger daughter, whose words only have meaning in the group as the expression of something that is common to all in some degree. This awareness is expressed by one person out of her single and separate self-discovery but it is valid because it springs from a challenge discovered though not yet fully accepted in common. It is the previous sense of common involvement that has made her decision possible, and has therefore brought about her function as prophet for the whole community. She speaks with authority, but not her own. It is derived from the body in which she speaks, but not officially, for the symbolic source of authority is still her father, and the authority is corporate and not to be appropriated to any single member. Here is, then, a charismatic authority. It is her personal conversion that makes her a prophet, but she only is one in virtue of her membership of the group. Yet it was because she had lived to a great extent 'in the wilderness', not fully involved with the day-to-day concerns of the family, though supported by its existence, that she had the kind of mind that could see a coherent vision, and get others to see it.

But the prophet is, inevitably, also a judge, a scandal and an offence. She is a scandal and an offence to those who have refused to share in the community awareness, but prefer to turn to the symbolic centre as the only source of authority—as long as it says what they want. (If it does not, they will say that it is no longer the true head, and look for another, or try to assume the headship themselves.) Therefore she judges, not by passing judgment on anyone but herself but precisely by judging herself and choosing the real (the spirit) at the expense of the unreal (the flesh). Her clear judgment of herself involves others and they are judged, falling to one side or another of the division made by the sword of the word.

But there is a further complication in this situation. The elder daughter's husband is both the most intelligent and the most perceptive person present. He is aware, as the others are not, of the importance of formation, yet he sees it in relation to its end. He thinks in political terms, of the breaking down of barriers, of service and equality and responsibility for what is made by those who make it. He wants to be free to work for the things he believes in. Yet he realizes that to force freedom on people is in fact often to imprison them more securely. It demands of them a hypocrisy that conforms to the behaviour appropriate to the structures that express freedom, while using them as protective and offensive rather than reconciliatory. Because he knows all this he is the person best fitted to make a decision which will be for the good of all, and he could do this and let the others feel it was in fact *their* decision. This means that he is well suited to the exercise of a formative authority, just because he knows what formation is for. He is the kind of person who could be the source of both symbolic and actual authority, in practice, for the sake of a community not yet sufficiently aware of itself to be able to be in touch with authority as diffused, and expressing itself in the charism of prophecy.

And this is precisely why he will not, at this juncture, take any part. To use his unusual insight and gifts to assist the 'right' decision now, would be actually to deprive the situation of its nature as an opportunity for true transformation. The 'right' decision would be one according to the Law, not according to the Spirit. Yet to refrain from exercising his power of teaching and guiding *may* mean that the *wrong* decision will be taken, one which does not create community. It takes a lot of understanding and humility to sit back and let people take real decisions, when it would be so easy to help them to take a right but not fully committing decision. If this young man succeeds in doing so it is at least partly because he, also, has been formed by living in a formation community that was geared to transformation, without knowing it.

At this point the mother of the family feels it is time to intervene. She is delighted and touched by her younger daughter's sudden awakening, and the evidence of idealism and a real determination to grow up. She is also feeling disillusioned by her elder son's selfishness, and conscience-stricken at the realization that this is very largely her own fault. She is, as usual, tolerantly cynical about her father's transparent attempts to safeguard his own comfort under the guise of concern for others. But just because she is moved with real affection and compunction, and under no illusions about the moral value of the arguments put forward in support of traditional values, she is determined not to allow herself to be stampeded into a decision which is contrary to common sense and the obvious interests of the family. To move to yet another old, large, and shabby house, with rather less money to run it, is a prospect she personally finds depressing, but this actually confirms her in her opinion that it is the right thing to do. It is what her husband really wants—she doesn't know that he is in fact ceasing to want it, even now. It is what her father needs, the selfish old so-and-so. It is what her elder daughter needs, and here all her protective feelings are uppermost, together with a certain distrust of her son in law. Her younger daughter's idealism will come to no harm by a few years storage. Her younger son will not be exposed to children among whom physical strength is more important than brains. He isn't particularly strong, and is the sort of child who is liable to be bullied, being a natural non-conformist.

All this she explains to her family, with tactful modifications, and with a great deal of affection and humour and real concern.

They can all see that she really does want to do what is best for all of them, and what she says is realistic and fundamental and represents all that has so far made this family the very successful thing it is. She really does care for all of them, much more than for herself. There are hints of less pleasant motives, such as jealousy of her son in law, and a desire to manage her husband (for his own good, of course) which is mixed with a certain lingering resentment of him because her life has been to a great extent flattened and subdued to his needs. But these are minor influences. Her main motive is sheer, unpossessive motherliness. These people need to be cared for, and she can do it.

This was the framework of her own conversion, long ago. It was in embracing her vocation as a mother that she was able to leave behind her desire for a gay life, and channel all her energy into service of her family. That is the extent of her achievement, and its limitation. She has no other language but that of motherly concern, and there has been nothing in her life that might have provided a formation by which a 'new' conversion, with a wider language, might have come to her. So the community which she has made, out of her conversion, is not one *into* which she can be converted, at least for the time being. She does not even feel it *as* a community, but only as hers, her child, to care for, and she has no sense of the stirring of new life that is going on in it. And the irony of it all is that it is she herself, by her love and care, who formed this community to a point where it is potentially capable of creating a new community, one which will not depend on the support of its external structure, but can develop new structures according to the needs of its developing life.

Her appeal is all the stronger because it really is an appeal. It is a rational, humble, and not at all self-righteous statement of what she deeply feels. She does not play on their loyalties or present herself as a martyr. She simply asks them all to put aside both prejudice and irrelevant idealism and do what is clearly the sensible and kind thing, especially for the sake of those who are not very well able to cope with the tougher side of life.

It is an absolutely straight and unloaded plea, and it has a considerable effect.

It has a most unexpected effect on her eldest daughter. She has been listening all this time, tossed and turned and perplexed and curiously excited. From being a formless threat to her peace of mind the uncertain future has come to seem, perhaps, something to be coped with. For a while it seemed that she was to be exposed to the world, and this frightened her although her fear was tinged with eagerness. But the fear was uppermost, although it was struggling against a sense that she must not be a drag on the others, least of all her husband. When she hears her mother, in her usual reassuring and affectionate way, stating her own case, and appearing to offer her exactly what she thinks she wants, she suddenly finds the prospect much less attractive. The fact is that her encounter with herself, the conflict between love and fear, has already given her a greater definition, a greater sense of herself. And this newly aware self is beginning to feel itself capable of giving.

For the first time, she speaks. She reminds the others, to her own surprise, that within ten years or so their parents will be elderly, the youngest boy well into his 'teens, her sister grown up. There will be no longer any need for a big house, and her mother will find the work too heavy. Another move will be needed, in fact. This very obvious thought strikes a chill, and does not please her mother, who dislikes both the awareness of the approaching end of her *raison d'être* as mother, and the evidence of rather brutal commonsense in her hitherto dependent daughter. But the girl's husband is delighted, and his own anxious tension relaxes. The very tactlessness of her way of showing that she does not need to have her life arranged for her is endearing to him. But he feels very sorry for his mother in law even while he is sharing with his wife a new sense of community. He lookes across at the older woman, and meets her eye, and she realizes that he knows how she feels, that he is not sympathizing with her, but congratulating her on her daughter. A little of the fear and anger goes out of her. He has this power of forming people, giving them what they need in order to begin to know themselves without fear. The slight, scarcely noticeable message of understanding brings her back into the community. She laughs, at herself, looks half ruefully at her husband and realizes that he is in it too. Her look, and her few words, are a confession and a plea, and his smile is the confirmation of a reconciliation. In a culture part of whose protective formation is an avoidance of clear-cut and committing gesture their liturgy is a very slight one, but it is a language that works.

What has happened, without any conscious pushing, is that the practical decision which the family is gathered to make has become comparatively unimportant. It doesn't really matter, now, which course of action they finally choose. It wouldn't matter if it were announced that, after all, there was to be no new road, and they could stay where they are.

It doesn't matter, that is, from the point of view of the creation of community now, through the encounter with a situation demanding decisions. But it still matters a lot in another way, because the setting in which they choose to live as a converted-created community will affect the way they are able to work out their conversion. Some structures are better able than others to express the reality of community, and indeed it is the awareness of this fact that has made the terms of the decision to be taken in this case. So the actual choice made will, in the long run, radically affect the future spiritual development of all the members of the family. But this does not alter the fact that what matters at the point of decision is not the content of the decision, for the conversion event *has* no content, but is a commitment to the unknown—this is what makes it a converting decision, and not just a matter of deciding to behave differently. The occasion of the decision, and its working out, are not its content. They are the necessary frame for it.

What has happened to this family is something more important than a practical decision, however wise. Out of an existing com munity, accidental in origin, conditioned by the life of the flesh, worked out and supported by the Law, they have been creating community in the spirit. It didn't happen all at once. It was prepared through the years, begun in the relationship of father and mother which had in it at least as much of real self-surrender as might serve to grow into something more. In all these years there have been constant little crises, and some bigger ones, in which an encounter was an invitation, and a challenge, and a choice was made. Not always a good choice. There were periods of estrangement and depression, when only the external structure of the Law kept the community in being. But the sense of direction was never wholly lost.

This common and not very drastic family problem is one of a series of events that make up the history of this family. Yet this event, and the others, are not part of an unfolding process happening *to* the family but actually *are* the family, they bring it into being *as* a community and determine its quality and character as a community.

But this community-creating event could not take place without the continuous history, with recognizably belonging events and traditions, rules, language, customary gestures, of this community as it happens to be.

The formation, in fact, conditions or even prevents the transformation, as in the case of the individual. But in this family setting it is easier to see the interdependence of the structures of formation and the occurrence of transformation.

But there is one element in this family situation, the community conversion event, that is absent or at least easily overlooked in studying individual conversion, of whatever kind. This is the function of ritual as providing the occasion of transformation. Ritual may seem an odd word to use in this context, but it is the realistic one.

The family I have described have an important decision

to make. If one person is making a decision he can make it wherever and whenever the occasion for it arises. The encounter that demands his decision is one that just happens. But a community decision can't happen like that. When a group of people is involved it must somehow be explicitly stated that a decision is to be made, and what it is. If it is one concerning the whole group it can either be decided by their leader, or leaders, and communicated to the rest, or it can be decided together. In either case there has to be some point at which the group signifies its consent to the action decided upon. If it does not, it ceases to be one group, and splits up.

This communication *can* be by letter, or to each singly, but unless the members then tell each other, somehow, the identity of the group is likely to be very vague. It isn't really a community, in fact, but only a system.

But the normal thing is for the people concerned to come together, and either make their decision or signify their assent to the one made in their name. And when people do something together, on purpose, and *mean* something by it, which is not fully expressed by what they actually do, this is ritual. The family I described simply came and sat around in the sitting-room and talked. But they came for a purpose, and because they had been called together for that purpose, by someone whom they recognized as having authority to do so. They came with the intention of making a decision about the family's future, and therefore their action was in itself an expression of membership in the family, and of a sense of responsibility towards it—even if that were regarded as a responsibility for making the rest conform to one's own wishes. This is ritual.

The creating of a community, then, means the point at which the accidental (in the flesh) community becomes the on-purpose (in the spirit) community, by conversion, mutual self-surrender and faith. And this occurs, and can *only* occur, at a point which is arranged, and ritually established and expressed in some way. This seems inescapable from the nature of community living as

such and the pattern which conversion takes. The movement towards decision which gives definition to the individual is an interior process, and must always be so, however many people are
doing it at the same time. But when the area of conversion concerns community life, and the community is aiming at creating
itself—coming into being as itself—then the process of encounter/
conflict, repentance/self-discovery, surrender/faith has to be
ritually expressed.

This means in practice that it is ritual of some kind that bridges
the gap between formation and transformation, because it concerns both. It is related to the nature of the formation that is going
on, and indeed is the expression of this formation in a language
which is intelligible to all the community. The family in my
example met in their sitting-room in a fairly informal way, and
this expressed the kind of family they were, and the way they
were used to living and thinking together. It expressed the un-
work-a-day character of the occasion—it wasn't in the kitchen,
or casually over a meal. It was not totally informal; I would suppose
that they all saw to it that they were reasonably clean and tidy
before they came. But it was not stiff, they were not awkward
in each other's presence, as if sitting, unaccustomed, in the best
front parlour. They sat easily, in a room they were used to. All
this showed to each one the nature of their relationship and also
the nature of the occasion.

But ritual is also related to transformation, because it is the
situation expressed by the ritual with which the converted community has to deal, in working out its conversion.

But as soon as ritual is under discussion the question of the
function of various members of the community comes up, and it
is at this point that the most serious misunderstandings can occur.
The various functions of people in a community are part of the
language by which the community understands itself. Yet it
seems clear that in the transformation event the particular roles
are not important, as I tried to show in the case of the different
expressions of authority in the family. The converted commu-

nity consciousness is a consciousness of the whole, and that whole is personal, in the same sense that I said that the whole person was involved in transformation when it is individual.

It is still individual, but the encounter is a community one, and that does not mean an encounter with a lot of separate people, severally, but with them as sharing. The encounter is with the thing shared, which is oneself, also, but not possessed, only known in its sharedness. And it comes to definition *as personal* in this encounter, by which it is transformed.

The transformed community is so in virtue of something which is not, cannot be, a function of any one member. The converted consciousness is unaware of separate roles, as the family, in the end, was unaware of particular contributions to the decision but only of the achievement of community. Yet this conversion only happens when there is ritual, and that means differentiation of function, however rudimentary, if only in the fact of one or other summoning the rest to the rite. But function is not fixed, the symbolic leadership can find expression in the charismatic authority. And neither can do more than provide the material for actual transformation.

In practice communities seldom seem to be able to hold both these necessities in balance. They tend either to play down the ritual, the differentiation of function, and assume that the community only is, at all, in so far as it is a converted one, expressing its identity, therefore, in an almost purely charismatic fashion. Or else they emphasize the setting for transformation, expressing ritually the self-awareness of the formation community, knowing that its purpose is transformation, but so accustomed to being *in via* that it loses much conviction of the likelihood of ever getting there, at least recognizably. Charismatic expression of communal authority is not likely in this setting, for authority is more clearly articulated through defined functions, which are symbolic but also actual.

If we are ever to reach a fuller understanding of what community is, and discover a language for it that is able to embrace both these different kinds of community awareness and transcend them, it seems necessary first to find out in more detail what are their strengths and what are their weaknesses, as means to full Christian development.

I have therefore followed the pattern of the rest of this book and have chosen to describe and discuss examples of the ideas I am dealing with. In this case, as in that of prophecy, it seemed more convincing to describe actual communities showing these two kinds of self-understanding—the predominantly formation-minded one, of people who come together in order *to be* converted, and the predominantly transformation-minded one, of people who come together because they *are* converted. The former is represented here by Benedictine monasticism, the latter by the 'Separatists' who later formed the leading part of the colonists who sailed in the *Mayflower*. The fact that one belongs to the Catholic tradition and the other to the Reformed is not accidental, though it would have been possible to find examples of each kind of community that reversed the position. In fact, communities of either tradition have been founded according to one or another of my two patterns, and they seem to have shown the same characteristics, regardless of their official creed. But their later histories were often modified by the character of the Christian tradition in which they stood, therefore they are less easy to study for my purposes. My two examples show two tendencies in what amounts to the theology of the Church, and they should be useful in clarifying the underlying differences between the Catholic and the Reformed approach, in the light of what has been discovered about the relation between formation and transformation.

CHAPTER VI

THE COMMUNITY OF THE TRANSFORMED

THE language which the early Separatists (true Elizabethans) used to describe the Church of England recalls with remarkable force St Paul's description of the unconverted behaviour of some of his converts: 'A huge masse of old and stinkinge workes, of conjuring, of witchcraft, sorcery, charming, blaspheming the holy name of God, swearing and forswearing, profaning of the Lord's Sabbath, disobedience to superiors, contempt of inferiors, murder, Manslaughter, robberies, adulterye, Fornication, covenant breaking, false-witness-bearing, lying . . .' It is a fairly comprehensive list, and the remarkable thing is that this particular diatribe (including the oddly inconsequent use of capital letters) came, not from a Puritan, but from one of the Anglican scholars who later helped to prepare the Authorized Version of the Bible. But it expressed fairly well the opinion of those who eventually 'separated' themselves from it. If many people, not already convinced Puritans, held this opinion of the—just about—established Church, it is not surprising that some of the more zealous felt that the only thing to do was to get out of it.

It is interesting to notice that all those who joined the Separatist movement at any stage of its peculiar career were, without exception, 'of the vulgar sort of people' as the local bishop described them when one of the earlier leaders, Browne, was jailed for holding meetings.

Browne's basic idea was that, contrary to Calvin's notion, there was no need to wait until the State took action to reform the Church. And Browne's doctrine was one that underlay the whole movement, although he himself eventually deserted the cause and went back to the Church of England.

Browne's notion was not reform, but revolution, a totally new creation by which God's kingdom was 'not to be begun by whole parishes, but rather by the worthiest, be they never so few'. These worthies were to *separate* themselves from all 'the ungodliness and wicked fellowship, and to refuse all ungodlie communion with Wicked Persons'. The idea was not new, several reformed sects on the continent had the same idea, and indeed it is characteristic of all new communities that are based on the idea that *conversion is the normal condition of membership*.

It is this basic idea, that the true Christian community consists only of those who have been converted—the 'saints'—that gives its special character to the Separatist movement. The same character and the same kind of development is to be found, modified by historical circumstances, in other communities founded on this principle, whether Christian or not. The earliest Christian communities had this character and the problems created by it can be seen in the way St Paul, and the writer of the Pastoral epistles, tackled them. (Paul did so more successfully than the Separatists, for reasons which will become apparent, I hope.) Other examples can be found among many medieval sects, especially the millennial ones, and also in the beginnings of several religious orders, though not all.

The special characteristics of such a community are all connected with the fact that conversion is an interior event, in which whatever formation has preceded it appears irrelevant and even hostile to the new understanding. In particular, all the structures —the articulation of authority in the accidental community out of which conversion occurs—are seen to have no relevance to the awareness of community created by conversion.

The Brownists grouped themselves in independent congregations, each of which elected its own pastor—and got rid of him if he didn't reach the required standard of holiness. It was the Spirit moving freely in the congregation who chose the pastor, and therefore he was expected to show evidence of his calling by his behaviour. He had no other claim to office. Fixed structures of authority were 'human inventions', not warranted by scripture, and this is a good description, for the structures of authority in a community *are* inventions that express a human understanding of the natural, human, unconverted man and his needs. They are formation structures and have no place in the immediate transformation event. This the Separatists saw very clearly. All authority in the community was a charismatic authority, even the pastorate was a free election, depending on the spirit-endowed quality of the holder of office. And since membership of the community itself was only for the converted its members were expected to show in their blameless lives the proof of the reality of their conversion. It seems the logical thing to expect.

'Put off your old nature which belongs to your former manner of life and is corrupt through deceitful lusts, and be renewed in the spirit of your minds, and put on the new nature, created after the likeness of God in true righteousness and holiness.' And if those who were separated were expected to prove their election by their holiness, equally it was clear that only those who were blameless could be admitted. There was no question of supposing that the Church could possibly include the whole baptized population, as Calvin did.

From this principle, that the Church is a 'priesthood of believers', a community of 'saints', sprang the necessity for frequent and earnest examination of conscience. This soon extended to the examination of other people's consciences, but the unpleasant side-effects of this zeal should not be allowed to obscure the real earnestness and faith of those who were called to separation. The very real sense of vocation they had was one that did indeed create community and they were prepared to suffer a great deal rather than go back to a life which they felt to be incompatible with their conversion.

John Robinson is a good example of a man who was driven, step by painful step, into separation. He did not want to leave the Church of England, but the intransigence of the authorities under King James made it impossible for him to go on, for he could not, in conscience, approve of the ceremonies in which the Church expressed its identity. He went on preaching, however, until he was eventually excommunicated. Then he knew that all hope of reform from within was gone. This caused his moment of decision, though it took him two years to reach it. When he had made up his mind, he went on with unshakeable faith to the end. He evidently felt that his salvation was at stake, and indeed the true conversion decision is one for or against Christ.

It was the presence of pastors and teachers of this quality that gave power and coherence to the groups of Separatists, and they needed this sense of mission, this assurance of grace, for they were hated and persecuted wherever they turned up in England. Among all the accusations hurled at them—most of them of quite random maliciousness and totally without foundation in fact— one basic motive for antagonism becomes clear: these people, who were speaking with the voice of the Spirit, were people who had no authority to speak at all. They were 'vulgar persons' and had no legal or financial prestige. They were the people whom the social structure of the time had left 'in the wilderness' which is where, as I have tried to show, the power of transformation does occur. But these vulgar persons, being consistent in their thinking, concluded that if the Church was an assembly of people freely called by the Spirit and, therefore, dependent on no office holder, its members all equally had the right to make decisions affecting its day to day management. They wanted, in fact, government by consent. Starting from the psychological fact that formation structures are irrelevant to the actual transformation event, they concluded that these structures were also irrelevant to the working out of transformation, in practice, and that others, more in keeping with the converted nature of the community, should take their place.

At this stage they had given up any idea of imposing their converted patterns on the unconverted—of reforming the Church from within. This problem was to return to plague them later, as it always does in the second generation of such a movement,

but for the moment it seemed quite simple to transfer their converted community consciousness to the sphere of everyday life.
The perilousness of this undertaking is not apparent at first.
People in love, or in the first throes of conversion, are apt to
bind themselves to types of behaviour which seem not only possible but imperative, as the only adequate expression of their new
self-awareness. So these little groups of persecuted people demanded, as a matter of course, the right to rule themselves according to the demands of the Gospel, all the congregation
consenting. The English authorities, using the same words, but
understanding them in their normal, unconverted sense, naturally interpreted this as a flagrant attack on the principles of mon-
archic government, and since James was especially touchy about
anything that seemed to infringe his rights as God's anointed, the
full fury of political fear backed by moral rationalization was un-
leashed against the Separatists. This is the normal impossibility
of translating converted language to unconverted ears. 'The un-
spiritual man does not receive the gifts of the Spirit of God, for
they are folly to him, and he is not able to understand them because they are spiritually discerned. The spiritual man judges all
things, but is himself judged by no one. For who has known the
mind of the Lord so as to instruct him? But we have the mind
of Christ.'

They remained stubborn, or at least many of them did. It was
not only the spirit of contradiction that gave them the 'obstinacy'
of which the established Church complained. They felt themselves to be misunderstood, and indeed they were. Their language of conversion used words such as 'freedom', 'people',
'government', but the words glowed with the understanding of
them that belonged to the converted community. They felt that
they *were* free, not merely that they *should* be free. If the authorities treated them as dangerous rebels and put them in prison
that merely showed that (since they assumed they shared the
same language with their persecutors) the Church of England
exercised a 'tyrannous' power, and was acting as the willing agent

of Satan. They had no choice but to be 'disobedient', their conversion demanded it.

They demanded 'freedom of religion' and they were not being
in the least inconsistent if, later, they denied it to others. To
accuse them of hypocrisy is to misunderstand the psychological
relation of formation to transformation, as the Separatists themselves, indeed, did. Their right to freedom was, in their minds,
based on a fact, the fact of their free election. They *were* free,
and they expressed this conviction in the language of their conversion. And in expressing it they also limited it. The freedom
they thought of was a freedom they knew, expressed in the language they knew. It was not an abstract principle to which they
subscribed but an experience to which they testified. But because
it was expressed in their particular conversion language it was not
capable of expressing any other kind of experience. 'Freedom',
to them, meant *their* conversion experience, and anybody else
claiming freedom, who did not express it in their language, could
not have any true claim to freedom as they understood it. The
conviction with which they withstood attempts to suppress *their*
freedom was the same conviction with which, later, they persecuted those who used another language of faith. It was not hypocrisy, but rather a wild consistency, that ordered both reactions.

Their basic mistake, in the light of what I have discussed so
far in this book, seems to have been to transfer the type of awareness which is proper and inevitable in the context of transformation, wholly and untranslated into the formation context. They
did this because they were unaware of the relation between the
two, but assumed that the tremendous and undoubted reality of
the conversion experience left no room for any values but those
belonging to the converted state. Several centuries before Freud,
this is hardly surprising, yet St Paul could have warned them.
The Corinthians to whom he wrote the passage quoted above were
converts—baptized, practising Christians. The Separatists could
(and no doubt did) quote with confidence and indeed smugness
the bit that assured them that 'the spiritual man judges all things,

but is himself to be judged by no one'. But the sentences that follow this might have shown them that the fact of an undoubted conversion does not constitute a 'spiritual man' who can therefore claim full freedom and autonomy. 'But I, brethren, could not address you as spiritual men, but as men of the flesh, as babes in Christ. I fed you with milk, not solid food; for you were not ready for it, and even yet you are not ready, for you are *still of the flesh*. For while there is jealousy and strife among you, are you not of the flesh and behaving like ordinary men?'

The Separatists, even at this stage, were certainly given to 'jealousy and strife'. They kept it up even in prison, and the strongly worded row over the flighty habits and daring clothes of Thomasine Boys, wife of the imprisoned convert Francis Johnson, scandalized not only the enemies of the Brownist group but the brethren themselves. Thomasine was a kindly, if 'bouncing' girl and she adopted the child of another leading Brownist, Penry, who had been hanged, drawn and quartered for his faith. Because she would not give up her 'excessive deal of lace', which offended the poorer Sisters, she was abused and slandered, and so was her husband, who was not loth to fling a few texts back again. The 'Millinery war', so called because of Thomasine's affection for her 'showish hat' and refusal to wear 'sober taffety or felt', was both a scandal and an entertainment that only a sentence of deportation to America was able to end. Their ship bound for the colony never got there however, but returned to Southampton when one of the other vessels foundered. The prisoners managed to escape and reach Amsterdam, where they were no sooner organized into a new congregation than 'jealousy and strife' began again. The scripturally salted invective which the combatants hurled at each other makes marvellous reading, even if it is not very edifying.

Yet this sort of thing is to be expected in any community, and the trouble was not that this sort of thing happened but that both sides assumed that they *must* be right, and the other side children of the devil. The necessity for this conclusion arose naturally from the premise that the called were people of blameless life. To admit that one was not blameless was to deny the validity of one's call, and the utmost rigour of scripture must be employed to enforce the opinion that one was indeed one of the 'saints'.

It was this that made the Separatist congregation much more than normally 'factious'.

The period in Holland was an important one for the Separatist church in many ways. They were in a foreign country, and therefore they tended to hold together. They had neither power nor influence to tempt them to abuses, indeed they were so exceedingly poor that many of them suffered acute hardship and some, in despair, returned to England, preferring to risk gaol in their own country rather than starvation on foreign soil. The 'factious' behaviour in Amsterdam led to a great deal of splitting up, but eventually a congregation settled at Leyden, and it was there, under the leadership of John Robinson (whose painful conversion I mentioned earlier) that this very poor little congregation showed what a community could be like when it was truly living according to its deepest ideals. They 'lived together in peace, and love, and holiness', and even if this description comes from a partisan source it seems to have been fairly near the truth. Another ruling elder, William Brewster, was a great help, because he had a gift of eloquence and of prayer, and could 'rip up ye heart and conscience before God', a sort of one-man dramatic catharsis which certainly does have the effect of purging by pity and terror, and allowing the spirit to get to work. And when the unruly power of the spirit was let loose by the word of William Brewster, prophet, there was John Robinson to guide the working-out of the spirit in accordance with the true needs of the community. He could be 'very plain' when he felt it was necessary, and he did not hesitate to point out that it was not much use to be always noticing other people's failings if the critics were 'remisse in themselves and not so careful to express a virtuous conversation'. He was trying to build a community, and discouraged people who were 'close and cleaving unto themselves,

G

and retired from ye common good'. But in spite of his scoldings his people loved him, for he really cared for them, and it is significant that they described him as a 'commone father unto them'.

As father, he used his commonsense and his worldly shrewdness, as well as his converted community awareness, in the service of his people. For he knew with his heart if not with his head that these people, sincere and whole-hearted as they were, and prepared to suffer for their faith, were still in many ways 'babes in Christ', and needed the milk he could provide for them.

John Robinson preached for several hours every Sunday, as was the custom, and while he certainly took his texts and his message from scripture he himself records that he was beholden 'to the great volume of men's manners which I have diligently observed and from them gathered no small part thereof, having also had in the days of my pilgrimage special opportunities of conversing with persons of divers nations, estates, and dispositions, in great variety'.

Robinson was probably one of the most truly saintly of all the 'saints', and he gave its character to the little Leyden congregation, which never numbered more than about three hundred. But that was a lot, considering the tendency to split up which had hitherto been one of the most obvious characteristics of the Separatists. Robinson, in fact, so far forgot his earlier and more rigid views as to allow that some other Christian congregations, although in grave error about many things, nevertheless 'grounded their practice upon the word of God', and on one occasion he allowed his congregation to take communion with another Church—that of the Scottish (Calvinist) Church in Leyden, an offshoot of the Dutch Reformed Church. This scandalized the brethren at Amsterdam, who held strictly to the Holy Discipline of the Separation. Yet it was this comparatively lax Separatist who actually held his congregation together 'as a father' through many difficult years, and made it possible for them to preserve in great measure the quality of their conversion. It really was true to say of them, 'to the honour of God and without prejudice to any, that such was ye true pietie, ye humble zeal, and fervent love of this people, towards God and his waies, and ye single-hartednes and sinceir affection one towards another, that they came as near ye primitive pattern of ye first churches as any other church of these later times has done'.

In other words they were a real community, and what was more they were truly a converted community, because they had as their leader a man who was able to give them what they needed. What they needed was threefold, and they found it in one man.

First of all he was the symbolic centre of the community. In theory they didn't have one. In theory they were all equal, and so indeed they were, as spiritual men. But the fact that they thought of him as a 'father to all' shows the place he really occupied in the consciousness of the community. He represented to each member the wholeness of the community, without in any way subtracting from the individual's own sense of responsibility. On the contrary, he increased it, by the love he showed in his obvious concern for each one, whether he was reproving or encouraging. It was by providing a focus for the community's self-awareness that he held it together. The community was able, by means of this symbol, to *know* (not merely to *say*) that it did not create itself but that it drew its being from something that created it, *as* a community. The Leyden community called John Robinson 'father', and thereby expressed their awareness of the kind of relationship that the community has to its source, which he symbolized.

If Christian theology has always used the word 'father' as the most fitting one to describe God, this is not because fathers are kind, forgiving, generous, careful and far-sighted, and therefore give us a good sort of idea of what God is *like*. Fathers in general may be all these things, and it may be helpful to think of God as having these qualities—but this way of thinking is a *formative* idea, which helps to develop an understanding of what kind of behaviour belongs to the relationship for which man is formed. But the transformation of man is not brought about because God is merciful or whatever, but because he is *Father*. It is the discovery of a relationship, in which the qualities of the persons concerned are quite irrelevant. The two lovers in the second chapter were not converted to each other because either of them was kind or unselfish or forbearing or compassionate. These qualities formed their approach to each other, and the learning of them made their encounter a fruitful one, but the occurrence of transformation brought them into a relationship to which all these admirable things were quite alien and meaningless. So to call God 'Father' is not to acclaim his qualities but to bear witness to an experience of relationship. It is to cry 'Abba, Father', because of an awareness that is of the spirit. But the ability to do so, to witness to the fact of a community being created in the spirit, depends on the existence of a pre-conversion community which is of a kind that *can* be converted. And such a community must have some sort of symbol which *means* the community to its members. It need not be a human being. It can be a statue or a picture or an ideal of a golden age, or just a memory. But it must be something at least vaguely imaginable. And most often it is a human being, because a human being is a person, and the symbolic centre must be personal.

When a conversion occurs, the community comes to self-consciousness as related within itself by and in its source, but the moment of conversion is not describable or realizable except in terms of the symbol that formed the community's self-definition in the moment towards decision. This symbol, therefore, is personal in its nature, since it is the 'person' that comes into being in the movement towards decision. But it is also symbolic, that is, it has an imaginable form which can be grasped by the minds of the people in the community—minds which work in the world of appearances, the flesh. And in practice this happens most easily when this symbol is embodied in an actual human being who is in some sense the head or leader of the community. In a family, or any secular community, the head or leader is himself the symbol of the community's self. He is their link between their converted self-consciousness and their efforts to know and communicate this self-consciousness in the ordinary events of life. He is the 'language' of their conversion, to a great extent. This is why leaders like Lenin or Juarez or Mao Tse Tung have so much influence. They are the converted community's own self-awareness.

But for a Christian community this is not so in the same way. The Christian's conversion is in Christ, who is the person who comes to definition as the community's self-awareness—an awareness of relatedness to the source of the community's life, its generation by the Father. This is presumably what we mean by talking about Christ as the Son—in a relationship of being-begotten-by-the-Father. And it is also what we mean when we talk about the Church as somehow or other the body, the very being (which is what 'body' meant for Paul) of Christ. Its personality comes into being as *Christ*, who is its self-awareness, its relatedness to the Father. But the *source* of the community's life also *is* the life that makes it a community at all, therefore the source and the person in whom this source is known are the same kind of thing. The Father and the Son have the same nature, and this nature is community-creating, in human beings. All this is simply a matter of experience and observation, even if it has to be analysed in a rather special way. I don't want to push the thing, or to seem to be developing the material artificially in order to make it show what I want it to show, but it does look as if, seen from this angle of what-it-is-that-makes-community, the mystery of the Trinity makes ordinary psychological sense. There remains the link-up, the power that breaks out in the breakdown of the Law, the power that transforms, that draws and defines the personality in the movement towards the decision that transforms, and in the light of which the material of formation becomes new, converted, recreated. This power is the self of the community in its creation, it is the creator of community, and its life *as* community, shared life. It is the sharing, in the community, of the life whose source makes the community *be* itself, by its self-awareness which is Christ—which is as near as I can get to explaining how a community in the Spirit comes about, and what makes it come about.

But this isn't enough, in practice. There has to be something that people's minds can latch onto in an immediate sort of way, as people seize on the image of a human leader. He is the symbol, and that's quite straightforward. Christ is the focus of awareness of the Christian community, but unless he is very vividly present to the *imagination* of the individual the symbol can't work, as such. And a strong imaginative picture, although useful as part of the *formation* for conversion, is irrelevant to the converted consciousness because what the Christian community is the body of is not a man wandering around Palestine, doing good and looking pious (or not, according to taste) nor yet an enthroned Byzantine Emperor, still less a kind of super boy-scout-with-a-beard. The Christ whose body is the Christian community isn't imaginable in that way at all, in fact to say that he is the symbolic centre is to use the word 'symbol' in a rather special sense, to mean something that gathers together into one word or phrase or act a whole complex of feelings and hopes and ideas and intentions and gives them a unity and a reality that can somehow be 'turned on' by using that word or gesture. This is part of the function of converted language, whose words and gestures are symbols in this sense.

But since the converted community is still in process of becoming what it is—still consists to some extent of 'babes in Christ' —there is a great part of its communal awareness which is still *un*converted, and it therefore uses the converted language hesitantly, and with varying assurance and meaning. In this situation, which is the continuous and normal one of any community (broken only by moments of acute self-awareness reached at times of crisis, ritual or accidental) it is necessary to have what might be called a symbol of the symbol, only the first use of the word is the more ordinary one. It means something which is acting as a sign or reminder of something else. But in the case of the sym-

bolic centre of the community it is normally not *just* a reminder
as a picture or relic might be. The symbolic centre is a human
being, who is also a member of the community. So he himself
is sharing in the life of the community, and it is in virtue of this
membership that he can become also its symbolic centre, a reminder of the meaning of its existence and a symbol to focus the
desire of the community for its further transformation. So his
function is formative, with a transformative purpose built into it.
But he becomes manifestly unnecessary, *as* symbol, insofar
as transformation is actually achieved.

Which brings me back to John Robinson, who was such a success as symbolic centre, because he knew how to be a formative
influence tending towards transformation. His office as pastor
made him the symbolic centre, but since the office in a community of the converted depends on the visible qualifications of the
man to fill it, he would not have been effective as symbolic centre
unless he had also had the kind of authority which I described (in
Chapter V) as belonging to the son in law. It is a *personal* authority. This is the second of the three roles he had to fill, and which
have to be filled in any community.

This kind of authority is a personal quality. It does not depend
on appointment or official status of any kind, nor does the person
concerned have to be in any particular relation to the symbolic
centre (which is, as centre, the source of authority, but sometimes
only symbolically). Personal authority simply comes from certain
qualities of insight and foresight and grasp of character, which
enable their possessor to make decisions with more certainty than
other people, and to convey his own certainty (with or without
supporting reasons) to others. It is personal in the sense that it
belongs to him, as a person, and cannot be separated from him,
though he may choose not to use it. The young man in the family
in the last chapter had this kind of authority and deliberately
did not use it, at least at that time. Such abnegation is unusual,
and indeed usually unnecessary. Personal authority is needed in

any community in the process of formation, and without it it gradually falters and falls apart. (It may be held together for some time simply by the authority of its symbolic centre as such. But a long-standing inability on the part of the person who is the symbolic centre to live up to his office inevitably leads to a weakening of the power of the symbol, and its eventual uselessness.) Of course personal authority can be misused very easily, and it is especially liable to misuse by attempting to keep the community at a formative level, in order that its own authority may continue in being. Just because personal authority, like symbolic authority, ceases to have any meaning in the transformed consciousness, someone who is gifted with personal authority is especially tempted to substitute his own decisions for the personal, converting, decision of the people over whom he exercises his authority. It is especially hard to avoid this, because the kind of behaviour that follows a truly converting decision in the community, and one that is the result of following a strong lead, may be just the same. Also it is part of the burden laid on a person with this authority that he must often actually be the one who presents the material for decision. He must decide when to do so, and when it is too soon. He must know who is capable of responding and who is liable to be frightened off. He must use his authority to build up the courage of the rest so that, with his support, they may accept a challenge. It is so much easier to decide *for* them —easier for them, and easier for him. And so often it seems not only easier but safer and more responsible. And often it is the right thing to do. So the life of a person who has such authority is itself a long series of particularly agonising decisions, in none of which he can have sufficient certainty of his ground to be sure that he has in fact decided rightly. It is scarcely surprising that in practice this kind of authority is abused more often than not, either by rash or self-seeking leadership, or by trying to keep the community permanently below the decision level—for their own good, of course.

John Robinson appears to have been one of those rare leaders who knew when to demand a true decision response, and when to gentle a worried or cantankerous 'saint' over a difficulty, without demanding a decision at all. His success in exercising authority made him also effective as symbolic centre. He was not, and could not be in such a community, the 'symbol of the symbol' in the sense that his people thought of him as representing Christ. He was rather the symbolic centre in the sense which belongs to a secular community, which is, after all, what any community is in its unconverted capacity. To put it very simply, he gave them the feeling of knowing who they were. He did this by exercising his authority in a way which made them think of him as 'father', and so relate him unconsciously to their community-awareness as people of God.

The third kind of need that the Leyden congregation found fulfilled in John Robinson was the need for the assurance of the Spirit's presence and leadership by means of charismatic gifts.

The place of charismata in a Christian community is an important indication of the type of self-awareness which it has. In the early Church it was taken for granted that the presence of the Spirit in the community would be made evident from time to time in special and sometimes startling ways, such as healing, prophecy or 'speaking with tongues'. It is generally assumed nowadays that this was a special dispensation for the reassurance of the young Church, and that the work of the Spirit is now to be expected rather in the activity of the Church's institutions. The Church itself is a prophetic body, a healing and teaching body, and so there is no need, normally, for these peculiar manifestations of power. I am not concerned, here, to comment on this view, but rather to point out how the occurrence of charismata is related to the concept of formation and transformation which I have been examining. Charismatic gifts are, by nature, unofficial. They cannot be laid on to order, they do not inhere in any office, though an office holder may possess them. Like prophecy, which is itself charismatic, they occur in the 'in

between', in the desert. The more unusual ones are most liable
to descend on 'in between' people, and are particularly liable to
erupt in times of uncertainty and danger, when the structures of
formation are weakened and disrupted. I discussed this in connection with individuals who were prophetically inspired, and
noticed that their followers, if any, were usually people who were
socially or religiously 'outcast' in some sense.

This state of being outcast, lacking the security of formative
structure, is the condition that makes the outbreak of
charismatic expression of community self-awareness particularly
likely. The family I described in the last chapter were thrown
into this state by the threat of the disruption of their former way
of life. It was under this threat that they achieved a new self-
awareness, at least partly by means of the perhaps temporary
prophetic charism of one member, on which the family's fate
acted in a particularly clear-cut way, because of her own
personal and temperamental condition which made her a suitable 'subject'. The early Church was in this condition, and so
were the Separatists, in their early days. In both cases (and in so
many others with a similar history) a low social position, lack of
legal influence, and financial insecurity created the 'wilderness'
condition, and the charismatic phenomena followed. In the case
of the Leyden community these were limited and comparatively
moderate, though the elder William Brewster evidently had considerable powers. There was nothing like the feverish prophecies (sometimes by rival prophets) that had characterized the
Amsterdam congregations. But there seems little doubt that the
Leyden community possessed a charismatic character in a wider
and less peculiar sense. Their sense of being guided by the
Spirit was both real and sober, and it kept them going through
grave hardship.

Much of this sense of being a community in the spirit can be
attributed to the personal influence of John Robinson, whose
whole-hearted devotion to his people was evident. He was more
than the symbolic centre, he had an authority beyond that per-

sonal authority which consists in a mixture of brains, intuition and a forceful personality. He was *holy*, he was a spiritual man in the full sense, even though the limitation of his language of conversion led him, sometimes, into unwise and intemperate attacks on those who seemed to him to be the enemies of true religion. He was so really transformed that he lived in great measure 'in the spirit' and people felt this. It gave him the power not only to make shrewd and far-sighted decisions but to inspire in his people a response of love that was itself transforming. In him the gift of the spirit was not an occasional or startling affair but a permanent type of awareness of life, which he was able to share with his people to a great extent. In this way his real authority was available for use in the service of the spirit—a formative authority, naturally, but one which was exercised by a man so spirit-endowed as to 'provoke' transformation almost as a matter of course.

It seems fairly clear that the hard-pressed, worried and insecure Leyden community owed its character and its immense fortitude (nothwithstanding continued outbreaks of 'factiousness', and the tendency of the teenagers to be attracted by the habits of the jolly, easy-going Dutch) to the combination of qualities in one man. They are interlocking qualities, though they are separable. Pastor Robinson was a good 'father' (that is a good symbolic centre) because he had personal authority, and exercised it as a spiritual man. It was the courage and faith that he formed in them that made some of his congregation dare to decide to take the risky course of emigrating to the New World.

Their position in Holland was becoming more and more difficult. Their economic condition was bad, but a worse worry was the fear that they would gradually be absorbed by the Dutch. The second generation problem was already beginning, as the children grew up and were found to be not automatically converted. The problem was not faced in Holland; rather the notion of founding a new life in the New World postponed it, for only those families that were especially fervent and courageous were likely to go. Whether they knew it or not, the decision to emigrate was a decision to try to preserve the conditions for a converted, charismatic community.

After several years of complicated and fruitless negotiations with the Virginia Company and the New Netherlands Company, the Separatists in Leyden finally arranged matters with the Merchant Adventurers Company, a loosely organized collection of men who were willing to finance the new colony, in the hope of making money out of it. They had no interest whatsoever in the religious convictions of the colonists apart from the fact that these people seemed prepared to face hardship and difficulty for their convictions, a fact that made them a hopeful commercial proposition. And when delays and trouble and more 'factiousness' had so discouraged the congregation that only a small number were finally willing to go the number was made up by 'strangers' who were simply Englishmen, of whatever faith, who were willing to settle the new colony. So in the end only about fifty 'saints', including children, undertook the risky venture, though others intended to follow later. And John Robinson stayed behind, with the hope that he would rejoin his flock at some future date.

Before the colonists left the whole congregation spent a day in prayer and preaching and 'abundance of tears', and no wonder. John Robinson's farewell to them was typical of him: 'I charge you before God and his blessed Angels to follow me no further than I follow Christ', he told them, and begged them to be as ready to receive God's revelation 'by any other instrument of his' as they had been willing to receive it from him. This shows very clearly both that he did regard himself as God's instrument, and that he took it for granted that he had no permanent claim to be the mouthpiece of the Spirit for them. It was only in 'following Christ' that he was a leader for a Christian community.

His notion of his role among them is shown also in a letter that reached them in England, where they were delayed by more quarrels and muddles. He offered them advice, making it clear that he was fully assured of their 'godly wisdoms', but to encourage them in what they were doing, 'not because you need it, yet because I owe it in love and dutie'. His advice was that they should repent of their sins, and pray for patience, since they were sure to be tempted by some 'evill daye' to 'take offence at ye Lorde himself'. Considering the conditions of sea travel, and the unknown difficulties that awaited them in the New World, this seems sound advice. He also warned them to avoid the pursuit of private profit, but to work for the 'general convenience'. This contempt for personal profit seems to be characteristic of converted communities, and recalls the communism of the earliest Christian community. It is interesting to notice that it revived, among the Separatists, at this crisis of danger and decision.

The story of the trials and dangers of the voyage, and of the early days of the colony, is a fascinating one, but it is not relevant here except in so far as it demonstrates the particular problems that beset a community of the converted.

There seem to be two possible courses that can be pursued by people whose community depends on being called or Separated—that is, on the conviction of election. One is the logical following out of the idea of conversion as a completely Spirit-directed affair in which no human agent or organization has any right to interfere. The other is a gradual accommodation of the notion of a converted community to the necessities of continued existence, without actually abandoning its principles.

The first is well shown by the strange and funny and also pathetic history of James Smyth. The other is shown by the actual history of the New England colony as a social organism with legal powers and a tradition of its own.

James Smyth was an intelligent and adventurous thinker, a Cambridge graduate. He had been one of the original 'saints', as their pastor at the Separatist meetings in Gainsborough. When they were later driven out by persecution he came to Amsterdam, to be a thorn in the flesh of the other leaders of the Separatists. Even John Robinson found him a trial, because he upset people with his wild ideas when he, Robinson, and other good pastors were laboriously trying to build up the morale of their exiled congregations.

For James Smyth had a ruthlessly logical mind. Like the other Brownists he rejected all fixed offices in the Church as 'human inventions', not warranted by scripture. The Church was a 'priesthood of believers' under the direct rule and inspiration of the Spirit. Where was the pure word of revelation to be found? Only in scripture, of course, which was God's word. But one day James Smyth announced to his bewildered congregation that he now realized that the English version of scripture, being the work of fallible men, could only be a 'human invention', and might lead the faithful into error. Only the original Greek and Hebrew were reliable sources in which the true Christian might search for God's word.

The next stage of the argument loomed up, inevitably, and to a man of that period—unacquainted with theories of inspiration the apparatus of scholarship needed for modern exegesis—it was a monstrous one. Even James Smyth could not bring himself to admit that Greek and Hebrew might also be a human invention, and liable to error. Without the means of working out this problem as later scholars did, Smyth had only two alternatives—to conclude that there was *no* certain source of God's word available to man, or to assert that God *had* literally spoken in Greek and Hebrew. The former was spiritual suicide for a man whose life was founded on faith in Christ, the latter clearly took some swallowing, yet it had to be accepted. But an abiding uneasiness and lack of conviction in adopting this conclusion is clear. James Smyth continued to hold that the original scripture was God's revelation, but he thought it best not to use it in worship. His congregation henceforward relied solely on the free movement of the Spirit at the meeting. That congregation must have been devoted to this truly charming and dedicated man, for they followed his unusual teachings without demur.

But that was only the beginning. The next theological bomb-shell caused much wider reverberations. Pastor Smyth came to the conclusion that since baptism was an act of faith, and no baby could possible make such an act, no one in his congregation was lawfully baptized, and indeed no Christians had been lawfully baptized for centuries.

Smyth and his congregation debated painfully about this, for it was difficult to see how they could put the matter right if no real Christians existed, therefore no Church which could baptize. The course they finally adopted satisfied them, though it aroused rage and derision among the other congregations. They met together and 'unchurched' themselves, and when they were thus free of all religious allegiance they started from scratch. Smyth baptized *himself*, and then the others. (This feat earned Smyth the title of 'Se-Baptist' or self-baptizer.) After this they elected Smyth and all the other officers to their previous positions. So the congregation was, outwardly, exactly as before, and this did not worry them at all. Their new and 'lawful' baptism constituted them a new creation, a purified and perfected people. The continued use of what was in practice their former organization did not worry them at all, and this is consistent with the fact which I have already discussed—that behaviour in working out conversion is not necessarily outwardly different from previous behaviour. The difference is in the converted consciousness. The 'language' of conversion uses the same words as the unconverted language referring to the same type of structure, but it has a new significance, is a different 'language', in the community consciousness of the converted. Smyth's little congregation, inspired by his faith and persuasive personality, evidently did have a strong community awareness, as converted, which made them able to withstand a great deal of furious reproach and argument, much of it well grounded in scripture.

But this happy state of affairs did not last. James Smyth was one of those rare people who are so deeply honest that they do not become attached to their own opinions as to possessions. Continued study convinced the poor man that he had been wrong in his idea that no previous baptism was valid, and with his usual recklessness he told his congregation of his new discovery. This was too much for many of them. They really had been converted to his view, to the extent of basing their lives blindly on his assurance. And it had worked. They *knew* themselves to be reborn, purified. The congregation split up, in the end, and half went back to England and formed one of the earliest Baptist congregations, maintaining Smyth's former doctrine. The rest stayed with Smyth, because their faith was founded in him as the symbol of their community consciousness.

It was partly as a result of this that many of the Separatists moved to Leyden, for they feared the spread of such wild ideas.

The end of the story is sad and moving and very interesting. In the four or five years that remained to him James Smyth continued to care for and pray with his tiny congregation, meeting in Jan Munter's bakery. And he studied and prayed, and did not hesitate to tell other people the results of his study and prayers. He had had plenty of opportunity to observe the fierce intolerance, the smugness and quarrelsomeness of strict Separatists— always justified from scripture, very dogmatically interpreted. In the end he came to the conclusion (and it was published after his death) that it was sufficient for salvation for a man to be a 'penitent and faithful Christian'. He denounced the endless bouts of godly criticism in which he himself and others had indulged. He admitted that people might think him 'inconstant' in thus renouncing old ways, but 'I will every day, as my errors shall be discovered, confess them and renounce them . . . I profess I have changed and shall be readie still to change for the better'.

James Smyth died in loneliness and poverty, mainly from malnutrition. His few followers eventually joined a Dutch Church, and disappeared as a separate body. But their pastor had died content, assured of salvation because God was merciful. He had followed out the implications of his conversion with unwavering

courage and with astonishing results, when one remembers the
religious temper of the times. He realized, or very nearly realized,
the huge problem of what scriptural inspiration really means. If
he could find no solution he can hardly be blamed. And he
came to believe that doctrinal formulae are not relevant to the
salvation occurrence which transforms, but that what is needed
is penitence, and renunciation of all one's cleverness and virtue.

He was perfectly right and perfectly consistent, for he was
working out, in his own painful life, the distinction between formation and transformation. He saw, even more clearly than the
other Separatists, what *really* pertains to salvation and what does
not. What he did not tackle was the problem of how you get
people to the point of transformation.

This was the chief worry of the New England Saints. When
the bishops of the Church of England at that period were trying
to justify to their Puritan critics the delay in reforming the manifest abuses, they appealed to the need to retain 'harmless' beliefs
and ceremonies to which many were attached, lest the 'weaker and
ignorante' should fall away from the Church. Having rejected
many of the beliefs and nearly all the ceremonies, the Separatists
had the task of somehow keeping the 'weaker and ignorante'
from falling away from the congregation of Saints.

At first sheer necessity and hardship kept the community together. It was only when the first rigours were over, when proper
houses were replacing the first rough cabins, when the settlement
really was settled and sufficiently numerous to require a central
government and a code of Law, that the weakness inherent in the
concept of a converted community became apparent.

The trouble was not only that the colony did not consist
solely or even mostly of Saints. The nucleus of Saints took it for
granted that they had the right to impose their notions on the
others, but the rigorism that characterized their government was
not due mainly to a need to control the unconverted. It arose

from an inability to distinguish between the *language* of conversion and that of ordinary unconverted life.

The words of their language of conversion were scriptural words, and indeed scripture was their community culture, the language in which they understood their nature as a community. But since scripture expressed their conversion they assumed that it must automatically provide a rule of life applicable to every contingency. This, for them, resolved the paradox of their situation as a community of the perfect, who were yet manifestly in need of the normal regulations and structures that any community requires. The regulations culled from scripture were to fill the place of the Laws of England, and this would preserve their character as Separated, a congregation of the elect. In fact of course, they were using (with modifications) Jewish legal and social structures to perform the functions that any legal and social structures are intended to perform, which are purely formative. The result of transferring the Jewish legal code to their own period was naturally harsh, harsher in some ways than the actual Jewish code, for they considered it reasonable, 'on occasion', to use torture to extort a confession. They were, however, less free with the death penalty than was the Jewish law, at least in theory. The death penalty was dealt out for sodomy, and flogging was a normal penalty for other kinds of sexual sins. But the Saints' penalties were far less harsh than those of English law at that time and they were also more tolerant, in the matter of heresy, than the other Puritans. They never went in for witch-burning, whereas in other parts of New England witchcraft was punishable by death. But as time went on they, too, began to try to enforce orthodoxy by law, levying fines for non-attendance at meetings, and beating those who denied what were considered to be necessary doctrines. Since this did not make worship any more popular they were soon fining people for talking against their pastor or the 'Holy Discipline' in general. When this state of affairs is compared with the life of the Leyden congregation the change seems tragic. But it was probably inevitable.

John Robinson never did rejoin his congregation in the New World, and when news of his death reached Plymouth there was deep and real grief, and a sense of irreparable loss. He had been a powerful symbol, keeping alive—even in his absence—hope and courage of an almost eschatological kind. With his death something was gone that could not be replaced. But even if he had crossed the Atlantic, and (even less likely) had been replaced by an indefinite succession of men of equal calibre, the degeneration in spiritual quality was bound to follow, though it might have been less evil in its manifestations. For 'evil' is the only word to describe the results of trying to treat an ordinary secular community as if it were, or ought to be, a group of the totally converted. The failure to translate, or rather to realize that translation was impossible and should not be attempted, led not only to the use of scripture as the source of the legal code, with all the barbarities implied. It did something much worse than impose a penal system belonging to a civilization a few thousand years out of date. It demanded in everyday conduct the proof of being saved, just as it demanded from pastors and officers in their conduct of the Spirit's election. People's rights, as members of the community, depended on their status as members of the Church —that is, as saved, since this was a Church of believers. This did not become a legal enactment (probably the number of 'strangers' made it impossible) but it was certainly part of the consciousness of the Saints. It followed that all behaviour must be such as was fitting for saints, and not only tearful and loud public confessions (more familiar to us as sessions of self-criticism) but the usual rigorous condemnations of other people were normal. The doctrinal and ritual quarrels, the splits and feuds, the back-biting and accusations of heresy, are almost too involved to be unwound, and all of them show the basic assumption that correctness of doctrine and behaviour are the essential proof, to oneself and others, of being saved. 'Deviationism' and moral failings of any kind, were proof not of being *unconverted* but of having *fallen* from one's conversion, and being therefore in a state of reprobation. This was such a terrible thought, especially in connection with one's own children, that any amount of harsh discipline and punishment was used in order to terrify the young and wayward into that outward conformity that would prove their right to be regarded as members of the Church. (The difficulty of controlling the behaviour of the children and young people during the five or six hours of the Sabbath services was a constant worry to the Saints, and their records refer to it frequently. They usually employed one person to attend exclusively to this, and it appears to have been indeed a full time job during worship. Various 'godly widows' are mentioned as being successful at it, and praised for the zeal with which they plied a stick on those who talked or fidgeted. Girls, apparently, were the worst, being given to giggling and even flirting in the meeting.)

Hypocrisy is inevitable under such a system, and smugness and talebearing equally so. Also the fears and passions which might not be openly expressed or indulged could be legitimately worked off by hounding those whose behaviour branded them as the devil's children. This bred the atmosphere so well evoked by Shaw in *The Devil's Disciple*, where the wretched little base-born Effie is treated as a scapegoat for the repressed passions of her self-righteous 'family', and the pastor, half strangled by the rigid moralism of his congregation, can only find salvation by embracing a hope of martyrdom which is his way out of an intolerable spiritual impasse.

One tiny and (almost) amusing instance of the passion for finding proof of spiritual status in outwardly verifiable signs arose from the assumption, common at the time, that a baby was always born precisely nine months after conception. So any couple whose child was born even a few days before nine months after their wedding might find themselves in the stocks for fornication. But it was also believed that a child was born on the same day of the week as that on which it had been conceived. George Willinson, in *Saints and Strangers*, records that this 'led to great embarrassment at times, for many a child was unhappily born on a Sabbath. Some ministers were disposed to question the propriety of baptizing children born on that day. One pastor loved to thunder on the subject—until his wife presented him with twins one Sabbath, just after the morning service, when it was the pastor's custom to retire for what the congregation had always presumed was rest and meditation.'

The satisfaction among the thundered-at congregation must have been considerable.

This kind of thing is of course not confined to seventeenth century New England, nor to Puritan sects. It happens wherever the community's existence is determined by membership of a group that has certain moral standards built into it as part of its *raison d'être*. They don't have to be Christian ones. Communist states in their early stages demand behaviour that proves a correct ideological state of mind. The Israeli kibbutzim, founded by devoted enthusiasts, find it harder, sometimes, to generate a like enthusiasm in the second generation, and in some cases actively discourage their teenagers from going on to higher studies, in case they become disinclined to return to a life which seems meaningful to the converted, but is not self-evidently worthwhile to those who do not share the language of their parents' conversion.

Catholic communities have been, on the whole, less prone to this particular misconception of the relation between formation and transformation, for reasons which will, I hope, become apparent in the next chapter, but the malice and snooping that characterize groups of 'devout' wherever they occur, are not difficult to find among Catholics. Mauriac had a sharp eye for this particularly nasty aberration of religion, but it is not only in France that it occurs, and it seems inevitable that it will occur wherever a faith or ideology blurs the distinction between formation and transformation. The legal systems of most Western nations are still suffering from the same tragic mistake, and the anger and anguish over legal measures dealing with such things as homosexuality, abortion or divorce betray the sturdy roots (much less rationally worked out than among the Saints) of the same desire to find in outward behaviour proof of spiritual quality, and enforce spiritual health by law.

Another consequence of the same attitude is the respect for material prosperity as proof of the Lord's favour. Victorian tracts and improving books recount, over and over again, moving tales of the poor boy (or girl) who withstands temptation, continues virtuous and industrious through lurid misadventures, and is finally rewarded with prosperity and/or a rich husband/wife. The Puritan respect for wealth is odd, when one remembers the early contempt for rich clothing and fine furniture, and Robinson's exhortations to shun private profit. But it is the inevitable consequence of assuming that a community-consciousness grounded in the conversion experience, and expressing its assurance in a language which resounds with the certainties of conversion, can transfer the mental concepts that express this consciousness, untranslated, into the context of secular life, and apply them to its organization. Without the converted awareness, without the light of self-knowledge in Christ (whether he is explicitly recognized or not) what assurance can people have that they 'belong' in the community unless they can find convincing proof of it in their own lives? The sins of other people are such an assurance, hence snooping and witch-hunting in all its forms. Material prosperity and 'good luck' are such an assurance, hence the moral value attached to worldly success, and the whole scramble for position and financial security to which our educational system (product of a crypto-Puritan ideology) is wholeheartedly dedicated. Success is the charism of the secular community that is not content to be secular but doesn't know how to be anything else. It proves to the community and to the individual that he really belongs, that he has what it takes.

The Separatists, like so many other communities of the converted, failed to create community once the first generation had died out. The early community awareness failed to grow and be rediscovered in later development because the members assumed that, since all members were converted, community already existed. They thought and legislated accordingly. The real encounters, the conflicts that lead to self-discovery and conversion, no doubt occurred between many individuals, or in families, but it was not realized as part of the process of community building. If you assume you already *have* a building you lose interest in the architect's plans for it. Everyone's energies were engaged, therefore, in trying to understand everything that happened *as if* real community in the spirit existed. It was like trying to behave *as if* you lived in a house, with doors and stairs, when you are really camping in a field. The result looks lunatic to the outside observer, though it seems perfectly consistent to the deluded, as they mount their imaginary stairs and meticulously lock non-existent doors. That is the tragedy of such enthusiastic groups, whose real piety and charity dwindles to pious practices and charitable acts, both measured out by the teaspoonful, and carefully noted.

The reasons why this swift degeneration follows have been examined, but in the process a new idea seems to be emerging, one which will assume increasing importance. The realm of the secular is normally held to be, roughly, the sphere of life in which religious ideas are not directly operative. But from the analysis of the Separatist movement it appears that the secular should perhaps *include* the sphere of religion, in so far as religion is formative. This means that we could safely stop worrying about the border between secular and religious, for the specifically religious is concerned with the formation of human life *towards transformation,* and secular influences can do this too, and increasingly do so, as understanding of psychology increases. The distinction, in that case, will not be between secular and religious, which can happily fade into each other, if they are allowed to, but between the secular and the *sacred,* which is not the same as the religious. The sacred is purely that area of consciousness which is concerned directly with transformation, either in creating the immediate occasion for it, or in expressing its immediate results. With the beginning of a new notion of what secular and sacred could mean, and their relation to the previously explored concepts of formation and transformation, it should be possible to look with new eyes at a community which is not formed *by* conversion, but *towards* conversion. In the new understanding that arises from this chapter it seems that what I am going to describe is a community that is both religious and secular, in the full sense of both words.

CHAPTER VII

THE FORMATION COMMUNITY

THE Separatists, like other communities of the converted, failed in the end to create community because they assumed this wasn't necessary. To the early Benedictine communities the notion of creating community, in the sense in which I have used the phrase, was not considered. But they saw life in a community as a means to salvation, and salvation, as I have suggested, means that community is created.

At first sight the set-up looks very similar: a group of people, dissatisfied with the lax and only nominally Christian behaviour of their contemporaries, withdraws from them in order to lead a life which is intended to be a close following of the Gospel. This description could apply equally well to the Separatists or to the first Benedictine communities. The difference is not to be found in the type of life they envisaged as proper to Christians, either. If the Separatists had been celibate, and had spent some hours of each day singing the psalms, or if the earliest Benedictines had brought their families with them and perhaps spent rather less time in vocal prayer, the 'feel' of the two communities would still have been totally different.

The real difference lies in the condition of membership. The Separatists assumed that conversion—'being saved'—was the condition of being a Christian at all. The Benedictines came together in order to work towards salvation, of which there can be no assurance until the moment of death which is also the moment of judgement.

The way the two groups thought about conversion is a good indication of the basic differences in their approach. To the Separatists, conversion was the experience of grace, the knowledge that one was saved, and must therefore live a life that expressed this knowledge. If one lived up to this knowledge, eternal life was assured. To the early Benedictines, conversion meant a decision to work *towards* salvation by turning away from all that might endanger one's soul. To choose life in a monastic community was a way of turning away from the danger of worldly distractions and involvements, and in this sense it meant a conversion. But this conversion carried with it no certainty of salvation, only the opportunity to work for it. Clearly, neither concept ties in exactly with the idea of conversion that I have been digging out so laboriously. How are they related?

Benedict himself did not set out to found a religious community. When he left his studies in Rome and wandered off into the hills, he seems to have had only the vaguest idea of what he was looking for, in terms of a way of life. He knew what he *wanted*—he wanted God. Nothing else interested him except as a means of discovering God more and more completely. Benedict, in fact, had been converted, in the sense discussed in this book. Of the occasion of his conversion nothing is known. He had been brought up in a devout Christian family, and sent to Rome to study, sometime in his teens. It can fairly be assumed that a serious and sensitive boy from a Christian family, introduced (even with a housekeeper-cum-nurse to keep an eye on him) into a city as basically and openly pagan in its values as Rome was, despite its Christian veneer, would either gradually abandon the more inconvenient of his Christian principles, or be obliged to assert them in a strong and personal way against the challenge of the cynical and corrupt city. The consensus of opinion seems to be that Benedict did not stay very long studying in Rome, since his later writing betrays only a slight knowledge of the Greek and Latin literature which made up the university studies of the time. This makes it easier to suppose that the conflict and decision that finally drove him into the wilderness was indeed the direct outcome of his confrontation with a corrupt society, scarcely affected by the Christianity whose centre the city was supposed to be. The supposition that Benedict's decision was a truly converting one is borne out by the fact that he did not go home, or tell his parents where he was going. It seems likely that they hoped that he would distinguish himself in some respectable career, perhaps as a lawyer, perhaps even as a priest. But in any case they clearly regarded the corrupting influences of the city as a routine hazard, and not a very serious one, or they would not have sent their son to study there.

Benedict might well have come morally unscathed through his studies, and attained distinction in a career, without surrendering to the vice around him. But he was not concerned simply to avoid gross sin, though it was probably the contact with it that forced him to a decision. He probably had that deep, 'instinctive' notion, common to people who are sensitive to the working of the Spirit in themselves, that a good and blameless life could never satisfy him. He wanted something more, and to call it 'God' is to give a name to the source of those queer, restless feelings, those unexplained discontents, those longings and nostalgias that have no clear object but that come to most people. Most of us dismiss these feelings as a distraction from the duties and necessities of living, but some people—deliberately or reluctantly—allow themselves to recognize them as a fact, to wonder about them, perhaps name them, and try in some way to discover their source. If it is possible to name the source the search becomes purposeful instead of aimless. Whether the name proposed by one's familiar language is 'art' or 'freedom' or 'God', the naming of it makes it possible to direct one's energies to the cultivation of the kind of pursuits indicated by the use of such a name. This is yet another way of considering the notion of what leads up to conversion and the function of language (in the wide sense of the whole system of the words and gestures of self-understanding and communication) in promoting and working out transformation.

Benedict called the source of his desires 'God', and set out to find a life that would make it possible to discover more and more fully this deepest reality of which he was so vividly aware. It is not surprising that he went off, literally, into the wilderness. It was not in the official structures of the Church, however important they undoubtedly seemed, that he could find his salvation, but outside the city, in both senses. The idea that God was most completely to be found in solitude, far from the houses of men, remained with him all his life, even when he himself had abandoned the eremetical life in obedience to what was clearly God's will for him. In the language of his conversion the hermit's life stood for nearness to God, complete conversion, the total salvation experience, in fact. This unformulated idea is at the back of his references in the Rule to the eremetical life as one to which some of the monks might be specially called. The intuition that somehow transformation occurs 'in the wilderness', in the in-between states where the structures of the Law break down or do not reach—this feeling, common to all who pursue holiness, is here expressed by the concrete symbol of the life of a hermit, actually and physically in the wilderness, actually and physically outside the community structures. But even so he would never have suggested that the experience of a definite call to the hermit's life was a conversion in the sense in which the Separatists understood it. Salvation, for him, was on the other side of death, and this view of the matter was one he shared with his contemporaries, and has been the normal Catholic view throughout most of the Christian centuries.

Yet it was not the view of the earliest Christians. John writes of eternal life not as a future hope but as a present possession: 'I write this to you who believe in the name of the Son of God, that you may know *that you have eternal life.*' A few sentences earlier (1 John 5) he says: 'He who believes in the Son of God has the testimony in himself. He who does not believe God has made him a liar, because he has not believed in the testimony that God has borne to his Son.' In other words the experience or 'testimony' of eternal life *is* the experience of God, which is verified in oneself, and of which Christ is the revelation: 'And this is the testimony, that God gave us eternal life, and this life is in his Son.' The argument is circular, and could go on indefinitely. What John is describing is the experience of the creation of community, in the sense described earlier. John seems to be scarcely interested in the end of the present world, which is simply the full and unclouded expression of what, in fact, already is, for those who believe: 'This is the judgement, that the light has come into the world, and men loved darkness rather than light' (John 3). Judgement is not something coming at the end of history, or even at the end of human life, but it is the acceptance or refusal of Christ, encountered in the present, by faith: 'This is the victory that overcomes the world, our faith. Who is it who overcomes the world but he who believes that Jesus is the Son of God?'

The idea that faith is what brings people into knowledge of God, or 'eternal life', or salvation, or whatever phrase describes the transformed existence, has perhaps become less odd and arbitrary after the analysis of the occurrence of transformation which forms the first part of this book.

Paul, writing some time before John, and much more taken up with the notion (common to all the early Christians) that the end of the age, the last day, was imminent, still makes it clear that salvation is not a future event, at the end of the world or of the the individual's life, but a present experience of what will soon become totally apparent. The odd and mystifying word 'justify' means, for him, to bring into a right relationship—a relationship of love. So he says, 'Since we are justified by faith, we have peace with God through our Lord Jesus Christ. Through him we have obtained access to that grace *in which we stand,* and we rejoice in our *hope* of sharing the glory of God'. And a little further on, 'we also rejoice in God through our Lord Jesus Christ, through whom we have *now* received our reconciliation'. And this doesn't simply mean that our sins are forgiven, as if sins were an extra that could be scraped off, leaving the real person nice and clean. It means a total personal revolution, a complete change of the mode of existence, from the estrangement and muddle of sin to sharing in the life of God: 'So you must also consider yourselves dead to sin and alive to God, in Christ Jesus'—not only in the next life, but now. Paul is concerned about the relation between eternal life as it is known now, and as it will be when it is totally revealed, and discusses it mainly in terms of a transformation of the body, wondering how this can come about. But this puzzle never obscures the central fact that salvation is already present, in Christ, and that those who are in Christ, by faith, have eternal life *now*, are saved *now*.

With this kind of understanding of salvation the earliest Christian communities regarded themselves, as the Separatists did, as a community of the converted or saved, an eschatological community, whose full glory would very soon become apparent. But time went on, and the end of time did not come, and the self-consciousness of Christianity changed. And it is interesting to see why the early Church did not, in spite of the similarity of its ideas about itself, go the way of the 'Saints' in New England. After describing the gradual changes in the Church's structure, as charismatic authority and gifts gave way to authority residing in the fixed offices of the community and gifts mediated through the sacramental system, Bultmann sums up the development in this way (it should perhaps be noted that the word 'transformation' is used here in its ordinary sense and not in the special sense in which I have used it throughout this book):[1]

'This development, the outcome of which lies beyond the boundary of the New Testament, though it is presaged within it, is ultimately *a transformation in the Church's understanding of itself*. Originally the Church conceives itself as the eschatological people of God, the Congregation of the saints, those who are called out of the world and divorced from it. The Church senses this transcendant character of itself by the gifts of the Spirit which are at work in it. But the Spirit is the

[1] *Theology of the New Testament*, 2 vols., London, 1952 and 1955, Vol. 2 § 53.

earnest money or the pledge of the coming glory, the eschatological fulfilment. Hence, the Church lives in hope of the fulfilment and documents its transcendant character in its ex-
clusiveness and by the conduct of its members as 'strangers'
in the world.'

(This last sentence shows very well how the language of conversion both expresses and limits the working out of conversion.
'Documents', here, means a way of recording and expressing
something. The self-understanding of the Church, its language
of conversion which is that of an eschatological community, conditions its behaviour.)

'While the consciousness of being a non-worldly society belonging to the other world and filled with its powers does not
actually get lost, it nevertheless suffers a peculiar transformation.
In consequence of the delay in the expected parousia, *the transcendant character of the Church* gradually comes to be seen
not so much in its reference to the future as in its present
possession of institutions which are already mediating
transcendant powers in the present: a sacramental cultus and
finally a priestly office.

'Of course, *that reference to the future* does not get lost,
but it, too, becomes peculiarly modified. The future salvation
toward which hope is directed comes to be seen less in the
completion of the history of salvation and the transformation
of the world at the dawn of a new age than in the future life of
the individual beyond death. Certainly the traditional picture
of the end-drama continues to be passed on . . . Still, the most
important thing in the picture of the future is the expectation
of the resurrection of the dead, and the last judgement; that
is, interest is concentrated upon that which is decisive for the
individual. . . .

'The more the Christian's way of life comes to be understood
not as a demonstration of the new (eschatological) existence

but as the condition for achieving future salvation, the more this reference to the future loses the meaning it had in Paul; the dialectic relation between indicative and imperative [between what a Christian is and what he ought to do about it] is surrendered. Then the effect of baptism is limited to forgiveness of sins committed in one's pre-Christian period . . . When . . . the knowledge is lost that the future so qualifies the present that believers exist eschatologically now, understanding of the paradoxical nature of the Christian situation gradually disappears, and *the Church has changed from a fellowship of salvation to an institution of salvation* [my italics] even when, and particularly when, it holds part of the traditional eschatological conceptions. Its transcendance is understood no longer as pure reference to the future, but primarily as a sacramental quality. The Spirit is no longer the power that now and again breaks out in the "gifts"—the words and deeds and conduct of the believers—but is a power immanent in the institutions, particularly in the sacramental cult; it is the office-bearers' equipment for office. The officers have taken on the quality of priests, while it is only through their mediation that the Spirit is indirectly at work in the layman . . . But there is still another way in which this reference to the future is modified: the eschatological tension relaxes. The expectation of eschatological fulfilment is not simply given up, but the fulfilment of the hope is pushed forward into *a time that lies in the indeterminate distance.*'

This long quotation (apart from the tedentiously over-simplified description of the Spirit as available to laymen only 'indirectly' through the clergy) makes admirably clear just what is the difference between a community conceived of as transformed, and one conceived as a means towards (a far off and mysterious) transformation. It also makes it clear why the Separatists, and other similar groups, failed to develop in the same way. Coming later in history than these first Christians, they could look back and see this development, and see it as a degeneration from the primitive idea. Therefore *they explicitly rejected this kind of development* as a betrayal of the Gospel. They deliberately barred the door that led to the only way forward for the second generation. The only alternative was to try to *pretend* that they were preserving what in fact cannot be preserved in that form. They failed for the same reason that many marriages fail, when the existence of the marriage is held to depend on the continuation of the feelings and behaviour that characterized the first experience of passion. But on that analogy, Benedict's community was founded on the apparently odd assumption that passion is something that may (if you're lucky) occur as the result and crown of a marriage entered into without it.

Benedict himself was converted in a very full and clear way and if the conclusions drawn by the second chapter of this book have any validity his experience was the spiritual equivalent of the passion that 'converts' a couple to each other, or rather to the 'thing', the spirit, in each other which comes to awareness in their encounter. (Benedict's language of conversion, being Christian, provided for behaviour more directly connected with the cultivation of holiness in a very wide area of living. This is why a religious conversion is normally capable of leading to a change in behaviour amounting to what we call holiness, whereas the conversion through sexual passion normally does not, even though it may be just as intense and real and complete as the religious one. The language of sexual conversion as such hasn't a large enough vocabulary.) Yet when he consented to be the leader and father of a group of men who, at least vaguely, desired what he desired, he took it for granted that the thing that had made him what he was could only be found at the end of the long journey of life, and his community was ordered on that basis.

The confusion is again one of language. Benedict was aware of his new and absorbing relationship with God. In its pursuit he had sought out a lonely cave and lived there in considerable hardship, for several years. The life he lived, a transformed life of

H

unusually clear awareness of the nature of that which is encountered in the salvation occurrence, was so deeply satisfying and absorbing that, consciously at least, he desired nothing else. He would have been the last person to suppose that he was unique, or that others could not share and even surpass his experience, but the language of Christianity as he knew it did not include concepts that could have made it possible for him to see his transformed awareness of life as in fact identical with the eternal life towards which, he hoped, he was travelling.

This is not to say that the theological words and concepts that could express it did not exist; they did. 'Language', again, in this context means the total of awareness of life as conscious experience and as capable of being communicated. This language can be both more and less than the actual word-language of a particular culture, for the words of a culture only become part of its total language when they are working as symbols of a well-articulated complex of feelings, memories, hopes, desires and are in sufficiently frequent and familiar use as parts of living to have acquired the symbolic value that could make them part of the total language of that culture. It seems that it has happened quite often in the history of Christianity, and no doubt of many other cultures, that some words remained for long periods purely intellectual, having no symbolic power, and therefore virtually inoperative at that time as communication of meaning to people living out their Christian commitment. But sometimes they come into full use again later.

After a false start with a monastic community who really had no intention of changing their lives in any inconvenient way, Benedict found himself, somewhat to his own surprise, at the head of a group of men who simply wanted to learn from him how to be good Christians. That was how they, and he, thought of it. Most of them were very simple people, shepherds and peasants, but this was not the reason why he treated them as people for whom salvation was a long way ahead. He assumed that it was far ahead because it was so for all Christians. That being so, he ruled them, and later wrote the Rule for them, as people in need of *formation towards salvation,* people not yet transformed. In the first community—or rather communities, for there were soon too many monks to be accommodated in one monastery—there were many local peasants and artisans, as well as a few of the shepherds who had sought out the young man in his hermit's cave and listened, enthralled, to his teaching. There were also some better-off young men, sons of wealthy families, who brought badly needed financial support and above all the land on which a stable life could be established. There came also some children, and this is a very good indication of the way Benedict thought of monastic life. In a community assembled for the purpose of formation it was perfectly acceptable that children should be included. Not only the children but everyone there was in process of formation, all alike were looking forward to eternal life as their reward; therefore the fact that a child cannot make a fully responsible decision did not worry anyone. So fathers of noble families brought their sons to Benedict to be educated as monks, and there was nothing in the least odd or harsh in this notion of dedicating children to a fairly austere life at an age when they could not possibly know what they were in for.

Nowadays we don't do this, and are inclined to regard such an action as unjust or fanatical or superstitious, but this is simply another example of the confusions that arise from applying one culture's total language to the interpretation of a culture that used quite a different one. The idea of moral responsibility as something that comes with age, or that can be modified, is a comparatively new one. And the accompanying idea that people should not be expected to honour undertakings whose content they don't fully understand is fairly new also. Both ideas arise from the notion of a fully moral decision as something involving the whole person, consciously. The modern notion of a responsible decision is one that comes near to regarding decision as a converting event. This aspect of it is not explicit, but although unexpressed it is sufficiently near the surface to make us regard with revulsion such things as child marriages, or forced marriages, or even arranged ones, and to look with suspicion on death-bed repentances or conversions that occur in moments of danger or under the influence of strong emotion. This notion was altogether absent from the consciousness of an earlier age. (Centuries after Benedict, both Normans and Saxons took it for granted that Harold's oath taken over relics he didn't know were there was binding because they *were* there, not because of the fact of his oath. His intention was irrelevant.)

This emphasis on the importance of moral responsibility may or may not be due to the growth of an awareness of the spiritual significance that decision can have. What seems clear is that the culture in which Benedict founded his community did not have it in this way. No one would have thought it right to force an unwilling subject to take vows (that particular abuse came later) but vows were simply the outward expression of an intention, and the degree of awareness of what that intention involved was not a thing that anybody worried about, provided the intention was there, and was sincere.

The difference in approach does seem to be rooted in the understanding of Christian life as essentially progress towards salvation. If that is what life is, then there is no decisive point in this life, there is only a good will and an honest intention to co-operate with grace, conceived as a God's merciful assistance towards salvation, not as the mode of life which *is* that of salvation. It seems likely that the radical modern reassessment of what salvation (religious or secular) could mean became necessary because this expectation of eternal life as something beyond death became hazier and hazier and less and less credible. Once death could no longer be *felt* to be the point at which salvation (or damnation) was to be encountered then the unsquashable human hope of salvation had to look for its symbol somewhere else, and develop a new language in which to express it: the language of Enlightenment, for instance, or of Evolution, or of Existentialism, or the Freudian heaven of sexual normality, or the Marxist eternal life of communism.

But as long as the symbol of eternal life can credibly and effectively operate in the form of the expectation of life beyond death then life this side of death naturally appears simply as a preparation for it. When transformation occurs, in the sense described in this book, its occurrence will be viewed and explained in terms of life as formation only, and the whole ordering of life will see it like that. This means that it becomes necessary to separate what is secular from what is religious. The truly *sacred* seems so transcendant that it cannot be regarded as a part of experience, it is something whose reality belongs in another world, and what is sacred in *this* life is anything that brings man into brief contact with it. It is not his life but another life, for which he longs and prepares himself and which he occasionally glimpses. In that case there must be an area of living which is explicitly concerned with this preparation, and with making possible those glimpses and hints that keep hope alive. This is the sphere of religion, and it seems possible that religion is necessary just in so far as the sacred is conceived of as something outside 'normal' human experience. Yet it has become apparent in the course of this book that many influences that nobody would describe as religious can create the conditions in which transformation occurs. A purely secular structure, in fact, can do the work normally ascribed to religion. On the other hand it is also clear that a religious structure of life can provide a language for conversion which ensures that the self-discovery leading to conversion, and its working out, are more far-reaching in their effects on the personality. This is not true of all religious structures. They can in practice narrow down the area of conversion disastrously. But the full language of Christian commitment is the one that is actually most far-reaching and radical in its demands on the converted.

This does not mean that religion is doing something the secular structure cannot do. It does mean that the frontier between religious and secular becomes very vague indeed, and need scarcely be considered, provided that the secular structure can provide the sort of formation that is needed for transformation The more clearly we recognize the sacred as a matter of not uncommon experience, and recognize how it occurs, and what are the optimum conditions for its occurrence, the better we shall be able to provide a secular formation which serves the purposes of religion. In that case religion needs to do two things; to provide a language in which the transformation-promoting qualities of the *secular* structure may be expressed, and to provide ritual occasions which will express the transformation-orientated character of secular living, and so bring about that encounter with the underlying reality of human life which constitutes the sacred.

But in a secular culture that is manifestly *not* directed towards transformation in any useful way religion has a much bigger part to play. It has actually to provide alternative *secular* structures. It doesn't call them that, but that is what they are, and the importance of the Church as a political (in the wide sense) institution, and of religious orders and communities within it, has been due to this fact. If formation precedes and conditions and works out transformation then it is inescapable that a body of people dedicated to bring about transformation must either find and use an existing secular formation which is suited to its purpose, or—if none exists—*make* one. Even the converted communities saw life as such a preparation, but to them the future fate of each depended on being saved *now*, and knowing and showing it.

The men who came to Benedict, attracted by his manifest holiness, were often poor men, but even they gave up something in order to come. They gave up the ordering of their own lives, and submitted to him. They gave up whatever small hope of worldly profit they might have had, and they gave up the normal desire for a wife and family. If they did this it seems only fair to conclude that their decision was often a true conversion, a true encounter with Christ. It meant repentance, not necessarily because they had all been great sinners, but simply because the encounter with Benedict's holiness made them discover the shabbiness and inadequacy of whatever previous attempts they had made at living as Christians. They knew themselves as sinners, and were converted, and the language of their conversion was the language of monastic life as Benedict showed it to them by word and example.

So, in some degree or other, the men who came to Benedict were converted, transformed men. Yet they were not treated as such. They came into a life designed, as Benedict said, 'for beginners' in the spiritual life, and the whole life was designed to foster a spirit of penance, demanding constant renewal of one's good intentions and humble prayer for the grace needed to go on to the end. And this life, designed for people who did not think of themselves as certainly 'saved', most certainly produced men of outstanding holiness, quite apart from Benedict himself. The 'religious life' Benedict created was an excellent *secular* structure, orientated towards transformation.

This is what we would expect, yet it seems to show that care has to be taken before we assume that language absolutely exhausts meaning in any simple way. It is clear enough that the effect of the kind of community life that Benedict created was to foster the type of decision which, as I have shown, is potentially transforming and often actually transforming. It is easy to see, now, the relation between such conversion decisions and the 'eternal life' that the New Testament offers. We are now engaged in working out a Christian language that makes this identification easier, but if Benedict's contemporaries did not see this clearly nor express it more than very vaguely, they nevertheless *meant* the identification, most emphatically. That was what their *life* meant, it was the unformulated 'feel' for this identity that made them able to persevere. So when it is regarded as axiomatic that language exhausts meaning it is perhaps necessary to suggest that this can only be true of what I have called the 'total language', which is the whole range of experiences and feelings and hopes and desires common to a particular community, expressed in word and rite and gesture, *even when* the fullness of that which is symbolized by each unit of communication could not possibly be expressed in a fully satisfactory verbal formulation by anyone engaged in using that total language. If this were not so there would be no possibility of development within a culture, no new ideas would ever come to expression—not even the idea that language exhausts meaning. Conceivably therefore, there is a greater degree of continuity, something nearer to an 'absolute' language proper to human nature as such—whatever that is— than might be supposed when one is baffled by the impossibility of properly interpreting one culture in terms of another. This idea is relevant to the understanding of the relation between formation and transformation, for it does seem as if the phenomena which make these concepts meaningful at all are of a kind that, in any culture, force themselves on the attention of human beings and demand that provision be made for them either as secular or as religious structures. When this demand is ignored the culture dies, from neglect of one or the other. It is arguable that the degree of success attained by any culture in its need to develop and continue depends on its ability to meet this demand in terms of language, in some way. This is why we can, with some assurance, translate the total language of another culture into that of our own, in certain very limited ways. So we can say, without much fear of bring proved wrong, that the spiritual progress of Benedict's first disciples did include the experience of conversion in the sense I have explored in this book, but that the working out of *this* conversion depended as usual on the language in which the converted consciousness expressed itself.

This language was a formation language, but it dealt with a type of formation that was explicitly devised to make transformation possible and likely (a religious one, in fact) and it worked effectively towards this end, *even though* the transformation experience was conceived as lying on the other side of death. Whereas the 'Saints' had tried to take the spontaneous behaviour springing from a transformed consciousness and impose it as a norm on lives still in formation (thus trying to impose not a religious but actually a *sacred* form of life), the Rule imposed norms proper to a sane formation *towards* transformation, but related them to attitudes of mind which are in fact proper to those in whom transformation is taking place, *in stages,* as it actually and observably does.

This practical efficacy (without an adequate theoretical understanding) is the reason for the huge and enduring success of Benedictine monasticism as a means of forming good and holy Christians. But the lack of adequate means to express what happens in practice is the reason for its limitations, and both successes and limitations are interesting in the way they reveal the interplay of formation and transformation. The success and limitations, and the reasons for them, are in fact the reasons for the success and the limitations of the whole Catholic tradition, but to see them on this small scale, undistracted by political influences of an ambiguous kind, makes their nature much clearer.

The thing succeeded just because the people concerned did not know (in so many words, though they 'felt' it) that what was happening was a life of the same kind as that towards which they looked with longing and hope, and Benedict avoided the pitfalls into which many of his predecessors had fallen, just because of this very failure adequately to express in words the fact of his own and his disciples' experience. This paradoxical statement needs some explanation, which is to be found by examining the heart of Benedictine monasticism—the Holy Rule. The composition of the Rule, and its unique character, were the result of a combination of different factors, and they can be considered under three headings: sources of various earlier monastic experiences; Benedict's own previous practical experience of founding and guiding first one and later several separate communities; and, not least, his own personality—a converted one.

The rule that Benedict composed lasted and worked when many famous ones had become no more than historical curiosities. It is true that no consistent and well thought out monastic rule existed before, but there were many precedents that Benedict might have followed. Although he did take ideas and even regulations from earlier forms of monasticism Benedict did not take any of them as a model or even as a basis for his own. In a sense his Rule was a reaction *against* earlier ones, and indeed he explicitly repudiated some of the wilder forms of monasticism which had been much admired in their time.

The earlier rush of fervent Christians into the desert, motivated by horror at the corruption in the cities of the decadent Empire, produced a crop of eccentric ascetics whose fame as the 'Desert Fathers' (although there were a few 'Desert Mothers', too) has rested much more on their oddities than on their holiness. Many of them *were* holy, as well as odd, like the two old hermits of whom the story is told that at the end of many years of shared life, without ever a disagreement, they decided it would be a good idea to have just *one* quarrel, to prove they were like other people. They tried very hard—but since one or other always gave way to the would-be quarrel-provoking demands of the other, they failed miserably to have even the mildest squabble, and finally gave up the attempt. But if many of them were really humble and fervent people, there was a danger in their way of life if it was conceived as a system rather than as the spontaneous expression of a personal need for freedom. If it is true that the outbreak of power occurs in the 'in-between' states, it is also true that this state is dangerous. For to be 'in the wilderness' means to be out of touch, unrelated to the structures of normal living, and this is the reason both for its efficacy, as sacred, and for its danger, as destructive. Mary Douglas suggests a correlation which ties in with the Bultmann passage quoted earlier:

'Where the social system explicitly recognizes positions of authority, those holding such positions are endowed with explicit spiritual power, controlled, conscious, external and approved—powers to bless or to curse. Where the social system requires people to hold dangerously ambiguous roles, these persons are credited with uncontrolled, unconscious, dangerous, disapproved powers—such as witchcraft and the evil eyes.'

But what about people who are not *pushed* into the wilderness—thereby making it likely that their resentment will induce them to use their power for evil—but who *choose* to go there, in response to what they feel is a call they cannot refuse? Mary Douglas describes a tribe who are deeply suspicious, as we all are, of people and things that don't fit recognized structures of living, but who yet centre their liturgy on a bizarre animal called a pangolin, that doesn't fit into *any* category of creature known to them. To them this creature is *sacred*, and they believe that the rites associated with the killing and eating of it have more power than any others. Also, the pangolin's power is released by its death, which it appears to undertake voluntarily since it comes freely to the village where it will be killed.

Power is released in the 'in between' states, but it is a dangerous power, and only becomes beneficent if the person whom it invades is sacrificed, given, voluntarily dedicated to death. This idea is presumably behind the veneration given to great ascetics and hermits, but this veneration can easily lead to a distortion, if the value of the life is seen as residing in its quality of being outside the City (the organization of secular life) without realizing the ambiguous nature of the power that breaks out there.

It is at least amusing to read about people like St Macarius, who could not bear anybody to distance him in feats of asceticism, so that if he heard of someone else's achievements in fasting or wakefulness he was cast into a fever of anxiety in case he should be beaten at his own game, and could not rest until he had proved his pre-eminence to his own satisfaction and everyone else's admiration. A pursuit of eccentric asceticism at the cost of humility could only make true transformation impossible, but a life which is totally unrelated, out of touch with the secular structures (whether expressed in a religious language or not) is in danger of this kind of misdirection because it has cut itself off from all values and standards but its home-grown ones. Being unrelated, it can become its own *raison d'être*, and this way lies madness, not holiness. Whether poor Macarius was mad, I don't know. But his prodigies of endurance don't seem to have much to do with the Christian notion of even the most unusual callings, for although prophets are, by definition, misfits, they are odd because they have been called to be so, and have surrendered to the call in love—not because they need to prove themselves better than and different from ordinary mortals.

Therefore Benedict's Rule rejected the unusual, and anything that would give people a chance to pursue oddness for its own sake. The life to which men gave themselves under his Rule was indeed and literally a life 'in the wilderness', where God might be found, but just because it was that there was all the more need to provide it with a framework of relatedness, and to ensure that the motive of action was surrender to love—humility, in fact, expressed as obedience both to a way of life as such and to the person who embodied the meaning of the community in his own person: the Abbot.

The fact that Abbot means 'father' is an indication of the kind of community Benedict was making. The Separatists in Leyden called John Robinson 'father', and he did indeed fill the role to which the name referred. It was his combination of qualities, however, that earned him the position and the title, and it died with him. But the idea of the 'Father' as the symbolic centre of the community, and therefore as in practice the source of its ordering and day to day decisions, is built into the Rule as one of its most important characteristics—perhaps *the* most important. A Benedictine Abbot may or may not be a person who has personal authority, though the chances are that the man elected will be one who does have it, but in any case he will be the symbolic centre in an unequivocal way. He actually does represent Christ for his brethren, therefore his existence (even if he isn't very successful in practice) not only gives coherence to the self-consciousness of the community but also defines the *kind* of self-consciousness it is—an awareness of life determined by Christ as Son, in the way which I tried to indicate in the last chapter.

The emphasis on obedience and humility means, in fact, that the encounter that creates the opportunity for transformation will be made in the frame of mind most suited to it, for it will grow out of a life in which attitudes of abnegation and self-surrender are regarded as normal. These attitudes are fostered by the type of secular structure as well as expressed by the language that makes this particular kind of secular structure specifically religious in nature and purpose.

This emphasis, which has become the distinguishing mark of Christian religious spirituality, was clearly at least in part a reaction against previous monastic mistakes. But the strength of this reaction, and the assurance with which Benedict selected and rejected elements of earlier monastic forms, picking out what he needed but giving a personal coherence to his Rule that makes it in no sense merely a compilation—was the result of his own experience of running a community in the years before he wrote the Rule.

There had been plenty of experiment and great practical flexibility and when Benedict finally put his ideas into writing the form of community life he was recording and encouraging was one in which various expedients had been tried and rejected. And both the elements he finally picked out from earlier forms of monasticism, and his own major innovations worked out and tested in practice, show him devising a type of formation which is perfectly designed to foster transformation.

There is great emphasis on community, and the norm of monastic life is regarded as life in one, stable community. This means that people have to tackle relationships and use them, rather than escaping them. Later forms of monastic life based on the Rule found ways of evading this aspect of community life, in order to emphasize the 'in the wilderness' aspect of the Christian vocation, which is indeed important. But it seems likely that Benedict, who had left his own beloved solitude because he felt he was needed, knew very well that personal relationships are the very stuff of spiritual growth, and that often enough a longing for solitude can be an escape rather than a response to vocation. Whether he concluded that this had been an element in his own solitary life it is impossible to tell, but it seems clear that he realized that a call to an unusual type of life could only be 'real' if there was a very solid formation behind it, and that this could only be obtained in community.

He also realized that, in order to be effective, personal relationships must be freely entered into, or at least freely accepted. Hence the innovation of a period of probation, a novitiate, before anyone was allowed to commit themselves finally to the monastic life. The same set-up that, fully accepted, can lead to transformation, can lead to defensive isolation if it is felt as an inescapable and unwanted restriction of personal liberty.

But at the end of the period of probation the commitment to the chosen life was to be expressed by public vows, and this was a new idea. This, and the wearing of a common dress, are means of making clear to the person himself and to the rest of the world what kind of a person he is, and what he is for. The public and explicit expression of this consciousness is an immensely powerful force in directing the person's energies towards the goal for which the community exists—namely, salvation. And this concentration of energies means that the various encounters demanding decisions are likely to lead to converting decisions, even though this is not how they are conceived, and even though the goal towards which all this effort is directed is thought of as being beyond death.

The emphasis placed on prayer, in the form of vocal prayer—the psalms of the Divine Office—and of meditative reading, shows the same direction of mind. These are occupations that do not bring a man into relation with other men, but on the contrary withdraw him from them, into a temporary seclusion, a mental 'in between' state, in which he is most likely to be subject to the invasion of power. But the effect of such encounters with the spirit are carried over into the rest of life, as in the working out of any kind of self-discovery and conversion, and so their influence forms habits of mind towards further transformation.

The creation of a system of secular living with a religious expression that marks it so clearly as formation for transformation came about because Benedict himself was living a life almost wholly transformed. His transformed consciousness used a language that was Christian, and it was a notably scriptural kind of Christian language, and so his self-awareness was able to make use of concepts that expressed particularly well and fully the reality of life and the things that assist its discovery. But also his transformed self-awareness included his experience as ruler and guide of a community of men of all sorts and ages and temperaments, so that the specifically secular aspects of life were also within the area of this transformed consciousness, and shared in its wholeness and personal definition. It may well have been this fact that at least partly helped him to avoid the pitfalls into which earlier monastic systems had fallen, and into which later religious groups (including the Separatists) also fell. What so often happened was that people were converted, and then others were attracted by their example and gathered round them, and the founder then laid down as norms for their behaviour the kind of behaviour that seemed proper to *him*, as converted. These worked all right in the beginning, but proved impossibly hard later on, when what was needed was a secular structure (expressed religiously) to underpin and frame the experience of conversion. Benedict did not make this mistake because his experience as Abbot was *part* of his own spiritual growth, of which his early hermit life had been only the beginning. By the time he came to write his Rule he was a saint whose sanctity had been defined by the experience of authority over a large number of assorted humans beings.

But suppose he had been accustomed to use a language that

clearly saw conversion as a dateable and once-for-all event, the condition and the fact of salvation? In that case he could not have failed to have recognized his own early call as a conversion experience, and he would have been likely, when followers came to him, to legislate for them in terms of this experience, trying to repeat it in them. He did not do this because he thought of his experience as simply *part* of his progress *towards* God, not as a norm of awareness for himself or others. This is what I meant when I said that the Rule was so successful just because it did not recognize the character of and conditions for transformation as an experience, or relate the experience to the hope of salvation.

But this happy mistake had other results which were not so happy. The trouble did not become apparent in Benedict's lifetime, nor indeed for a long time afterwards, but it eventually spoiled or at least endangered the success of the system as a formation towards transformation.

Since the reason why the effectiveness of the Rule for this purpose proved to have serious limitations is the same as the reason why the Catholic Church has also proved to have serious, even disastrous, limitations as an institution dedicated to the same ends, it may be interesting to see what these reasons are.

Benedict himself always saw the Rule as a method of training, a preparation for salvation. It could, and might, lead on to what he felt was a more perfect life, for the eremetical life still retained for him its value as a powerful symbol of the reality he craved. In practice, few monks did proceed to become hermits, and this worried nobody because it was clearly a special calling. And in practice there is no doubt that very many were so formed by the Rule that they *were* transformed, and did become holy, without ever wanting or needing to be hermits. There are plenty of encounters in a hard-working and close-knit community that can lead to conversion. But this was *accidental*, and its occurrence depended on the quality of life in individual members. As long as a good number of people were fervent and whole-hearted, it did not matter that salvation was seen as a reward at the end, and not something evident as part of normal experience of spiritual growth. But if there is no way to express the presence of a particular quality of life there is likewise no way to express its absence, nor will that absence be realized as a matter for concern.

In course of time Benedictine communities, like all other systems that have been in use for a long period, suffered a decline in spiritual quality. In a disturbed age the monasteries became obvious refuges for the sensitive or delicate, or for people who wanted to study, or who were disillusioned with the violent and vicious and power-grabbing habits of their contemporaries. They were not looking for God but for a bit of peace and quiet, and there's nothing wrong with that, in itself. The secular structure of Benedictine life was well adapted to people who wanted a regular, not luxurious but secure life, and the religious language that expressed its purpose could easily become part of the general Christian idea of the religious duty one owed to God. The observances of religious life were thought of as serving this purpose, and as being a good way of making sure one qualified for heaven at the end of the road. And since no other purpose was actually written into the Rule there was nothing anybody could put their finger on, and say 'that's not what St Benedict meant'. It was a good life, a safe and sane and human sort of life, and that was enough. But in fact what was intended to be a means (though the purpose was not explicitly expressed) became an end. It was not an end in the sense that people thought that this life was all that mattered, but that a life lived according to the secular structures arranged by the Rule, with careful attention to the specifically religious duties, was *itself* the necessary qualification for eternal life after death. So the observance of the Rule was no longer felt as the framework within which the encounter with God, the salvation occurrence, could take place but as itself the only kind of occurrence that had any necessary connection with salvation. The rest—gifts of prayer, special missions or callings—were extras. So they are, in one sense, but they are fairly common signs that something is happening, and the happening of this something is just what no longer seemed vital, though it was exciting if it did happen. It is interesting to notice how many of the Benedictines who got themselves canonized were people who did not remain in the cloister to which their vow of stability had committed them. Benedict himself did not come to sanctity by being a Benedictine; rather, his sanctity made Benedictines. Gregory was made a Pope, and became a saint that way, but he wanted to be a missionary. So Augustine went instead, not too happily, to barbarous England, and sanctity. Boniface went out from England to barbarous Germany and found martyrdom. It's true some Benedictine saints never left home, but discovered their ability to love in the succession of little, unnoticed decisions that convert over the years, as sometimes happens to married people. These are little happenings, less spectacular than martyrdom, which is an occurrence one can't help seeing. But martyrdom shows the nature of the calling that came to all these people, it reveals the *sort* of thing that was happening, and shows why some did need to go out of their monasteries in order to find the transformation they sought. They went out under obedience, as a following of their monastic vocation, but they went *out*, and it was in their *out*side life that their sanctity developed. It is no good saying that this was simply because the challenging nature of the outside work brought out latent courage and holiness, which were 'there' all the time. If qualities are not used they are not personal qualities. Potential holiness becomes actual holiness when it meets the challenge that provokes conversion. If it remains potential it is not actual and is not, therefore, personal holiness at all. So perhaps the occasional outbreaks of missionary vocation among Benedictines (rushing off to India to become Christian Hindus, for instance) are signs that the excellence of the formation the Rule provides makes people realize a need which cannot always find satisfaction within the framework of the Rule in its normal interpretation.

Once the Rule itself was felt to be sufficient for salvation the door was wide open for relaxation. If the Rule, virtuously observed, could fit people for heaven, then obviously it should be interpreted in a way which made it possible for people of good will to observe it without undue hardship, and this interpretation can show an increasing amount of latitude. This is what happened towards the end of the middle ages, as everyone knows, and it was an inevitable result of the failure to realize and express the relation between formation and transformation, and between salvation as experienced *now* and salvation conceived as a reward beyond death.

Clearly, many people realized that something was wrong, and there were many reforms, both mediaeval and later. The loss of fervour and brotherly charity, the laxity of life and compromise with 'worldly' values, were evident enough. The reactions among those who were really looking for God was strong, and some of them have endured. But they, too, often suffered from the failure of the Rule to express what it was for. Seeing a diminution in fervour, and consequent relaxation of ascetic discipline, they usually thought of reform and return to primitive fervour in *the same terms* as those that had led to the relaxation. They thought of the Rule as itself the condition of salvation, and therefore sought to make it more effective by interpreting very strictly various ascetical provisions in the Rule, such as silence, or a restricted diet, or heavy manual labour. But a Rule, strict or easy, is the secular structure of daily living, and its value lies solely in the way it helps to form people's minds, so that the challenge of decision shall prove a converting occurrence. The religious language in which it explains itself helps to make clear what the structure is for, and to provide special opportunities for the saving encounter. That is *all* that a formation structure, however excellent, can do, and when it tries to do more it distorts its own purpose and begins to die on its feet, though it may be a long time about it.

All this is not simply a simile for what happened to Catholic Christianity as a whole; what happened to the Benedictines is the same thing that happened to Catholicism, but the Benedictine developments show it on a small scale. The Church developed a formation structure, a secular organization, and this it had to do in the historical circumstances of its expansion. It was a secular structure explicitly dedicated to the transformation of man, and it carried out its task through its official structure, expressing what was happening in the form of sacramental rites. But the nature of what was happening was not expressed in terms of real occurrence, to human beings as wholes, in the present. It was seen as something to look forward to, whose coming was ensured by obedience to God—conceived as outside—and by his grace, also injected from outside. This is, of course, a fearfully crude distortion of Catholic theology at any period, but this is how most people *felt* about their lives as Christians (and still do feel). Even the deeply learned, who would never have expressed themselves in terms that lent themselves to such an interpretation, were influenced by this 'total language' of Christian self-awareness of a particular kind. It was natural, in this type of awareness, that the Eucharist—the rite which expresses most clearly the nature of the Christian community—should come to seem not a saving encounter with Christ *now* but a dramatic presentation of an action in the past, which yet had saving efficacy available as grace (from outside) now, in order to ensure salvation in the future. The structure, secular and religious, had usurped powers that do not belong to it, for no formation structure, secular *or* religious, is relevant to the transformation occurrence except as promoting it, framing it, and providing the setting for its working out.

And when you have a system of law and custom and religious ritual which is regarded as *in itself* effective of salvation then you have a secular structure which is claiming to be sacred. And once that happens, then the way is clear to every kind of legalism and casuistry and encrusted, arthritic ritual, all regarded as *sacred,* and therefore not to be touched by the hand of mortal man.

But if the formation structure is regarded as sacred, what happens to the real fact of the sacred, apprehended in the transformation-occurrence? What happens to prophets and saints? What happens to the Spirit which, although in theory able to blow where it likes, is in practice only supposed to blow down the organ pipes of an instrument contained in a well-built ecclesiastical edifice?

It's quite a problem, for the fact is that this structure really *is* designed to foster transformation, and therefore transformation does occur, however strenuously it may be resisted. The system continues to produce the results for which it was intended by its founder and his followers, and by those who, moved by that same inconvenient power, worked out a structure that could carry on in a larger and more organized way what had been begun in such an apparently haphazard fashion. So saints do occur, and even prophets. There is a depressing similarity about the things that happen to them. To put it briefly, first of all they are persecuted, especially by the godly and righteous, and then they are tamed. Sometimes the taming occurs in their lifetime, by absorbing them into the system and demanding uniformity in the name of humility. This often doesn't matter much, because a good version of the system actually releases the power it was meant to contain, so that the Spirit breaks out in visions and miracles. The painful submission is truly converting and the results are wonderful. This is one of the virtues of the system, even when it is misused. But often the taming occurs after the death of these odd and fascinating results of the system. They are canonized, which means they are explained in terms of the current total language of the Church's culture at that particular time and place. They are enlisted to support the system seen as a system-efficacious-for-salvation. So their odd behaviour is explained as *part* of the system, not as the power of the spirit manifested in the *breakdown* of the system, and this naturally makes the system itself seem extremely demanding and not really designed for ordinary people. So you get two systems, one for the advanced, who can manage these difficult skills and *therefore* qualify for heaven, and another, for ordinary people, who may, all the same, qualify—

partly by sticking to the system (at 'O' level) but also by the assistance and intervention of the successful 'A' level candidate. In this
way, when prophets and saints are not—as they sometimes are
—driven out altogether or personally suppressed, their function
as signs, as re-assertion of the community's real nature and purpose, is suppressed. They *should* remind the system that it is
only a system, and that it is in its death that it finds its true meaning. By being made part of the system, their power is neutralized.

The analysis in this and the previous chapter of two different
types of community devoted to salvation has shown two conceptions of how salvation happens, and the successes and failings of
each. If you think of salvation as a once-for-all happening, occurring in this life, you get great fervour, charismatic gifts and behaviour of various kinds (and I don't mean only the more exotic
varieties but hardy perennials like charity and peace) and an almost total disregard of ordinary hierarchies and formulations of
living, because these don't seem necessary or relevant. But you
also get, sooner or later, rigid standards of behaviour enforced
by snooping and tale-bearing and harsh punishment. You get,
consequently, hypocrisy and empty parade of piety and virtuous
behaviour, an emphasis on personal wealth and success, smugness
and callousness and bigotry and persecution.

If you think of salvation as something in the future, to be
attained by faithful observance of certain rules and participation
in certain ceremonies you get humility and hard work and
patience and a spirit of service, a respect for authority and for the
proper forms of community life, care for others and appreciation
of the material things that are necessary for life together and for
worship. But you are wide open to minimalism and tepidity,
to evasion of personal responsibility and flight from decision.
You are likely to be suspicious of anything unusual, to regiment
everything and everybody, censoring and flattening all evidence
of nonconformity. You get a preoccupation with the communal
buildings and possessions, with money and power. And—to

make sure nothing is left out of the system—blessings with everything.

But the odd thing is that both these very different ways of interpreting the Christian idea end up by making the same basic and disastrous confusion. They both confuse the sacred and the secular. One way imposes behaviour proper to contact with the sacred as the norm of secular life, the other treats secular life as if it were sacred.

How can we possibly find a balance between these, and restore both sacred and secular to their full meaning and effectiveness, not as opposed, but as both distinct *and* related?

CHAPTER VIII

THE MEANING OF THE CHURCH

THE ambitious title of this chapter is inevitable, and to call it anything else would not be modesty but an avoidance of the issues which have been raised by all that I have discussed so far. This is my reason. It is not an apology, but an act of acceptance of the unavoidable. It is not a claim to competence but an admission of previous failure to face facts—both a personal failure and a communal one.

At the risk of being tedious it seems necessary to begin by summing up the information gathered from each previous chapter, so as to show the direction in which the results appear to be pushing us. At the very beginning the technique I have used perhaps needs some explanation.

The trivial incident of a children's quarrel served to reveal the elements at work in even the most ordinary and minor kind of human upheaval. It was intended to show just how much a matter of everyday experience are the tremendous themes of salvation.

The technique of careful description of the whole human set-up was not, however, strictly necessary for a discussion of such themes. A bare outline would have been sufficient to provide an example of the concepts I wanted to discuss. But the point of beginning with these chunks of quasi-novel was not merely to provide illustration. My intention was to create at least a small degree of actual involvement in the situations described, so that the experiences referred to would *be experienced*. Then the words used to describe the nature of these events might possibly have the resonance of something like experimental knowledge. You could call this experimental theology, but whatever name it is given the idea arose from a conviction that much theological

242

discussion is wasted, not because the words used have no *possible* meaning but because the people who use them don't mean anything by them. They don't *know* what the words mean, even though they have almost certainly had precisely those experiences to which the words refer.

There is still one possible thing to do with theological words and that is to use them as purely mythological. There is nothing wrong with myth, and it is excellent as well as inevitable that we should use mythological language when we talk about things beyond our experience. St John's Gospel, for instance, uses the terminology of gnostic mythology, but the author was talking about real experiences, and his readers (some at any rate) knew this. The words referred to things they knew, and knew that they knew.

The trouble is that we now use a mythological vocabulary, and many of us reject it as mythology, but we have lost the experience-reference. We have lost the sense of the myth and also of the real human experience which the myth could express. What is left is not, as people hoped, an utterly purified residuum of timeless and absolute truth, but precisely *nothing at all*. No wonder humanists accuse us of being atheists with a semantic garment of Christianity.

Myth is wonderful and effective, because its symbols refer to a reality. When we recognize experience as related to the same reality of which the myth speaks then the myth becomes—not irrelevant but simply the *language* we use to communicate the experience. We seem to have lost the ability to recognize our most common experiences as having anything to do with the mythological vocabulary of our faith. My crude little 'human stories' are an attempt to assist this recognition, because I think that until we can make this link we might as well stop talking theology altogether. Nobody is going to listen, anyway, because the words don't mean anything human or humanly important.

The children whose conflict brought into play the whole drama of salvation were only two, but the idea that the result of their encounter, all being well, was something called *community* is not accidental. Community is not the common existence of a large group of people, it refers to the creation of a relationship, whose nature is not affected by the number of people involved. So the second chapter purposely created a situation that had no religious context, in order to see how community springs from encounter—a confrontation of the individual by something else, one involving a certain degree of conflict, which is the challenge of an 'otherness' recognized as dangerous and to be feared. It is this that creates the decision situation. The decision demanded is one involving self-surrender, a blind handing over of oneself in the face of a future which is blank. There is no conscious *content* to the conversion event. Transformation is a timeless occurrence to which all previous and succeeding circumstancs are totally irrelevant.

Yet it is these preceding and following circumstances that make possible the event, and determine its results. This is the area of what I called formation. Formation is all-important, but only in relation to that to which it gives way. Transformation is in the *in between*, it is unrelated, unstructured, eternal, self-sufficient, having no hierarchies, no morality, no past, no future, and no possibility of control or even of the observation of what is happening.

The occurrence of conversion in a sexual context also helped to show the nature of the act of surrender as one made in relationship, a relationship of love whose development creates the community we call marriage. It also helped to clarify the effect of transformation 'backwards', as it were, in providing the kind of accelerated and radically redirected formation which is the immediate prelude to transformation. The importance for conversion of a confrontation which induces an extreme form of self-knowledge became clear in discussing the symbolic function of nakedness, and the need for a 'liturgy' to frame and express conversion became apparent also. A sexual and non-religious type of conversion was intended to provide the essential de-mythologized vocabulary for a discussion of salvation, but it was necessary to show next how transformation happens when no single human relationship provides the occasion for conversion, but rather the encounter is with a whole situation, though it is necessarily encountered 'in' one or more individuals. This helps to show that even a sexual conversion is only accidentally related to the other person as he or she exists 'in the flesh', that the person is rather the means of encountering the demand for faith, and so creating community between the two, in their present and limited condition. In the case of the man who was converted, and lapsed, and was reconverted, the accent is on the self-discovery which is inextricably a part of the salvation event, although it is itself a process of formation. It is again the retroactive effect of the occurrence itself, bringing about self-knowledge and repentance.

One of the most important ideas that emerged from both these chapters was that the language of conversion is of crucial importance, because it determines the way in which conversion is worked out, and the area of living which it affects. Conversion affects the whole person, but a human being is a person only in the degree of this self-awareness, developed in the saving (or damning) encounter. And the effect of conversion is to convert the language of self-understanding, so that a whole area of ordinary living has a new type of awareness. This became even more apparent in the chapter on prophecy, when the nature of the power that is released in encounter was seen in its most typical form. The language of a prophet's conversion determines the action to which his conversion impels him, and delimits his effectiveness as a creator of community.

But this chapter also discussed the quality of 'in betweenness', of withdrawal from and irrelevance to the essential structures of formation. This had already appeared as a condition of transformation in earlier chapters, but the discussion of the phenomenon of prophecy showed that a certain personal ambiguity was an essential attribute of the prophetic calling, not only for the 'professional' prophet, but also, in due proportion, for part time or amateur prophets, who are no less called because their prophetic function is limited in its scope.

The outbreak of spiritual power occurs in the gaps, in the in between states, in the wilderness. But pure wilderness, totally unrelated existence, is not creative but mad, and it became clear that not only is formation necessary, but that a particular kind of formation is necessary, one which is explicitly at the service of transformation. This implies that the power which breaks out in the in between state is also at work in the structures which give way to it. In the family who had to decide where to live it became clear that the members of the family who responded to the challenge of the situation by a real conversion decision were those who were either already to some extent converted, or whose formation had been in the hands of such people, who therefore put love first in their scheme of things. The creation of community is a surrender to something which is shared, and the formation structure in which this sharing is worked out will necessarily be modified by the converted awareness of the members of the community. But it is also necessary, in creating community, to take into account those who are not yet converted, and to provide, in the formative structure, the support and help that they need, as well as the means for working out the converted community-consciousness in those in whom it exists.

This is the tension which any community has to deal with, and the two subsequent chapters examined two different ways of doing this, typical in their way of the two main Christian traditions, but not, of course, exclusive to either. The importance of language in working out this problem appeared even more strongly in the context of life in a fairly large group. The varieties of function in the group, types of authority and their relation to the community's self-awareness appeared as, in fact, part of the language by which the community understands itself. Both kinds of Christian community seemed, finally, to have been successful in truly creating community only because their actions in practice did *not* always correspond to their theoretical understanding of the spiritual condition of their members. Another idea emerged from the study of community living, which could not become clear from an account of individual cases of conversion. This was the relation of the concepts *secular* and *sacred* to the previously used concepts of *formation* and *transformation*. And I suggested that the concept of the *religious* (whether in the particular sense of religious communities normally so called, or of the area of ordinary living labelled religious) is really to do with the need for a particular kind of formation, which will make transformation more likely. In that case the religious is really part of the secular, and is distinct not in the area of life which it affects or discusses but in the fact that it directs life explicitly towards transformation, whereas the idea of the secular implies an approach which does so only accidentally. So religion is the organization of secular life for sacred purposes, and from one point of view it is co-extensive with secular life, just another way of describing (and therefore modifying) secular life. From another point of view religion fills in some gaps in the secular structure, where this fails to provide adequate formation towards transformation. In one way this distinction is unimportant, because in theory a good and humane secular structure is serving a religious purpose anyway, and all religion need do is to show what is happening. One can think of this as *describing* secular life, or as supplementing it *by* a description especially in ritual form. But in practice the notion that religion fills in the gaps is apt to lead to the idea that *any* secular structures which leave something to be desired as preparation for transformation should be replaced by others having an explicitly religious shape, rather than (if possible) simply being modified to make them serve their purpose better. In some cases (for instance in cultures of extreme and militant materialism) this may well be necessary, and this was certainly so for many centuries in the past. Nowadays it is less often the case, but the habit of duplicating secular structures dies hard, and it is seldom noticed how often the religious version suffers from precisely the same defects that marred the secular ones. The situation is in fact often worse, because the religious language which expresses the purpose of the structure is so clearly at variance with the reality, yet it seems that to admit the failures would be to deny the religious purpose of the structure. So an elaborate system of hypocrisy comes into being, with the best of intentions. (Hypocrisy is so often well-meant.)

On the other hand there is one area of living which is certainly formative but which is directly and solely concerned with the occurrence of transformation. This is the sphere of ritual, or religious observance, which frames the sacred. It is formative, it is structured, it is deliberate, but its sole purpose is to provide an occasion for contact with the sacred which is transformative, unstructured and spontaneous. The sacred, as I have suggested, is encountered solely in the breakdown of structure. Ritual is a sphere of living which is definitely religious, then, yet there is ritual which we think of as secular—parties, for instance, or the panoply of government or of justice, or the purely domestic ritual of a family meal. But if my definition of religion as a language that shows the direction of human life towards transformation is valid then these 'secular' rituals are religious also. Their purpose is to express the underlying nature of what is going on. Parliamentary pageantry is intended (one imagines) to produce a state of mind in which those charged with law-making will be acutely aware of responsibility, and humble in relation to it, and will make their decisions in the face of a community awareness which is at least implicitly a loving one. The same applies to the ritual of judicial procedure, though one hardly dares to say so. Celebrations and parties, large or small, express at least minimally a sense of belonging together, of sharing in life and hope. And all these have a clear relation to religious ritual normally so called in that they take people out of the routines of ordinary life, draw them in some way apart, for a while, so that they have an experience of community which can happen only accidentally in the course of their normal routine.

It seems, then, that 'secular' ritual has a religious purpose, and in that case ritual is religious because of what it is *for,* and not because of a specific type of religious language which it uses. But the use of a language which is *Christian* is the way to create a ritual which expresses a Christian notion of the relation between formation and transformation. Christian language is both formative and transformative, it describes secular concerns and focuses all of them on the sacred as their meaning and justification. And the point at which it explicitly changes the one into the other is a ritual one. When a whole community is in question this is necessarily so. Transformation can and usually does occur accidentally, in all sorts of odd ways. But if a whole community is dedicated to transformation it can't leave the occurrence to chance. The whole community is, in principle, involved, and therefore it must create deliberately the encounter which is at least potentially transforming.

This is what the Church is for, and what ritual in the Church is for, and the rest of this chapter will be an attempt to see how this can happen. Ideally, it would be best to start at the centre and work outwards, but in practice it is the nature of the centre which is least clear, so it will be best to start at the edges. Yet the edges, also, are not only unclear but impossible to define, therefore I intend to do what I can only describe as walking backwards towards the centre, relying on the magnetism of that centre to draw me there, but looking outwards, on the way, in order to see the view from that direction. And having reached the centre it should be possible to see the same view, but in a different light.

If there is no obvious edge to the idea of the Church it seems best to start with the only absolute limit it could have, which is that of humanity as such. This is 'the world' in the sense in which the prologue to St John's Gospel uses the word. 'He was in the world, and the world was made by him, and the world knew him not.' It means a world that is capable of responding to a demand, and therefore blameable in its failure to respond. This is not the cosmos, but the world of men. 'And this is the judgement

—that the light has come into the world, and men loved darkness rather than light.' But this world of men that God so loved is in a sorry state, is soaked through and through with a penetrating glue that seals people's eyes and ears, and congeals their movements and coats their sense of touch and fastens them in isolated proximity. So 'the world' and 'sin' are coextensive. But this extension is also the extension of potential salvation. 'God so loved the world that he gave his only Son, that whoever believes in him should not perish but have eternal life.' The occurrence of faith, the transformation occurrence, is liable to erupt anywhere at all in this extension, and its limits are only the limits of man's willingness to respond to the invitation. 'Men loved darkness rather than light.' The glue at least keeps them warm.

So if I'm going to walk backwards towards the centre the horizon is the limit of human life, and if I can't see that far the reason is that my vision is inadequate. All this is perfectly obvious, but it seems to be forgotten when people (especially ecumenical people) get together and worry about who belongs to *the* Church (or *some* Church) and who doesn't. All it seems to mean, *then*, is that anybody *could* be converted and *enter the Church,* and argument centres on what constitutes entering the Church, that is, where the Church, or some Church or other, stops. But unless everything I've observed in this book is nonsense, the occurrence of salvation is as common as the state of sin through which it breaks. The world is in its sins, but the world is also saved. In that case the Church, as a community of the saved, is coextensive with the world, as saved. Likewise, and no doubt to the same extent, the Church is the community of the un-saved, of the world. In that case, why worry? If salvation is going on all the time anyway, why give the world a new fancy name? But the name is, of course, the crux of the matter. To call the thing 'the world' is to refer to a huge mass of indeterminate beings, muddling along and (no doubt frequently) erupting into individual or group conversions that keep the whole lump reasonably human. To call it the Church implies that people have

an awareness of purpose in their existence, that conversion—
and so the creation of community—is what life is about, and that
human beings should be inclined actively to promote this process. And to call the process salvation immediately makes it clear
that there is something to be saved *from*, that people *can* be
saved from it, and that somebody is doing the saving.

In that case the odd situation arises that the Church in one
sense is co-extensive with mankind, but that the Church in
another sense is only those people who know that they are the
Church. Yet we can also say that people who know this can fail
to act on the knowledge, that is, they can refuse to be converted.
Do they belong to the Church? If we say they don't, we get the
Separatist's dilemma. If we say they do, we cannot, by the same
token, exclude *any* of the unconverted, even if they *want* to be
excluded, because after all they might change their minds.

But if we stick to the name as the crucial thing it becomes
easier to grasp though more difficult to practise. The Church
as a name for something only makes sense if it means what it does
mean to the people who use it. But to belong to the Church in this
sense implies without room for evasion that belonging to it means
fellowship or community with all the converted, and a responsibility for creating community for all those who are not yet converted.

So I have moved towards the centre a little way, not getting
further away from anyone else but, oddly enough, getting nearer
to them, since to accept that one is a member of the Church is to
accept community with all mankind, and the demands of this
relationship are limitless.

Yet if to belong to the Church means community with all mankind it means this in virtue of this named community, whose purpose is salvation. It doesn't just mean that *I*, as an individual, have
a limitless responsibility for others, but that this responsibility
exists because of the relationship of community in which I have
reached the awareness of this responsibility. So my conversion
in relation to the world means that I am converted in relation to

I

the Church, and my conversion in relation to the Church means that I am converted in relation to the world. And if I am converted, and the Kingdom of heaven is within me, I am also unconverted, and the Kingdom of this world is within me. If the Church is in the world the world also is in the Church, just as much.

It follows from this that when the Church is thinking about its task of transforming the world, it is thinking about transforming itself. And if transformation depends so fundamentally on formation, then the Church's job is to form the Church *for* transformation. And that means to form *the world* for transformation. And all this very involved explanation means in practice that the business of the Church, as people-who-know-they-are-the-Church, is to provide (within the limits imposed by the limits of the influence of her actual members) the type of formation that is suited to transformation. That means modifying the secular structure for the purposes of salvation. The Church cannot, even if it wants to, be a body that transforms, just like that. Transformation is something that happens, and nobody can lay it on to order. We can only create opportunities for it. Those people who act under the name 'Church' have this task of creating both the opportunities and the kind of more remote formation which make it likely or possible that the opportunities will be taken. And it does seem, increasingly, that at the remoter level this is *not* best done by creating duplicate formative structures which, of their nature, limit the reach of the formation provided, and therefore the effectiveness of that self-awareness *as* the Church, and *as* people-who-know-what-salvation-is.

No housewife who knew anything about bread would try to make it with yeast alone, as the Separatists did. She might, if her normal source of supply were obviously polluted, only make it with flour from wheat grown in her own back garden. But this would involve a great deal of work that would not necessarily improve the *quality* of the bread itself. It would obviously be only an emergency measure. The ordinary and natural thing is to get flour from the mill that serves the whole community, through local retailers.

This point scarcely needs to be laboured. What is less clear is the kind of influence of a formative nature that the Christian should seek to exercise on the secular culture. This is how the problem presents itself to most Christians, and yet in a sense to put it like that is to distort the issue. If what I have said about the overlapping spheres of religious and secular is true, then it is not a question of bringing Christian influence to bear on secular structures, if by that we mean that we count ourselves as outside them, even though taking part in them.

It is rather a question of realizing (in both senses) what we are, as Christians And that means realizing it as a community, that community whose limit is the horizon of humanity, but whose self-awareness as saved depends on those who have this awareness themselves—not as individually saved, in the revivalist sense, but rather aware of being people living in relation to salvation, as everybody is, even when they don't know it. This means that the Church is the world's prophet. Prophets, it is true, are separate and odd, but they are only separated by their prophecy. They don't belong anywhere, and yet they belong more deeply than anyone else to that community which it is their task to create —a converted, *real* community, in the spirit. If they came *in* from *outside,* from above, they would be no use. Instead they come *out* from *inside,* they erupt and disrupt and interrupt. And the inside that they must come out from is the inside of the community to which they are sent, which is *their* community, in whose guilt they are involved. 'I am a man of unclean lips and I dwell in the midst of a people of unclean lips.'

So the Church can only be itself when it is involved in the world, when it has a sense of sharing the world's need of salvation, and therefore responds to the demand for conversion not only in but *as* the world—which indeed is what it is. And in doing so it has a two-fold function. It has to use (and that means modify, because all use modifies what is used according to the purposes of the user) the secular structures in such a way as to get the best out of them as formation for transformation. This isn't strictly speaking the prophetic role, but it is the prerequisite of prophetic effectiveness. Jeremiah moved people—*and* made them so angry—because they knew he was one of them, a citizen of the same city, part of the secular structure by which they all lived. It was because he was *that* that he had a right to be heard when he spoke as the people's conscience.

John the Baptist was the son of a priest, very much part of the establishment. He was one of the people longing for a Saviour. That was why they listened—he spoke for them, coming out from among them.

Joan of Arc was French, and she spoke as a Frenchwoman, weeping for France's suffering, proud of France's election. Bernadette spoke for the poor and sick and despised because *she* was poor and sick and despised. And Christ was the prophet and the Saviour of his people because he, too, was one of them, and spoke with their voice, and died with their death.

So if the Church is the people who know that the world is saved, and say so, then it must be in the world, fully and wholeheartedly, it must be immersed, buried in it. It is only from this position of total immersion that the prophet has the right to speak, and the likelihood of being heard. As soon as he begins to think he *hasn't* got unclean lips then he'd better shut up, because he can no longer say 'thus says the Lord', but only 'I think'. The burning coal that purifies the prophet's speech is the fire of repentance, and the minute he stops repenting he is no longer pure. Only a penitent Church can speak the word of the Lord, and its penitence is real repentance for its real sins, which are the sin of the world, not for some private category of sinfulness which must be purged in order to make it ready to speak *to* the sinful world.

Sometimes, indeed, Christians talk as if all they had to do for the world was repent. But real repentance involves reparation; so the Church's repentance involves reparation, also in the world, and that means political and social involvement of all kinds, not as pressure groups on behalf of something called Christan values, but simply as part of the particular culture which is the world for us—retail.

A particular culture involves a particular set of ethical norms, a particular interpretation of what morality means. The Church's repentance necessarily involves her in trying to find ways of living which correspond with her repentant understanding of man's need for transformation. Her concern with moral behaviour is not a matter of trying to convince people that one particular set of ethical norms is better than another, but of helping people to see what morality is for. This is something that repentance does for people; they see their failures not as departures from a standard (however high and admirable) at which they are aiming, but as failure to love, which means failure to relate one's life to the reality apprehended in repentance and conversion. If this kind of awareness of the nature of goodness and of sin is kept in mind, morality and ethics slip into place as respectively the way in which we think about the *kind* of person (and his behaviour, which are the same thing) who is converted, and the means by which we hope to produce this kind of person. Ethics and morality are often treated as if they were the same thing, and they do overlap, but it is helpful to consider them separately, as matters which concern the Church *as a prophetic body*, since prophecy only speaks to the ears of people who have learned to hear.

Morality is concerned with discovering the kind of person who is able to hear, and repent, and be converted, and live. It is also concerned with the behaviour by which the converted work out their conversion, and so prepare the way for each new conversion—*both* their own *and* other people's. This kind of behaviour, both preceding and following conversion, springs from an interior response to love—drawing towards conversion and conditioning its working out. It cannot, therefore, conceivably be expressed as rules, except the one rule which isn't really a rule at all: 'Hear, O Israel: the Lord thy God, the Lord is one—and thou shalt love the Lord thy God with all thy heart and with all thy soul and with all thy strength.' Morality has no content, because its point of reference is the occurrence of salvation, the self-giving of faith, which *is* the act of loving the Lord our God. But morality cannot be simply a matter of interior attitudes, it only discovers its nature in its expression, and its expression is the command 'thou shalt love thy neighbour as thyself'. The moral formation towards conversion, and the moral behaviour that expresses that conversion, are both a matter of outward acts and words, religious ones, in the sense that they are related to the sacred, which is known only in the surrender of faith.

This is the point at which morality is controlled by ethics. Ethics is concerned with outward behaviour only. It is a language about morality, by which people can communicate about and agree on the kinds of behaviour which are morally good. Therefore ethics not only can be codified but obviously has to be, because you can't use a language whose words change their meaning according to the wishes of the speakers, as Humpty Dumpty's words did. ('When *I* use a word,' Humpty Dumpty said in rather a scornful tone, 'it means just what I choose it to mean —neither more nor less.'

'The question is,' said Alice, 'whether you *can* make words mean different things.'

'The question is,' said Humpty Dumpty, 'which is to be master—that's all.') On the other hand, languages do develop and change, adapting themselves to the needs of the time and place, but gradually, if possible, so that people can still, as the language changes, go on using it intelligently. But morality is not a language and does not change, because morality is what the language of ethics is trying to communicate *about*. Morality is an awareness of man's orientation towards a transformed existence, and this is not only a permanent part of human life, it is what human life, as human, really is.

The Church's responsibility, then, in the field of both ethics and morality is enormous. It is the work of people-who-know-about-salvation to hold fast to that knowledge and relate their lives to it, and it is in so far as the Church's life is seen to be actually and observably related to salvation that she will be able to influence the development and preservation of the ethical norms that express this relation. The frequent confusions and glooms that Christians get into about morals, among themselves and in relation to non-Christians, seem to happen because Christians see that morality is changeless and absolute, being concerned with the direction of human nature as such, and therefore assume that ethical norms can be changeless and absolute too. It seems, in a sense, an obvious deduction, and its flaws only become apparent when one realizes that ethics is, really, a language about morality, and obeys the rules that all languages obey. That is, it must make sense about the subject under discussion and also *to* the people who are discussing it. This sounds obvious, but it means, in practice, two things which seem contradictory. One is that ethical norms must *change* in order to mean something to people using them in all sorts of different cultural conditions, otherwise they won't make sense to people, and so cease to be a language at all. This is what happens to an ethical code which is given the force of morality itself. In different social conditions the units of the ethical language cease to relate to the kinds of behaviour to which they originally referred. They are not meaningful, then, to the people who use them, and communication breaks down. The other is that they must still express the unchanging moral direction, otherwise they won't make sense of their subject, and the language will cease to be *about* anything, it will be a nonsense language. This is what happens with situation ethics in its crudest form, because it uses the ethical 'words', but they have no content of moral meaning—and, again, communication breaks down.

But as long as we remember that ethics is a language we can make real progress, and the Church, whose very existence is concerned with morality, as the formation for transformation, is in an excellent position to guide the development of ethical norms

that really are about morality. But it is sometimes forgotten that
the reach of ethics as a language is far beyond the sphere
of private virtue or vice, for it is people in an 'accidental' community, in the flesh, whom it is the Church's work to guide towards becoming an 'on-purpose' community, in the Spirit. So
the ethical responsibility of the Church is perhaps *primarily*
political and social, since we have to build structures which sub-
serve the creation of community, and do not prevent or restrict
it.

Within this range of concern the Church has a special need to
bother about education, both on a national and a domestic scale.
The setting that can give a child emotional security and stability
is the foundation from which grows the adult who can, later,
meet Christ in his brothers and respond to that encounter not
by withdrawal and refusal but with the self-surrender of love.
This is so very obvious a part of Christian concern that it seems
unnecessary to mention it, and I do so mainly to show that it is part
of a *whole* concern. It has often been the case that the Church's
concern over education has simply been to turn out Catholics
(or whatever other brand name is to be stamped on the package)
with recognizable religious characteristics, as if *this* constituted
the Church's task in education. This is confusing formation with
transformation, and treating the sacred as if it could be
commanded by secular means. But if we can see that education
is part of the Church's ethical concern, (remembering that ethics
is language about morality in the same ways that aesthetics is a
language about art) we shall be even more deeply concerned over
education, although less inclined to see Christian education as a
matter of imparting facts about Christianity. That is a part of it,
but it loses its way if it loses sight of its end, which is transformation.

This, then, is the building up, the edifying of the world, for
salvation. It is a huge part of the work of the Church, this building up, but it only makes sense when one asks what the building
up is for. The Church is founded on a rock, and that is the symbol

of the security which is essential if people are to be formed for transformation. The global struggle to give people at least a minimum economic security, and to help them to find emotional security and stability, is the Church's work, because without this formation there can be no transformation. The Church is founded on the rock, but the Church's self is not the rock.

Having piled up the mountain through centuries of toil which is truly penitential (that is, having a converted awareness of the purpose of this toil, it is natural that a sense of terrific achievement should make the Church inclined to regard this impressive edifice, of natural human material hewn and lifted by man's own efforts, as all that is required. It is much, so very much. It is much to have made it axiomatic among civilized nations that human life matters, that the poor should not be oppressed, that the weak should be cared for, children educated, that love is worth more than power. However often these things are forgotten, however often the Church itself has forgotten them, these are the formation values she has laboured to establish and it is some measure of her success that it is her failure to live by these values that is the accusation most often flung at her. But is it enough to do this—would it be enough even if the Church herself never failed in her practice of them? Is the massive rock of solid human formation all that the Church is required to create?

'Get you up to a high mountain,
O Zion, herald of good tidings.
Lift up your voice with strength,
O Jerusalem, herald of good tidings.
Lift it up, fear not,
Say to the cities of Judah,
"Behold your God!"'

Quite a startling announcement, and if we hadn't all listened to Handel's Messiah quite so often we might be better able to realize what a shocking thing that is to say. But it is to say this that prophets exist. The mountain is there for the prophet to get up on, and prophets *are* shocking. They are offensive misfits, outlaws and nuisances. So how can the Church, on whom is laid the prophetic vocation of Christ, be the world's prophet, and therefore be all these irritating things that prophets are, if she is also totally involved in the world? Yet the Church can only say 'Behold your God' because Jerusalem *is* the city of this world. A conscience can only be upsetting and irritating because it is part of oneself.

All the same, it isn't enough to say that the Church has to be involved in the world, and that the Church must prophesy to the world. Both these things are true, although recently we have been getting rather tired of being told the first, and used to get even more tired of being told the second, because in neither case did anyone make it very clear how we were to set about doing either the one or the other. The first seems to take all the meaning out of belonging to a community called Christian, the other makes the idea of involvement in the world meaningless.

I think the clue to the resolution of this contradiction lies in the notion that the sacred is encountered in the 'in between' state. The involvement of Christians in the world is an involvement in the formative structures which the Christian insight recognizes as vital. For Christians, these structures should be religious, in the sense that they should tend towards encounter with the sacred. But the sacred itself is something about which the secular structures as such have nothing to say. Yet everyone knows it is there, or rather the experiences which the Christian can associate with the idea of the sacred are common to all. But the Christian is a person who, by his profession, is aware of the meaning of the sacred. It is the work of the Christian community, as prophetic, to announce the meaning of the experience of the sacred, to say 'Behold your God'.

But in order to do this the Christian has to be able to understand what he is saying with precision. He has the problem of communicating it to other people. He has to translate his language, which is *religious* (in the sense used here, of language relating formation to transformation) into non-religious language. But in order to do that he has to have a very clear understanding of the meaning of his *own* language. It is for lack of this understanding that many Christians, when they want to explain what they mean, can only go on using religious words. Their grasp of the meaning of these words is not sufficiently clear for translation to be feasible. Translation of *converted* language is not, of course, possible, as I suggested in the chapter on conversion, but the words that become the converted language have a meaning that can be used to communicate quite effectively, in the strictly religious (in my sense) context, and it is in this communication that they can become the language of conversion. Then, possibly, they can be translated (just as language, not conversion language) into concepts that can convey something in terms of another culture.

But if we are to translate into the language of 'another' culture, that means that we have a culture and a language which is different and Christian, and which therefore *needs* translating. And we do have this. We have, in fact, a cultic language, and it is this language that defines Christian self-awareness. This language is to do with the in between, it is not concerned with formation but with transformation. Many of the words and concepts we use in expressing the nature of Christian community are, indeed, words which are not necessarily connected with the sacred; they can be used, without translation, in talking to people to whom our specifically religious (in my special sense) vocabulary is meaningless. These are all words that deal with formation —words like patience, chastity, birth, justice, trust, poverty, belief, sorrow, fortitude, hope, sin, death. It is true that many of these words have extra resonances in the religious language which almost transforms them, and that when they become part of the language of conversion they are so changed as to be scarcely recognizable. All the same they do have a clear meaning that is common to all who use them, and this is because they are concerned with formation. They are to do with morality and ethics, with the facts of human experience, and provide a common currency of language in which to talk about formation.

But the words that relate to the sacred—redemption, conversion, salvation, God, Christ, resurrection, glory—are no use whatever for this purpose. They do have a non-religious meaning, but it is metaphorical, at such a wide remove from their normal religious usage by the Christian that they are rather worse than useless for purposes of communicating with another culture. The only way they can then be used is as the words of a mythology, and this is fine for Christians, among themselves, because they know—or should know—that mythology is a language that indicates a reality beyond the reach of any language. But people who aren't Christians and don't recognize the existence of any such reality (even though they may experience it) can hardly be expected to realize that a mythological language, as used by Christians, refers to anything but a myth. This leads to fearful confusions, because whenever Christians try to explain that their mythology is a language and refers to things that *can* be otherwise (though perhaps less adequately) expressed, they are accused of abandoning their faith. But this is entirely our own fault for going on using mythological words *as if* they referred to mythical realities.

Their proper use—apart, as I said, from private communication between Christians—is a cultic use. The reason for this is that in that case they are being used in a context which attaches the words immediately to the complexes of experiences and thoughts and hopes that are summed up in the gestures of the ritual, the total language of the cultic community.

In this context the formation categories are only indirectly relevant, though they are important, because they are the influences that produce the kind of people who form part of the cultic community.

The cultic community is the setting in which the converted awareness of the Church can become prophetic. The clarification

of her nature and mission which is achieved by the ritual encounter with the sacred is what is needed if the Church is to
know herself sufficiently clearly to be able to translate her self-
awareness into a secular language which is intelligible to the
world. This clarification is by repentance and conversion, and
this is what makes prophecy possible.

At this point on the journey towards the centre we can see the
Church's nature *as* the world and *in* the world and *for* the world.
We can see that the Church has a prophetic calling which breaks
through the necessary formation created by wide and morally
meaningful ethical concern. We can see that the prophetic calling comes to the Church in the cultic community and by it, and
that it is there that she learns the language that defines her, and
which she must use in carrying out her mission, but in a translated form. But what kind of translation is involved? The prophet
is there to call people to repentance, not to explain to them what
he thinks about life. The word he uses must be a converting word.

Yet, as I suggested earlier, the actual human words with which
he can communicate the message are all concerned, in this non-
religious context, with formation, and that is just what the
prophet is *not* talking about.

The apparent impasse is only apparent. The way ahead lies in
the realization that the language of the cultic community is about
things that happen to people, and that certain kinds of *behaviour*
are appropriate to such happenings. What the prophetic Church
cannot convey by words it can convey in the total language which
is the language of Christianity as life in Christ. It doesn't mean
that words don't matter, but that the words can only be translated and 'heard' by the world as the total language of sanctity.

The implications of this are appalling. It means that the
Church is only obeying her prophetic calling in so far as she is
clearly and unequivocally expressing the fact of Christ in her
whole life. Christ poor, Christ serving, Christ healing, Christ
suffering, Christ dying, and—but only through death—Christ
risen and glorified. A language that does not mean what it says

is a nonsense language. If the liturgy of the Church says things that the Church does not clearly and visibly mean in her total language of living—then the Church is talking nonsense, loud and emphatic and quite lunatic nonsense. It is nonsense to express repentance liturgically, and maintain in practice in the secular sphere, that the Church has nothing of which to repent. If the Church goes through a ritual that expresses the 'fellowship' of love, and does not show fellowship and love in its secular actions —not just the actions of individuals but the corporate activity that expresses in secular terms the transforming purpose—then this is nonsense. If we urge people to Mass, and don't emphasize that the language of sacrifice and self-giving is the secular word of this action, then this summons has the feverish urgency of the lunatic, and the whole affair has the character of self-absorbed and self-validating obsessiveness that characterizes lunatic behaviour, which is typically ritualistic. It has the sort of inner logic of the lunatic's world, of course. It provokes the kind of attitude that the fashionable and intelligent society of eighteenth century England had to madness. The kind-hearted were sorry, and kept away, advocating gentleness but segregation, and the less squeamish went to Bedlam on Sundays to laugh at the delusions of the demented creatures.

Christians must permanently run the risk of being considered mad, of course. But there is an odd kind of reversal in this. The real lunatic is mad because his world makes sense to him, but he can't relate it to anyone else's vision of the world, therefore he is cut off from other people. It is his cut-offness that defines him as mad, however real and truly human his personal insights may be. If he could, in the areas of living which constitute the common life, manage to relate and communicate, then he would not be mad, however eccentric his ideas and imaginings might be. So if Christians, however odd the roots of their behaviour appear to be, are related in their lives to the common concerns of the world, they don't come within the definition of madness, and if they are sometimes considered mad it is by people whose own inner coherence and existence seems to them to depend on the exclusion of many of those areas of living which are common human ones, and in which the Christian is engaged—suicidally, it seems to his critics. People who fear that their own safety will be endangered by the involvement in the needs of the poor and unhappy which is (or should be) typical of Christian behaviour actually regard Christian notions leading to such behaviour as a threat to *themselves*, and try to minimize it by describing people who behave like this as mad. This definition of madness—meaning people who do dangerous things—assumes that there is an insufficient reason for the dangerous behaviour, and it is the insufficiency of the reason that proves that the person is alienated, and does not operate according to values that are common. The argument turns on the *reason* for the behaviour. But if the reason is the following of Christ it is also, to people who are not afraid, *already* translated into the total language of love and service which ordinary people can understand without difficulty. The refusal to understand means that it is the fearful and withdrawing who are the alienated, not those whose behaviour they fear. *This* kind of accusation of madness is a compliment, and means that the Church, in some of her members at least, really is carrying out her prophetic mission. (It is sadly significant that accusations of 'madness' directed against Christians come more often from other Christians than from non-Christians. This must mean, surely, that the Church has failed to give that formation in security and love which is needed before people can respond to the challenge of the Gospel demand to leave all things.)

The prophetic mission of the Church belongs to the whole Church. Inevitably, only some individuals will carry it out fully, because of the uncertainty of the formation structures which are needed to bring people to the point of accepting the prophetic vocation. But if the call is to be made and heard at all there must be something built into the Church's self-awareness that makes prophecy possible. There must be something belonging to the

Church's nature as such, as a collection of people, that makes her prophetic character clear and possible.

It is hard to see how this can be, because of the Church's necessary involvement in the creation of formation structures and their interpretation in religious terms. The structuring of life means an official institutional existence, an articulation of authority and obedience, of teaching and learning. However fully we integrate ourselves into the world we have the work also of making clear the religious dimension of secular life, and that means a framework of formation. It means a tradition, so that formation can keep its goal in sight by having a continuously intelligible (and therefore changing) language...*about* it. It means continuity, so that people may feel the rock under their feet before they are asked to jump off it. It means a sense of belonging, to give courage so that the demands of the prophetic vocation may not frighten away the called before they have heard half the message. And you have to belong *to* something, and know it. Belonging, in this sense, does not come into the creation of community, but community presupposes it, for community is created in self-giving. A sense of belonging, as a feeling of human solidarity, is irrelevant to it, but it prepares for it and expresses it, and is therefore something that the Church can and should give. But the better she does this the less anyone feels like sacrificing it. The rock feels so nice and firm, nobody wants to leap into the void.

This natural desire not to be rocketed into the unknown is so great that it has sometimes persuaded Christians to treat as purely formative the one bit of her life which does most surely confront the Church with the demand to repent and be converted. From the mission of prophecy, translated into total language, we have to step backwards to the source of prophecy, where the language of religion is confronted by the reality it tries to communicate, and gains its power and meaning from that encounter.

It is perhaps necessary to repeat what I said in the introduction—that I am not talking in theological terms, but rather trying to describe the human events and reactions with which theology has to deal. For a certain kind of theology it may be sufficient to describe the Eucharist in terms of the presence and action of Christ. But this presence is not something on its own, unrelated to the people who take part in the celebration. At some point, somebody must ask, what does this presence and action mean in terms of the experience of people taking part? What is happening to them? What results should it, does it, produce?

Since this is the centre towards which I have been progressing, and also the point of this book, I shall hope to bring together in it the various strands of analysed experience that I have pulled out of the tangle of human life.

I know very well that because we are in the world, and all gummed up with worldliness which we can't altogether help, most of the time most people who form part of the Christian cultic community are not really aware of the fact that they are. 'Distractions' (wilful or not) means that in practice only a little of what the Eucharist is intended to do actually happens, and 'distraction' can be taken to include the fact that the present ritual does not clearly express what the ritual is actually for. So the ritual *itself* is to some extent a 'distraction', and so are the distortions of eucharistic theology which have infiltrated popular piety. If this were not so to some extent there would be no need for the Eucharist anyway, because we should have achieved an eschatological existence in which awareness of reality is total and uninterrupted. But to keep on saying this at every turn would be boring and is unnecessary, because the whole point of talking about the Eucharist in a book like this is the hope that the discussion will in fact make it possible for some people to be more aware of what is happening, and therefore more able to make it happen. So when I talk about what the cultic community is at, I am not saying that this is what everyone present is at all the time. Everyone knows that this isn't so. But this is what they are there *for*, and because of their knowledge of the total language of Christianity it may well be that many who appear to have only the vaguest idea of what is going on are actually more effectively involved in it than some who have a better grasp of the concepts that try to express it.

From the point of view of the ideas discussed in this book the most important thing about the Eucharist is that it involves both formation and transformation. It is framed in ritual, which is necessarily planned, ordered, deliberate, arranged beforehand, expected, structured, official and all the rest of it. Never mind how informal the 'shape' of the ritual, the very fact of a group of people gathering together and doing something religious, *together*, constitutes a ritual. Ritual doesn't have to be ritualistic, that isn't what gives it its character. Ritual is a deliberately arranged confrontation with the sacred. In that sense the silence of a Friends' Meeting is just as much ritual as the most encrusted of high Masses with incense curling around the fluttering draperies of any number of baroque ecstacies, and the whole lot drowned in music of high alcoholic content.

But the character of the framework—the ritual—which provides for encounter with the sacred is important. The words and gestures that are used express the community's notion of what the sacred is and what one should do about it. So a ritual that has very little in the way of self-definition can provide an extremely immediate and convincing experience of sacredness, but leave it unclear what kind of behaviour is required of those who have this experience. This definition must come from a non-ritual source, and runs the risk of being outside the area of conversion, and therefore of lacking the power and purposefulness that is proper to conversion behaviour.

On the other hand too elaborate a ritual expression can actually cloud the fact of the encounter which it is intended to frame so that no saving confrontation, in practice, occurs, but rather a salvation drama is observed. It may have been the failure of the eucharistic theology and liturgy of the Catholic Church after the Reformation to provide, *evidently*, a saving encounter that drove people to create the baroque ritual, and (especially) baroque architecture. To go into a baroque church is to be confronted with something that insistently demands a spiritual response of a decisive kind, quite unlike the contemplative mood of the gothic or the assured harmony of the renaissance classical forms. What the liturgy, as such, did not do, the setting tried to do.

In order to discover what qualities help ritual to achieve its purpose it is helpful to look at it first of all as a formative structure, which it is, and see what makes a successful one.

Formation is for the unconverted. It is designed to create conditions for the converting encounter. A ritual which wants to provide a good formation, then, needs to take into account the fact of unconversion. It should be intelligible in *un*converted terms. It should create a sense of belonging. It should not put up any unnecessary barriers, either intellectual or emotional. It must make everyone feel at home, safe, cared for, valued.

But these things are part of the more remote formation. It is necessary to have them, and to guard against their opposites, not only because they help everyone present to be in a relaxed and receptive frame of mind but because many people, at any given time, will be at a stage where these are the *only* ways in which the liturgy can help them at all. By means of this kind of help they may eventually take the next step towards the centre. If they are made to feel ignorant, unwanted failures they will never take that step.

The more immediate formation for conversion, a little nearer the centre, is concerned with discovering a sense of what the Church is for, of the relationship of its people to the sacred, and their responsibility in that relationship. The readings and prayers of a liturgical assembly are about this. This self-awareness is something that is expressed in words, and must be. The sharing of this awareness of the Church's nature and mission is still, in this dimension of liturgical action, a formative one, but the language is one that can carry the power of converted consciousness.

All this framing of the sacred, all this elaborate creation of a setting for encounter, is part of the task of the Church as prophetic.

The more remote formative influences of the secular are essential, but their purpose is to provide the mountain from which the announcement can be made—'Behold your God.' And this peak of the mountain can only be a vantage point for the prophetic announcement because it *is* a vantage point. It is solid, it is always there, it is a landmark. A landmark is something you can count on, it has been there so long that nobody bothers to ask how it got there. It is traditional, as a background to living, a point of reference and a guarantee that one is correctly orientated. Prophecy implies tradition and continuity, and the source of the Church's prophetic vocation is supported and backed by tradition: we refer to the tradition as the guarantee of its authenticity. You can't have prophecy without tradition, otherwise the prophet speaks for himself alone and has no point of contact with his hearers. He speaks a language that nobody but himself understands, and nobody is edified.

But if prophecy must take its stand on a solid and massively continuous tradition, the prophecy is also the thing that *makes* the tradition, for the tradition is a tradition about transformation, and the prophecy is intended to provoke transformation. So even the tradition is not purely formative, but suffers that retroactive effect of transformation, which defines it in relation to the salvation event. The very framing of the sacred suffers a sacral alteration, and becomes capable of mediating the presence of the sacred. It becomes, in fact, sacramental.

Yet the frame is not itself the sacred. Its purpose is to ensure that the sacred is encountered and not avoided. In order to do this the Church is called into the wilderness. The people of God have to be taken out of the reassuring structures of ordinary life, necessary as these are, and called to the top of the mountain which their efforts have piled up. It is an exposed position, abnormal and unrelated. It is a position that seems quite peculiar to other people who, seeing only the solidity of the rock, suppose that it is intended as a refuge. The people of God *is* a peculiar people in more than one sense.

This is one aspect of the ambiguity which seems to be the essential characteristic of the Eucharist. It is traditional and formal and has a definite history and development, and it has fixed roles and stages. The people who take part have come out of their ordinary lives, and will carry on with them, and will come again to church next Sunday, so that the thing is actually *part* of the continuity of their lives. And yet it isn't, it's quite different. In church they do and say things they don't normally say, which would indeed sound very odd at any other time. Yet here they are taken for granted. But it is odd, and it is the wilderness, and it is the bare and uncomfortable mountain top where the Church as prophet speaks to the Church as world and says, 'Behold your God.'

The lead-in to conversion is repentance, and this is provided for ritually. But it is not *just* a preparation for an encounter that has not yet taken place, a ritual purification before entering the holy place. That is a formative idea, and the formula of penitence is formative, certainly. But in this ambiguous setting it is *also* the *result* of the encounter with the sacred, working backwards to define the person as sinful and in need of salvation. The person who discovers himself in this encounter is already saved, but in his expression of repentance the penitent refers to and knows himself as in need of salvation. And both are true, at the same time.

This fundamental ambiguity at the heart of Christian experience is what makes this ritual action *really* a wilderness. Metaphors help to make one *feel* its wildness and remoteness, but the fact is not dependant on the feeling. The fact is a basic human experience that shows how conversion, love, faith, salvation or whatever you like to call it occur in ambiguous, 'in between' situations, and not otherwise.

But people don't like ambiguity. It is unsettling, it is unnerving, it undermines one's self confidence in the patterns of living. It is this dislike of ambiguity that has led to different interpretations of the Christian fact, resolving the ambiguity either by opting for transformation, as far as possible 'neat', or opting for formation, subsuming transformation *in* it as a sort of petrol that keeps the machine going. But Christianity has to be ambiguous because it is only the acceptance of this ambiguity that makes transformation possible. The Eucharist is supremely and bewilderingly ambiguous.

It is the embracing of ambiguity that brings about the transformation which is faith. This is what the Eucharist is designed to do. The fact that for most Christians it begins with a confession of sinfulness which can only reach its full significance if it means that the people uttering it are already in the presence of the sacred—therefore *already* purified—is only one example of this.

Mostly, Catholics at Mass think of themselves as present at, or even taking part in, a happening, which is a special sort of realization of the presence of Christ among them. They are involved in it in the sense that they want it to happen and pray for it and, as far as they can, they identify themselves with the machinery of the happening, so that they really share in it. This isn't theological language, it is an attempt to show how people usually feel, or try to feel, about what they do at Mass. But, again not using theological language, if we think of it in the terms used in this book, the happening involves them not because they *want* to be involved, but because if they take part at all they can't help being so. This happening is a *converting* event, and in so far as that is the real nature of the event, unless it *is* that it is, for the people who take part, nothing at all. If one is aware of what is happening then it involves decision, for or against.

That is easy to say, but it is difficult not to leave the matter in a metaphorical cloud, which is what we usually do. What is it about the Eucharist as an event that makes it a saving one? It isn't enough to say that it is an encounter with Christ, who makes the demand for surrender. This is true, at the theological level, but it doesn't explain why this business of saying words over some bread and wine, and eating it afterwards, should constitute an encounter with Christ except in a purely symbolic way. It isn't enough, either, to say that this is Christ's sacrifice, in which we are involved by a union of love, and through which we share in his glorified life. This is true, too, but it doesn't tell us what is the point of calling it a sacrifice, and how whatever it is is sacrificed, that is, 'made holy'. And it isn't even enough to remember that this is the new covenant, and that a covenant is an invitation that requires a response in order to ratify it, a promise that demands the obedience of faith for its fulfilment. This is true, and gets closer to whatever it is that makes the Eucharist a converting word. But it still doesn't show what the invitation is inviting *to*, or what obedience is demanded by the promise. And there still remains the puzzle of how the sacrifice idea, with its necessary association with death, fits into the much more understandable idea of a fellowship meal, which is a cheerful affair essentially concerned with living.

It may be possible to get a bit nearer to what is happening if we go back to that idea of ambiguity, which is uncomfortable and unsettling. First of all there is the scarcely defined ambiguity of the whole gathering; normal neighbours in an abnormal cultic relationship, everyday people who have a vague notion that they are unique—God's people and a nation of priests. This general sense of uprootedness is the setting in which people are asked to commit themselves to a whole series of irreconcilable assertions. We are so accustomed to them that they have come to seem quite cosy, but consider:

First of all there is the idea that the telling of a story about something that happened two thousand years ago is related to something happening now, of a different kind. The account of the institution is a perfectly straightforward bit of narrative, and refers to the meaning of the action it records only, apparently, as a symbolic action ('This is my body—my blood—do this in remembrance of me'). But (leaving aside the niceties of eucharistic theology) most Christians assume that there is some point in telling this story *now*, as more than a reminder of the fact

that their founder died. (Yet that, too, has an ambiguous significance, as we shall see.) The encounter is not with bread and
wine as symbols of Christ's historical death even if we think of
that death as a sacrifice, *nor* with Christ as a word meaning the
individual's experience of salvation. It is both, and both at once,
and *that* is what makes the encounter a saving or a condemning
one. The encounter is with the ambiguity, it is a demand for a
leap not from one fact to the other but 'in between', a self-giving
into a blank which is *essentially* a blank to the human mind because there is no way whatever in which the two concepts, both
perfectly easy to grasp separately, can be combined. All sorts of
ways have been attempted, especially the re-presentation idea.
This makes the Eucharist a symbolic drama involving all the participants, and effective because this dramatic involvement creates
in them a sense of identification with Christ's saving death, by
which they actually share in its efficacy. And since Christ is no
longer dead, but lives, this makes them sharers in his life as it is
in glory. This may be part of the way it works, but it is not the
thing that makes the Eucharist a converting event. This is part
of immediate *preparation*, the lead in for conversion.

Arthur Koestler's fascinating book, *The Act of Creation*,
aroused conflicting opinions, but one thing which it did was to
analyse with an almost obsessive precision the way in which a
creative mental act, one which really releases the latent powers
of the human mind, happens when the mind links up two ideas
which in fact are not capable, of their very nature, of having
any relationship at all. He shows how both jokes and tragedy let
loose emotion by the juxtaposition of irreconcilable entities, in
one way or another.

The occurrence of faith is precisely *this* kind of event. What is
produced by the encounter that provokes faith is not simply an
emotion, such as is provoked by a tragic or farcical situation, because the kind of things that are brought into irreconcilable opposition are not of that kind. They are of a kind that, in order to link
them without destroying either, requires a real personal surren-

der. This surrender is senseless—you *can't* make *sense* of this link up, that is why it seems so suicidal.

In the story of the two children it didn't make sense for them to forgive each other. Neither had got what they really wanted, and neither saw any prospect of getting it. Both were acutely aware of deep resentment which could never be worked off except on each other. To forgive was a leap in the dark, a leap in between the facts of their unhealed enmity and the fact of their mother's demand. Either made sense alone, but they didn't make sense together.

The two lovers had nothing to gain by committing themselves to each other. The fact of the security each already had made sense, and they could continue to enjoy it as long as their sexual relationship was not really loving. And the fact of their need for each other made sense, but it couldn't possibly be reconciled with security, for each was afraid of the other. The decision to love was made over against a void, in which they risked both their security and the satisfaction of their need.

The man who came up against the reality of poverty was faced by a demand that made no sense in terms of his normal life, nor of his possible effectiveness as a do-gooder. He could have done much more by writing a cheque. The conversion occured in the gap, when he surrendered himself to a vocation that had no obviously sensible content of any kind.

This is the pattern of all conversions, it is in this sense that conversion occurs in the wilderness where the certainties of the Law, the structures of formation, have broken down, and only the choice remains. The wilderness is framed by the ritual reminder of the vocation of the Church, and the need for grace and repentance. But at the point of encounter the framework breaks down. It provides the ideas which constitute the challenge, and thereby shows the yawning gap between.

This gap is a total blank, it is a kind of intellectual and even emotional blackout. As long as the two wires in an electric flex are insulated from each other the light stays on, and illuminates the room. But if the wires are allowed to touch each other the thing short-circuits, the fuse—the weakest point—blows, and the light goes out. This is quite a good analogy because when two powerful and essential Christian ideas are used together, as in the eucharistic irreconcilables, they give a steady intellectual light, as long as they are kept together but separate. And an appropriate emotion may accompany the thinking, for instance about the passion of Christ as an historical occurrence, or the goodness of human fellowship. But if the two ideas are brought together, allowed to touch, the light immediately goes out, and both ideas disappear, likewise the emotions. The much more powerful emotion that may replace them as a result of conversion is quite different, and it occurs afterwards. The immediate effect is simply total darkness. If the wires are separated and re-insulated the light goes on again, but every time we allow them to touch the light goes out—for the circuit breaks at its weakest point. In this case the weakest point is actually provided for, ritually, by the creation of the 'in wilderness' condition that withdraws people from the support and security of normal life. And it is in this total darkness, and nowhere else, that we can acclaim the light of Christ.

The ambiguity does not always present itself in the same conceptual form, it is true. It has no fixed form, even the poles of the space which demands to be filled with power are, at the moment of conversion, unclear. Indeed at that moment they are irrelevant. The sacrament is a means to the encounter with grace only by holding in tension the two irreconcilables, not by reconciling them. It does not stand *between* the believer and Christ, or bring Christ to the believer, but simply forces him to choose Christ, or reject him. And at the moment of choice the name by which we describe what is chosen—Christ—has no content either. The leap into the void means, in fact, so complete an encounter that the conflict, the sharp-edged dilemma of intransigent otherness, disappears and there is a meeting which is more like a fusion. I am not talking about emotions, but about events, for in the act of faith nothing whatever *is believed*, there is an identification of the believer with the object of his faith, so that he doesn't, at that point, believe anything. He just *is, in* it.

To the thing the believer is in we give the name Christ, because Christ is the self-awareness of the cultic community in which the conversion occurs. He is the symbolic centre, first as a separate symbol to which people can make conscious reference. This is the formative function of the Christ-idea, and it includes what little we know of the historical man, Jesus of Nazareth. But he is also the symbolic centre because he is the self-awareness, the personal life, of the community. He gives it its meaning, he is the thing that it shares. And this sharing comes about by the operation of that link-up between irreconcilables. The community of the unconverted comes to community in the spirit when the individuals who make it up are able to jump into the gap, because that is where they meet. They are made holy in this meeting, because this is the sphere of the sacred, this is the sphere in which Christ, priest and victim, is sacrificed outside the City. The leap into darkness is a leap into death with Christ whose death made no sense at all in terms of his mission on earth. For the ambiguity of the Eucharist is a presentation to the community, present in this time and place, of the basic ambiguity on which Christianity is based—that of Christ himself, who—like that odd animal who is sacred to the Lele tribe—belongs securely in no category whatever.

He cannot be thought of as a divine being, in human form, nor as a man seized by divine inspiration, but is a disconcerting complex that nobody has even managed to define satisfactorily, because the whole point is that you can't. He wasn't a priest yet offered sacrifice, he was ruler yet he ended up on a gallows. Master and servant, carpenter and king, a dead man who was known and recognized as living. A total failure and a total success. These are ideas to which we are well accustomed, so they don't easily feel contradictory. But if one reflects on any of these points it can be seen that while each member of each pair is clearly a true description, the truth of each one is a totally different mental and emotional 'area' from the other. If both are put into one sphere of thought they are *really* contradictory, really nonsense. For each has to be kept in its own proper sphere in order to be true, and the mental shift from one to another, if one really makes this move and doesn't merely slide over the top of both, involves a kind of psychological contortion. We are used to doing this, so we are usually not fully aware of what is involved —but try doing it in slow motion, and see what it feels like.

The eucharistic irreconcilables are the ritually presented and inescapable confrontation with the challenge that demands faith, and in response to which a man can be saved or condemned, by his own decision and no-one else's. The outbreak of power as a result of this acceptance of the irreconcilables creates community, it transforms the individual, converting him *out* of the formation community that built him, *into* the converted community that he must build. The ritual meal expresses both of these things, an abnegation of self and an acceptance of that same self, as shared, both given and received into and from the community. So the death idea and the fellowship idea—which are irreconcilable, since death is the one thing that makes fellowship quite impossible—act, here, as another (really the same) ritually inescapable confrontation with the gap in which the sacred is encountered. This confrontation creates the community which is prophetic—both involved and separated—and which as prophetic, must carry the message to the rest of the world, in a form which the rest of the world can understand.

And what is this message that converts, not by words alone, but by the total language which is the Word? What does it say? 'For what we preach is not ourselves, but Jesus Christ as Lord, with ourselves as your servants for Jesus' sake. For it is the God who said, "Let light shine out of darkness," who has shone in our hearts to give the light of the knowledge of the glory of God in the face of Christ.'

If we aren't preaching ourselves, even as transformed, how

do we preach Jesus Christ as Lord, and how do people acknowledge his Lordship? The whole point seems to be that the total language of Christianity is ambiguous, and by its ambiguity challenges its hearers, becomes the two-edged sword that cuts even to the division of body and soul. Because it says a lot of perfectly intelligible things, but they don't fit:

> 'But we have this treasure in vessels of clay, to show that the transcendent power belongs to God and not to us. Pressures assail us on every side, yet we are not crushed, we can't know what to hope for, but we do not despair; we are persecuted but not forsaken, struck to the ground but not destroyed.'

The contradiction, further on, seems even more radical.

> 'We are treated as imposters, and yet we are honest, as obscure and yet we are famous; as dying men—and see, we live! As men under punishment and yet not executed, as sorrowful, yet we rejoice always, as poor, yet we make others rich, as having nothing, and yet possessing everything.'

This is the genuine total language of Christian prophecy, the kind that people can hear. And the expected result of this is indicated in the next sentence—the normal result of the kind of wildly contradictory existence which is the real preaching of the Gospel:

> 'Our mouth is open to you, Corinthians, our heart is wide ... In return, *widen your hearts also*.'

The converting word of the Eucharist brings together formation and transformation, secular and sacred, not by mixing them up but by confronting us with them. Both—distinct and yet related—are necessary, both—together and yet unconfused—are effective for salvation. Both are presented to us—and this is the sacrament. It is the sacrament of the nature of man, whose awareness of himself as fully human is only in Christ, and this awareness comes by the annihilation of human achievement, the negation of sense, although sensible achievement makes it possible. The explosion of the power of the Spirit happens when the pathetic little spark of faith leaps between the poles of 'crucified' and 'Lord', and the world is consumed in the transforming love of Christ.

When it comes to the point, that is what matters to everybody, whatever they call it. When a human being is faced with the facts of need and pain and death, what use are the sensible things? 'Where has the professor gone to? Where has the well-educated fellow gone now?' says Paul, quoting Isaiah (my version) and he goes on to expand the idea, and show beyond a shadow of a doubt what kind of preaching is Christian, and what the Church is for, which is in the world, and in which the world is:

'Where has he got to, the man who is clever with the world's knowledge? Hasn't God made the cleverness of the world look silly? For since the world, by means of its knowledge, did not recognize God in the *wisdom* which is God, it was by the *foolishness* of our Message that it pleased God to save those who believe. For the Jews are always wanting signs and the Greeks go hunting for knowledge, but we preach Christ crucified— a scandal to the Jews and folly to the Greeks, but to those who are called—Jews or Greeks—Christ the power of God, Christ the wisdom of God.'